SACRA[...]TO PUBLIC LIBRARY

S[...]

D1107375

BATMAN '66 meets STEED and MRS PEEL

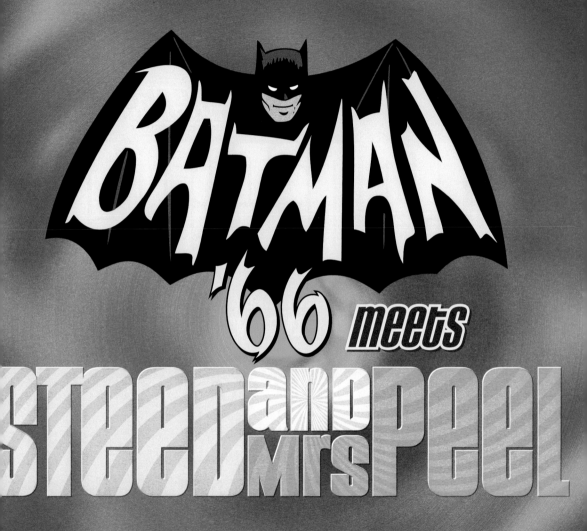

BATMAN '66 meets STEED and MRS PEEL

Written by
IAN EDGINTON

Art by
MATTHEW DOW SMITH

Colors by
WENDY BROOME
JORDIE BELLAIRE
CARRIE STRACHAN

Letters by
WES ABBOTT

Cover Art & Original Series Covers by
MICHAEL & LAURA ALLRED

Co-Published with BOOM! Studios

BOOM! STUDIOS   STUDIOCANAL   CLC CREATIVE LICENSING CORPORATION

BATMAN created by BOB KANE with BILL FINGER

Inspired by the 1960s *Batman* television series

Inspired by the 1960s British television series *The Avengers*

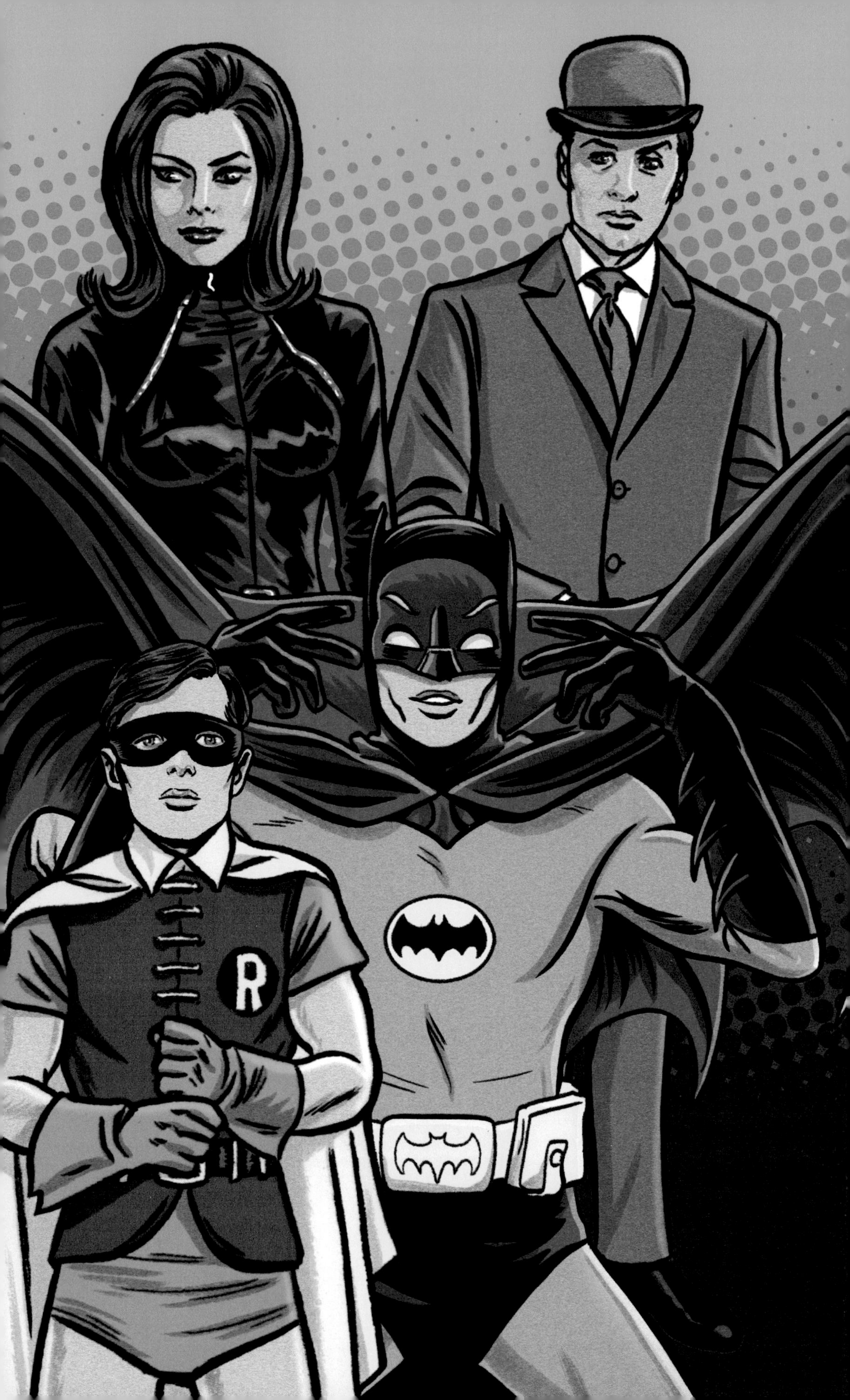
R

KRISTY QUINN
Editor – Original Series
JESSICA CHEN
Associate Editor – Original Series
CHRIS ROSA
BOOM! Studios Editor – Original Series
JEB WOODARD
Group Editor – Collected Editions
SCOTT NYBAKKEN
Editor – Collected Edition
STEVEN COOK
Design Director – Books
CURTIS KING JR.
Publication Design

BOB HARRAS
Senior VP – Editor-in-Chief, DC Comics

DIANE NELSON
President
DAN DiDIO
Publisher
JIM LEE
Publisher
GEOFF JOHNS
President & Chief Creative Officer
AMIT DESAI
Executive VP – Business & Marketing Strategy,
Direct to Consumer & Global Franchise Management
SAM ADES
Senior VP – Direct to Consumer
BOBBIE CHASE
VP – Talent Development
MARK CHIARELLO
Senior VP – Art, Design & Collected Editions
JOHN CUNNINGHAM
Senior VP – Sales & Trade Marketing
ANNE DePIES
Senior VP – Business Strategy, Finance & Administration
DON FALLETTI
VP – Manufacturing Operations
LAWRENCE GANEM
VP – Editorial Administration & Talent Relations
ALISON GILL
Senior VP – Manufacturing & Operations
HANK KANALZ
Senior VP – Editorial Strategy & Administration
JAY KOGAN
VP – Legal Affairs
THOMAS LOFTUS
VP – Business Affairs
JACK MAHAN
VP – Business Affairs
NICK J. NAPOLITANO
VP – Manufacturing Administration
EDDIE SCANNELL
VP – Consumer Marketing
COURTNEY SIMMONS
Senior VP – Publicity & Communications
JIM (SKI) SOKOLOWSKI
VP – Comic Book Specialty Sales & Trade Marketing
NANCY SPEARS
VP – Mass, Book, Digital Sales & Trade Marketing

BATMAN '66 MEETS STEED AND MRS. PEEL
Published by DC Comics. Compilation and all new material Copyright © 2017
DC Comics and Studiocanal S.A.S.®. All Rights Reserved. Originally published
in single magazine form as BATMAN '66 MEETS STEED AND MRS. PEEL 1-6
and online as BATMAN '66 MEETS STEED AND MRS. PEEL Digital Chapters
1-12. Copyright © 2016. All Rights Reserved. DC LOGO, BATMAN and all
related characters and elements are trademarks of and © DC Comics.
The Avengers and Steed and Mrs. Peel are trademarks of Studiocanal S.A.S.
All Rights Reserved. © 2016 Studiocanal S.A.S.®. All Rights Reserved.
BOOM! Studios™ & the BOOM! Studios logo are trademarks of Boom
Entertainment, Inc., registered in various countries and categories. All Rights
Reserved. Studiocanal logo ™ & © Studiocanal S.A.S.®. All Rights Reserved.
The stories, characters and incidents featured in this publication
are entirely fictional. DC Comics does not read or accept unsolicited submissions
of ideas, stories or artwork.

DC Comics, 2900 West Alameda Ave., Burbank, CA 91505
Printed by LSC Communications, Salem, VA, USA. 1/27/17. First Printing.
HC ISBN: 978-1-4012-6820-6

Library of Congress
Cataloging-in-Publication Data is available.

PEFC Certified
Printed on paper from
sustainably managed
forests, controlled
sources
PEFC/29-31-337   www.pefc.org

TABLE OF CONTENTS

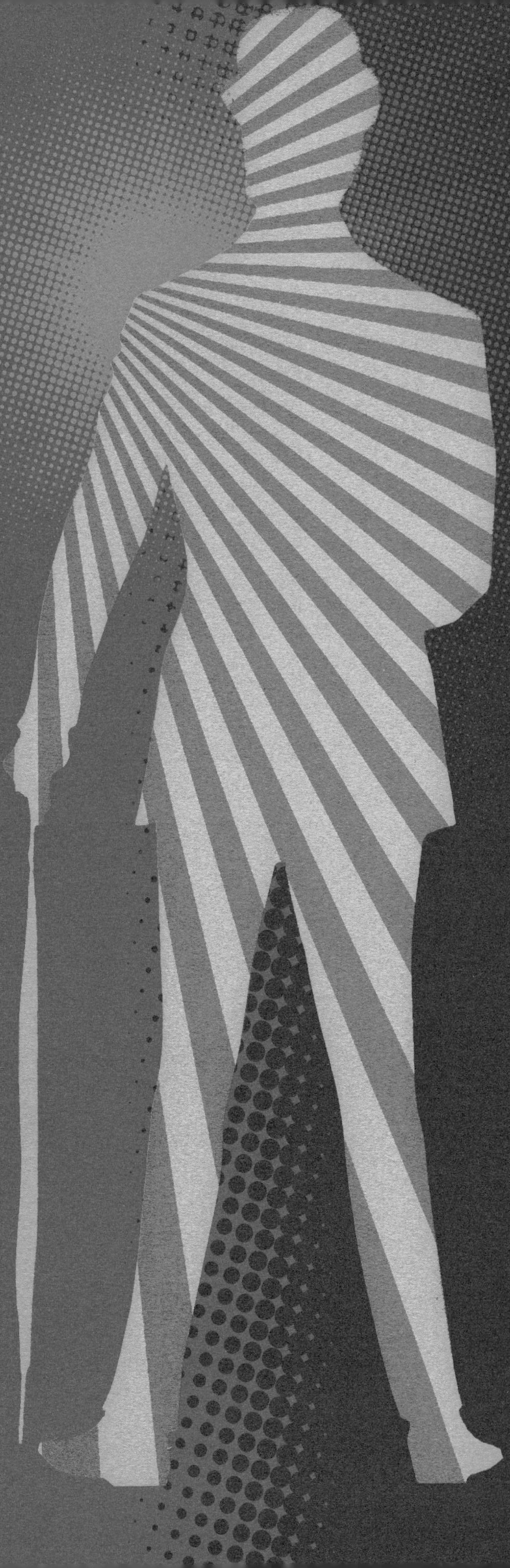

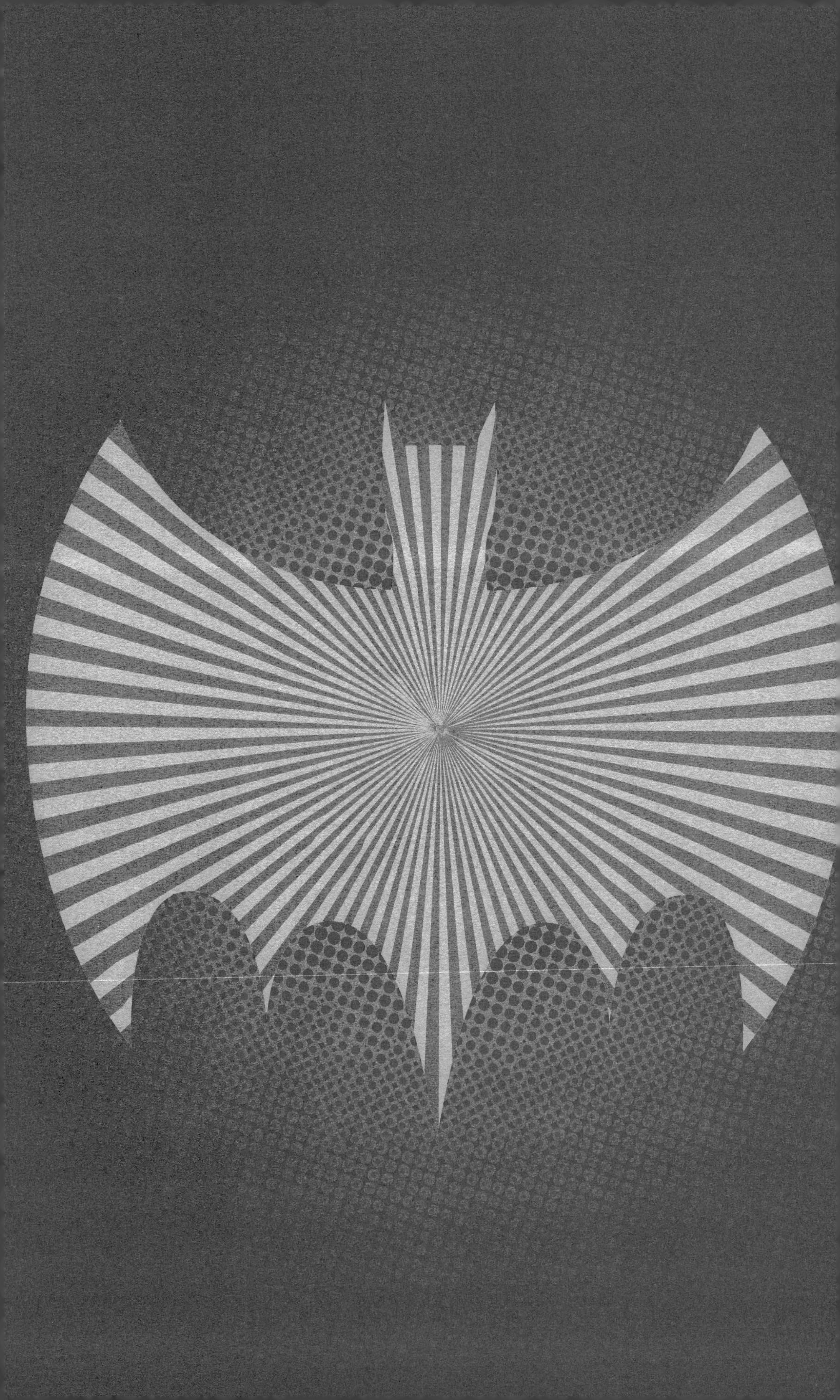

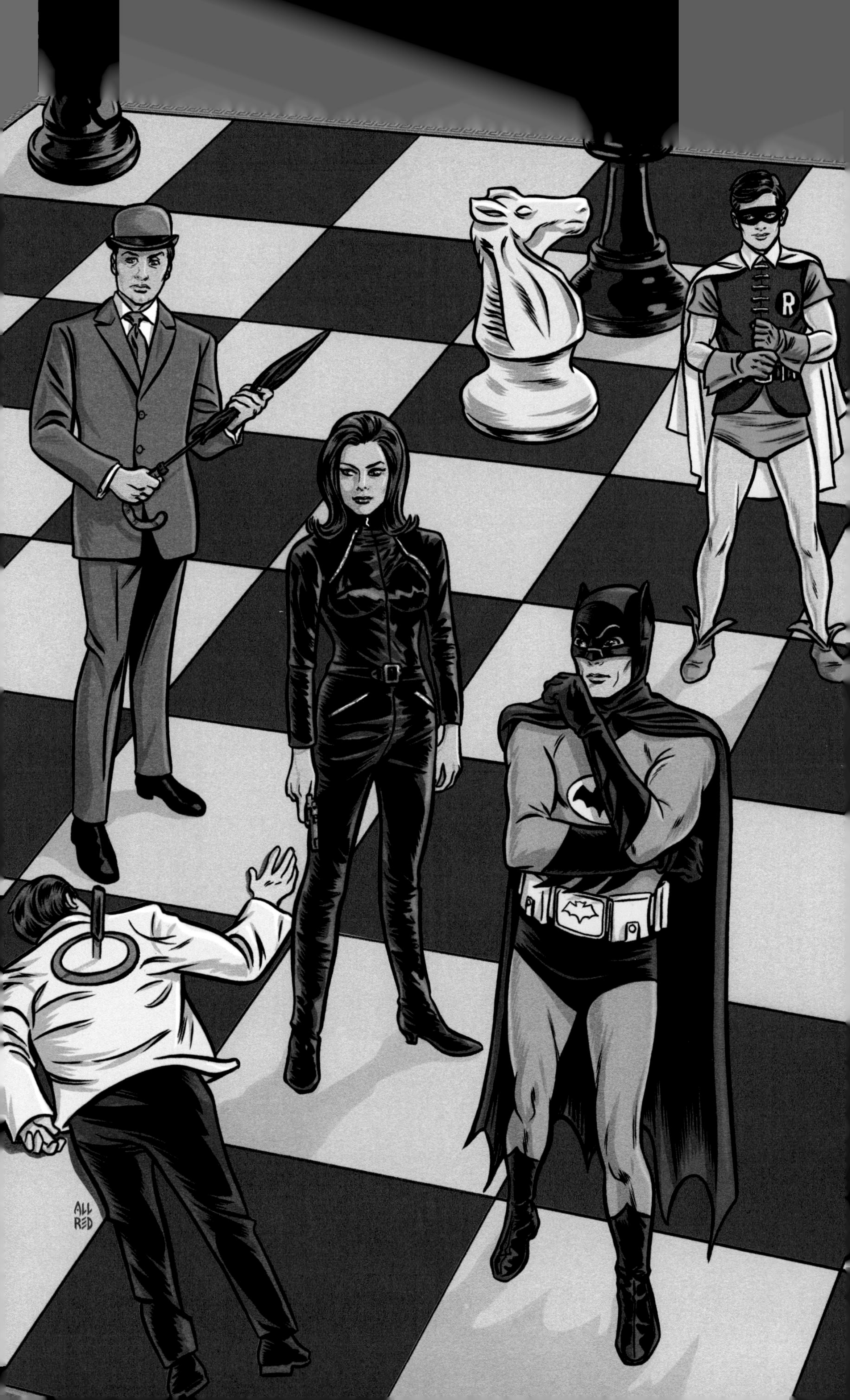
ALL
RED

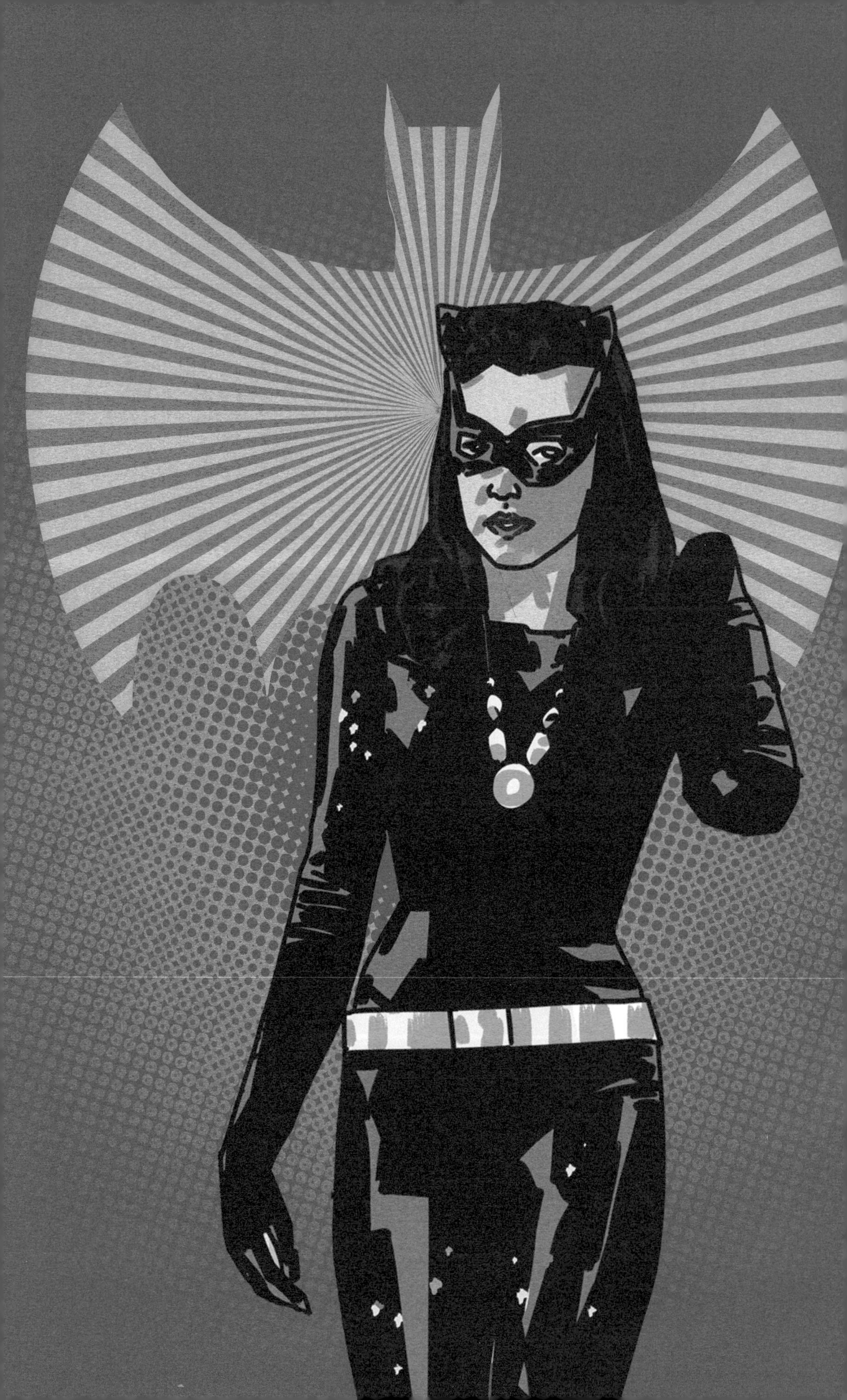

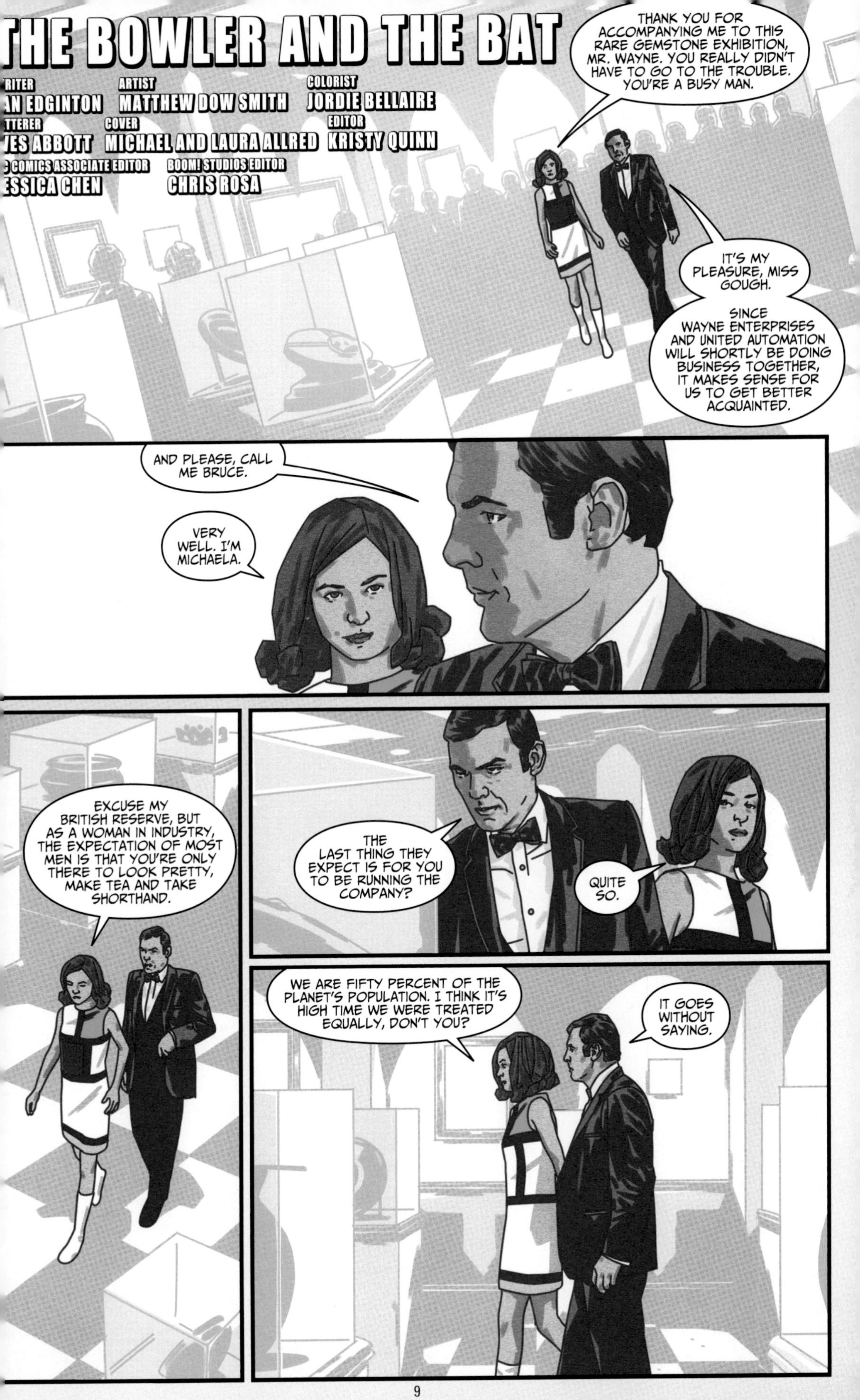
THE BOWLER AND THE BAT
RITER
AN EDGINTON
ARTIST
MATTHEW DOW SMITH
COLORIST
JORDIE BELLAIRE
TTERERER
VES ABBOTT
COVER
MICHAEL AND LAURA ALLRED
EDITOR
KRISTY QUINN
C COMICS ASSOCIATE EDITOR
ESSICA CHEN
BOOM! STUDIOS EDITOR
CHRIS ROSA
THANK YOU FOR ACCOMPANYING ME TO THIS RARE GEMSTONE EXHIBITION, MR. WAYNE. YOU REALLY DIDN'T HAVE TO GO TO THE TROUBLE. YOU'RE A BUSY MAN.
IT'S MY PLEASURE, MISS GOUGH.
SINCE WAYNE ENTERPRISES AND UNITED AUTOMATION WILL SHORTLY BE DOING BUSINESS TOGETHER, IT MAKES SENSE FOR US TO GET BETTER ACQUAINTED.
AND PLEASE, CALL ME BRUCE.
VERY WELL. I'M MICHAELA.
EXCUSE MY BRITISH RESERVE, BUT AS A WOMAN IN INDUSTRY, THE EXPECTATION OF MOST MEN IS THAT YOU'RE ONLY THERE TO LOOK PRETTY, MAKE TEA AND TAKE SHORTHAND.
THE LAST THING THEY EXPECT IS FOR YOU TO BE RUNNING THE COMPANY?
QUITE SO.
WE ARE FIFTY PERCENT OF THE PLANET'S POPULATION. I THINK IT'S HIGH TIME WE WERE TREATED EQUALLY, DON'T YOU?
IT GOES WITHOUT SAYING.

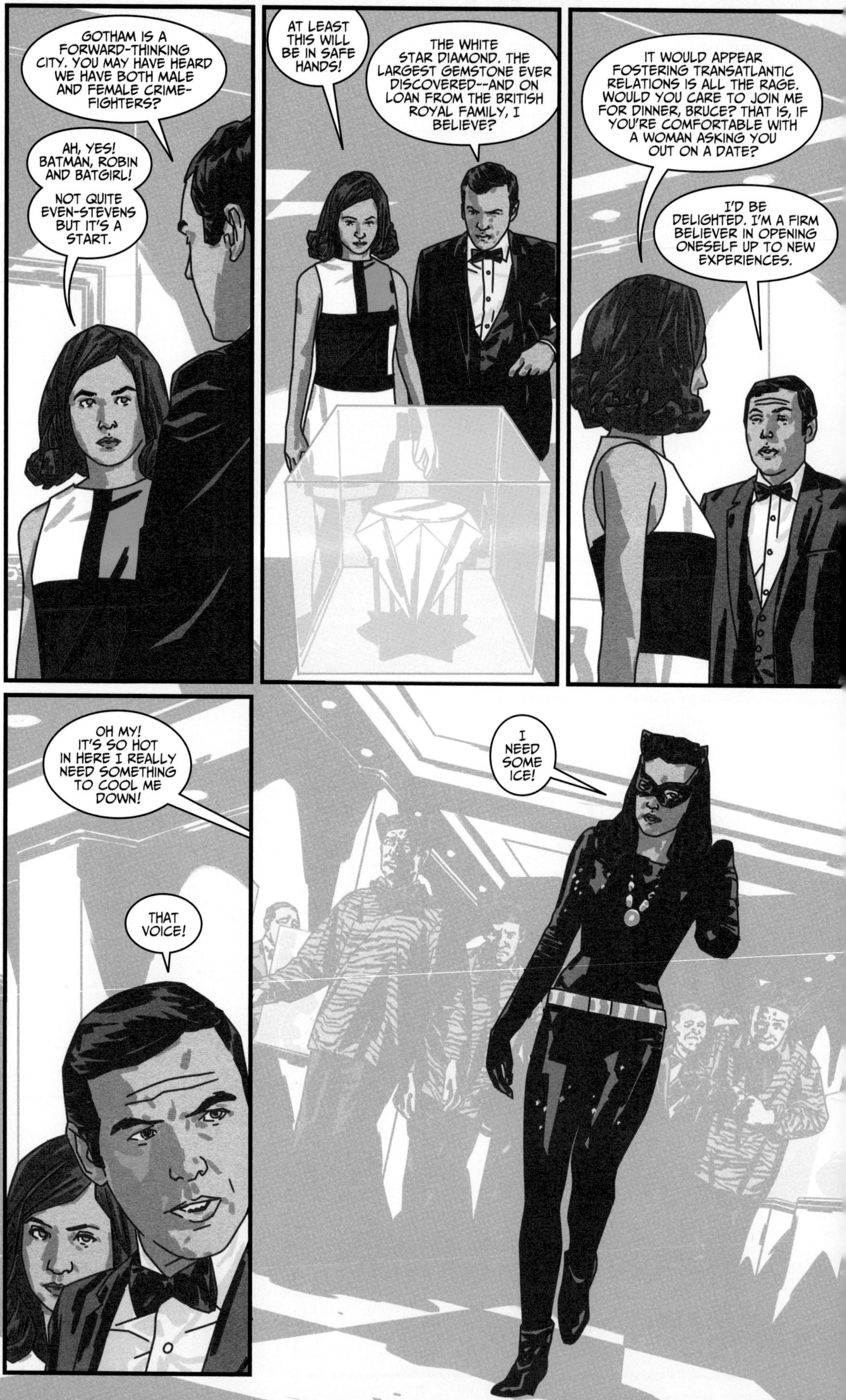
GOTHAM IS A FORWARD-THINKING CITY. YOU MAY HAVE HEARD WE HAVE BOTH MALE AND FEMALE CRIME-FIGHTERS?
AH, YES! BATMAN, ROBIN AND BATGIRL!
NOT QUITE EVEN-STEVENS BUT IT'S A START.
AT LEAST THIS WILL BE IN SAFE HANDS!
THE WHITE STAR DIAMOND. THE LARGEST GEMSTONE EVER DISCOVERED--AND ON LOAN FROM THE BRITISH ROYAL FAMILY, I BELIEVE?
IT WOULD APPEAR FOSTERING TRANSATLANTIC RELATIONS IS ALL THE RAGE. WOULD YOU CARE TO JOIN ME FOR DINNER, BRUCE? THAT IS, IF YOU'RE COMFORTABLE WITH A WOMAN ASKING YOU OUT ON A DATE?
I'D BE DELIGHTED. I'M A FIRM BELIEVER IN OPENING ONESELF UP TO NEW EXPERIENCES.
OH MY! IT'S SO HOT IN HERE I REALLY NEED SOMETHING TO COOL ME DOWN!
I NEED SOME ICE!
THAT VOICE!

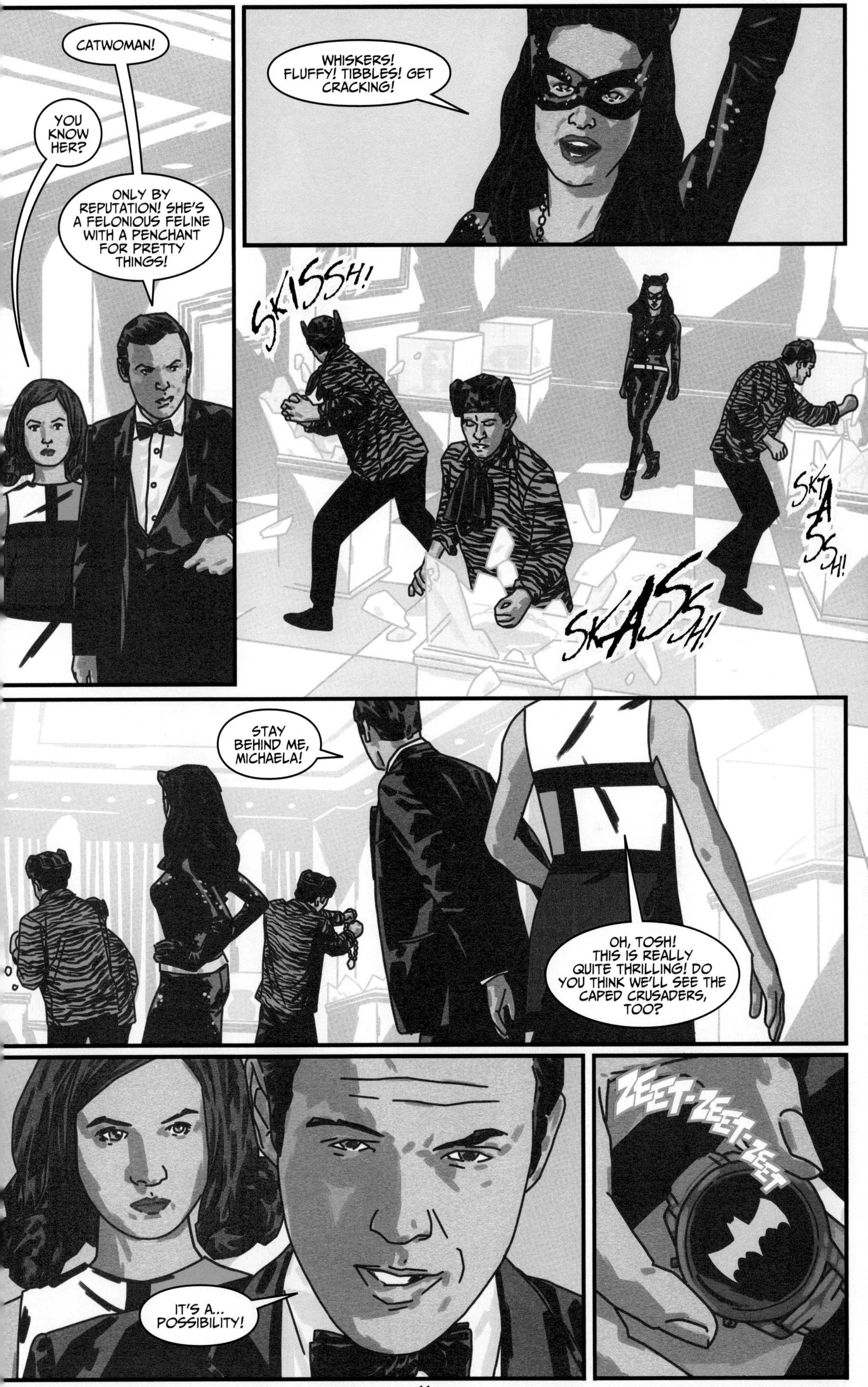
CATWOMAN!
YOU KNOW HER?
ONLY BY REPUTATION! SHE'S A FELONIOUS FELINE WITH A PENCHANT FOR PRETTY THINGS!
WHISKERS! FLUFFY! TIBBLES! GET CRACKING!
SKISSH!
SKASSH!
SKASSH!
STAY BEHIND ME, MICHAELA!
OH, TOSH! THIS IS REALLY QUITE THRILLING! DO YOU THINK WE'LL SEE THE CAPED CRUSADERS, TOO?
IT'S A... POSSIBILITY!
ZEET-ZEET-ZEET

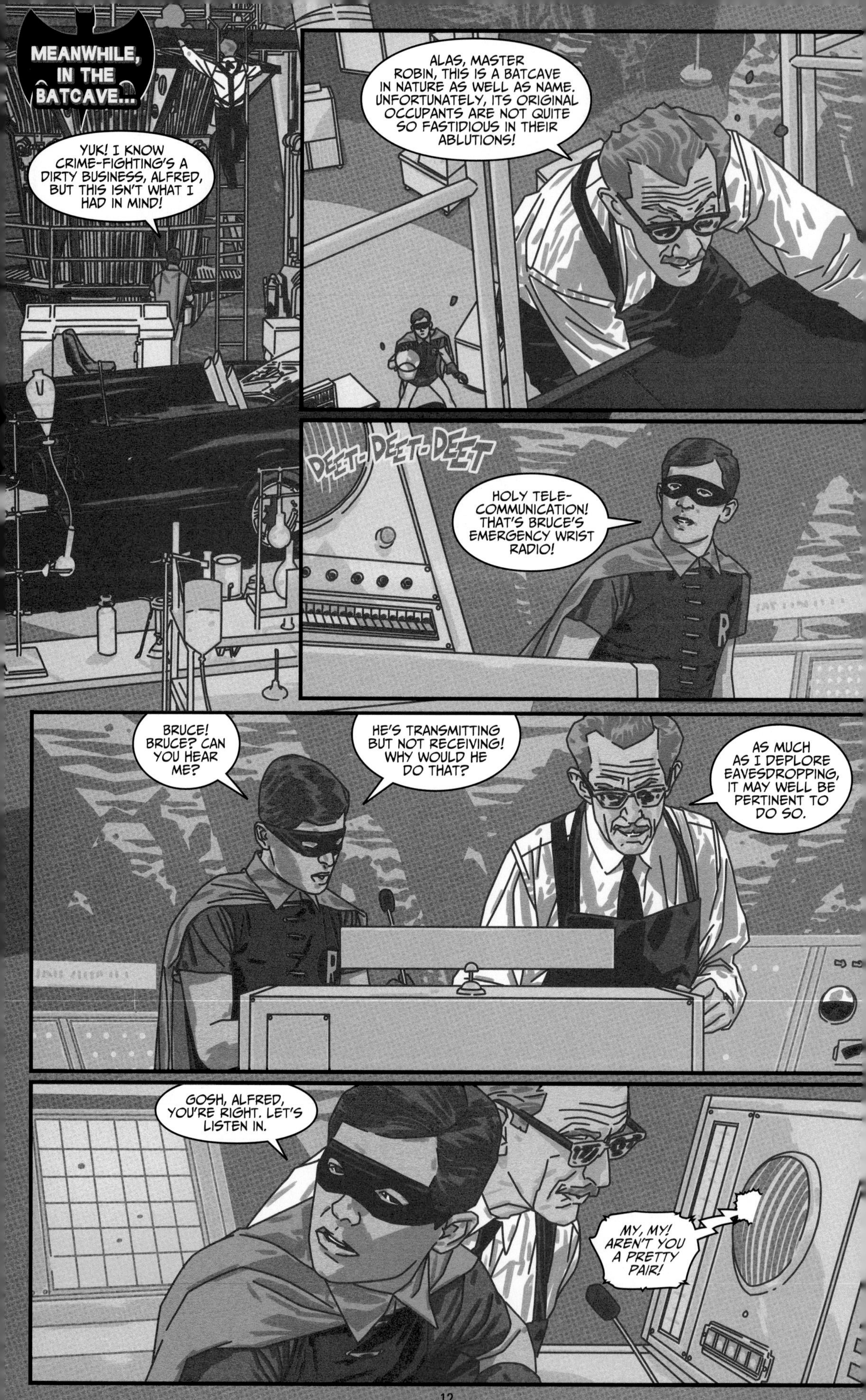
MEANWHILE, IN THE BATCAVE...
YUK! I KNOW CRIME-FIGHTING'S A DIRTY BUSINESS, ALFRED, BUT THIS ISN'T WHAT I HAD IN MIND!
ALAS, MASTER ROBIN, THIS IS A BATCAVE IN NATURE AS WELL AS NAME. UNFORTUNATELY, ITS ORIGINAL OCCUPANTS ARE NOT QUITE SO FASTIDIOUS IN THEIR ABLUTIONS!
DEET-DEET-DEET
HOLY TELE-COMMUNICATION! THAT'S BRUCE'S EMERGENCY WRIST RADIO!
BRUCE! BRUCE? CAN YOU HEAR ME?
HE'S TRANSMITTING BUT NOT RECEIVING! WHY WOULD HE DO THAT?
AS MUCH AS I DEPLORE EAVESDROPPING, IT MAY WELL BE PERTINENT TO DO SO.
GOSH, ALFRED, YOU'RE RIGHT. LET'S LISTEN IN.
MY, MY! AREN'T YOU A PRETTY PAIR!

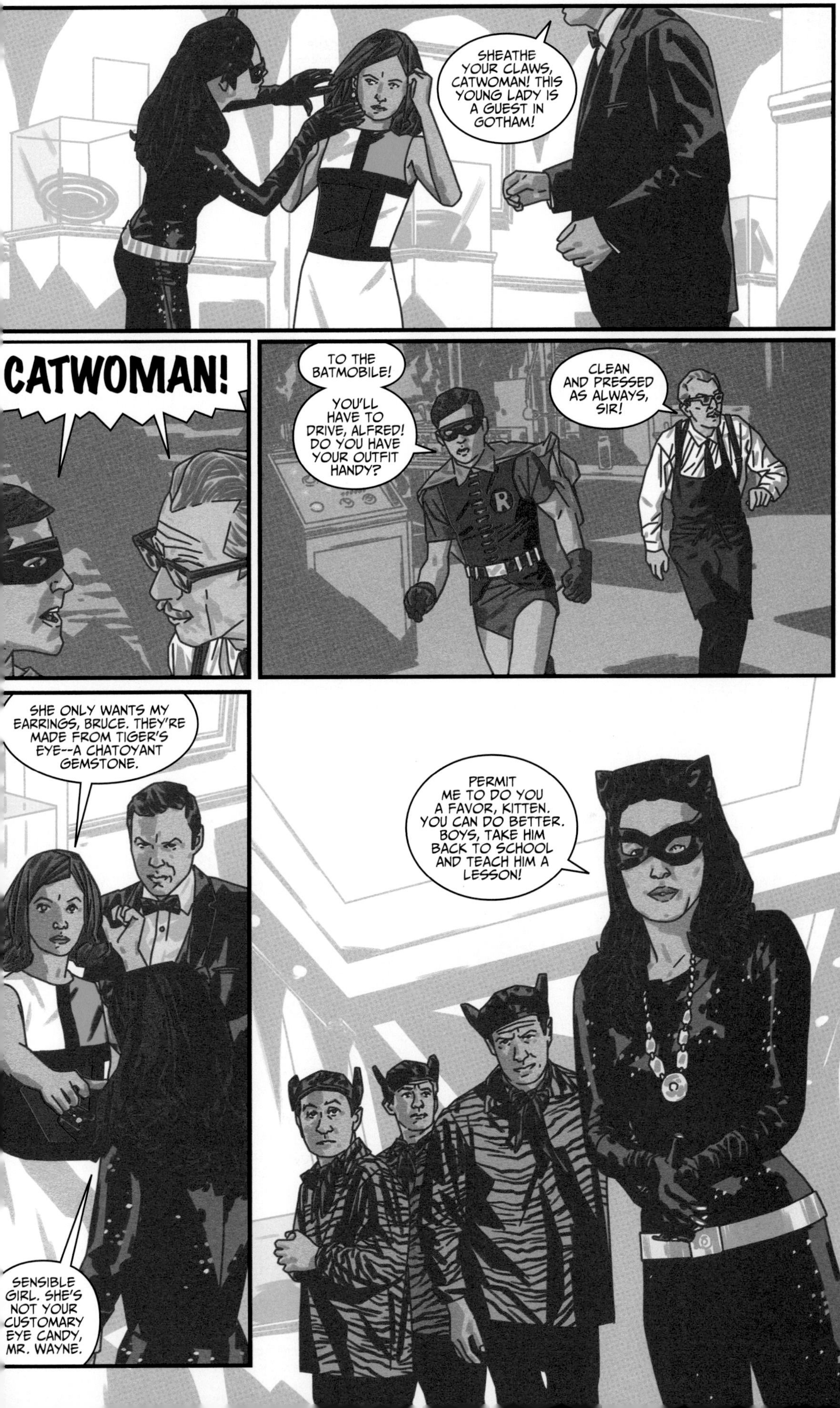
SHEATHE YOUR CLAWS, CATWOMAN! THIS YOUNG LADY IS A GUEST IN GOTHAM!
CATWOMAN!
TO THE BATMOBILE!
YOU'LL HAVE TO DRIVE, ALFRED! DO YOU HAVE YOUR OUTFIT HANDY?
CLEAN AND PRESSED AS ALWAYS, SIR!
SHE ONLY WANTS MY EARRINGS, BRUCE. THEY'RE MADE FROM TIGER'S EYE--A CHATOYANT GEMSTONE.
SENSIBLE GIRL. SHE'S NOT YOUR CUSTOMARY EYE CANDY, MR. WAYNE.
PERMIT ME TO DO YOU A FAVOR, KITTEN. YOU CAN DO BETTER. BOYS, TAKE HIM BACK TO SCHOOL AND TEACH HIM A LESSON!

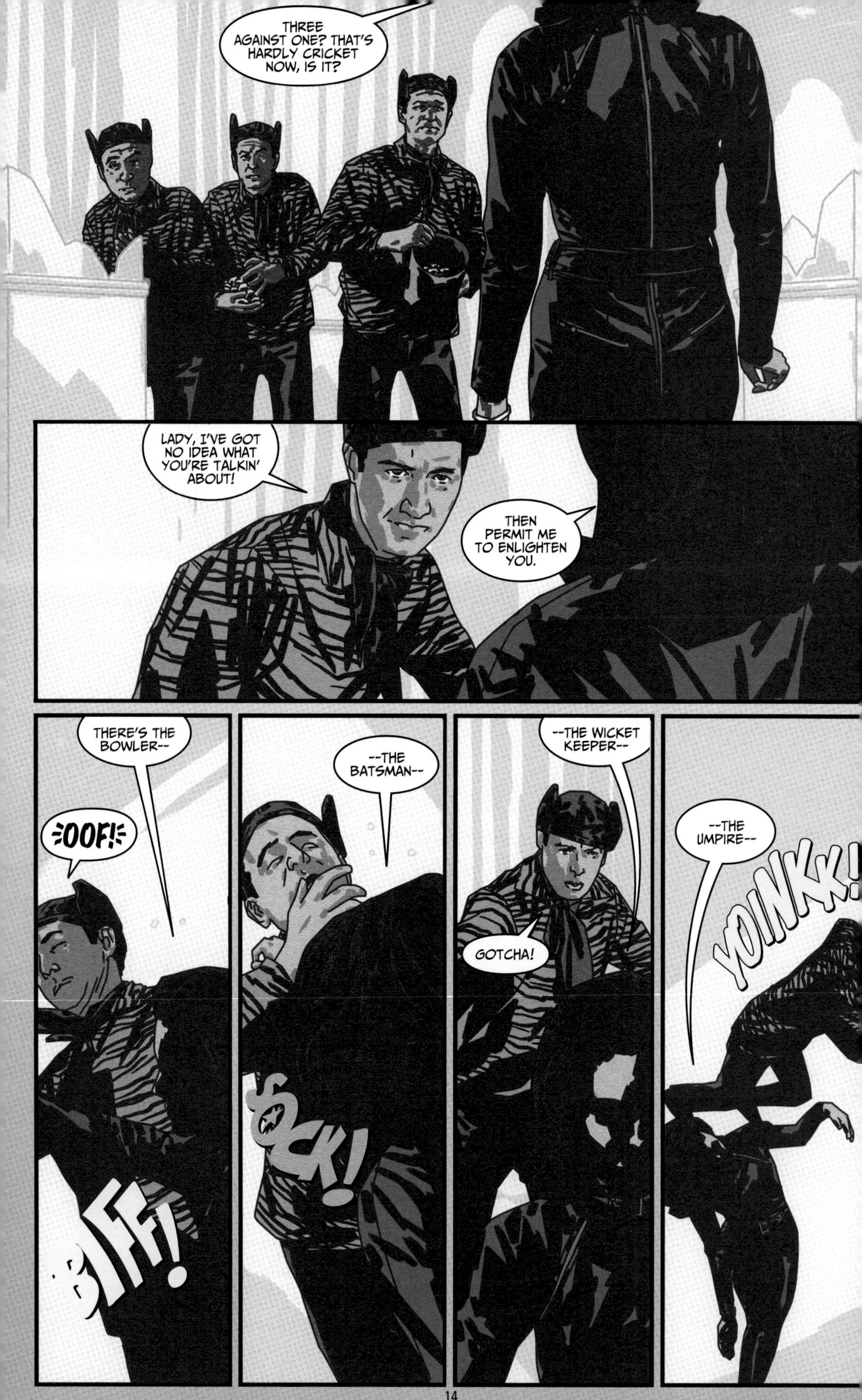

THREE AGAINST ONE? THAT'S HARDLY CRICKET NOW, IS IT?
LADY, I'VE GOT NO IDEA WHAT YOU'RE TALKIN' ABOUT!
THEN PERMIT ME TO ENLIGHTEN YOU.
THERE'S THE BOWLER--
OOF!
BIFF!
--THE BATSMAN--
SOCK!
--THE WICKET KEEPER--
GOTCHA!
--THE UMPIRE--
YOINKK!

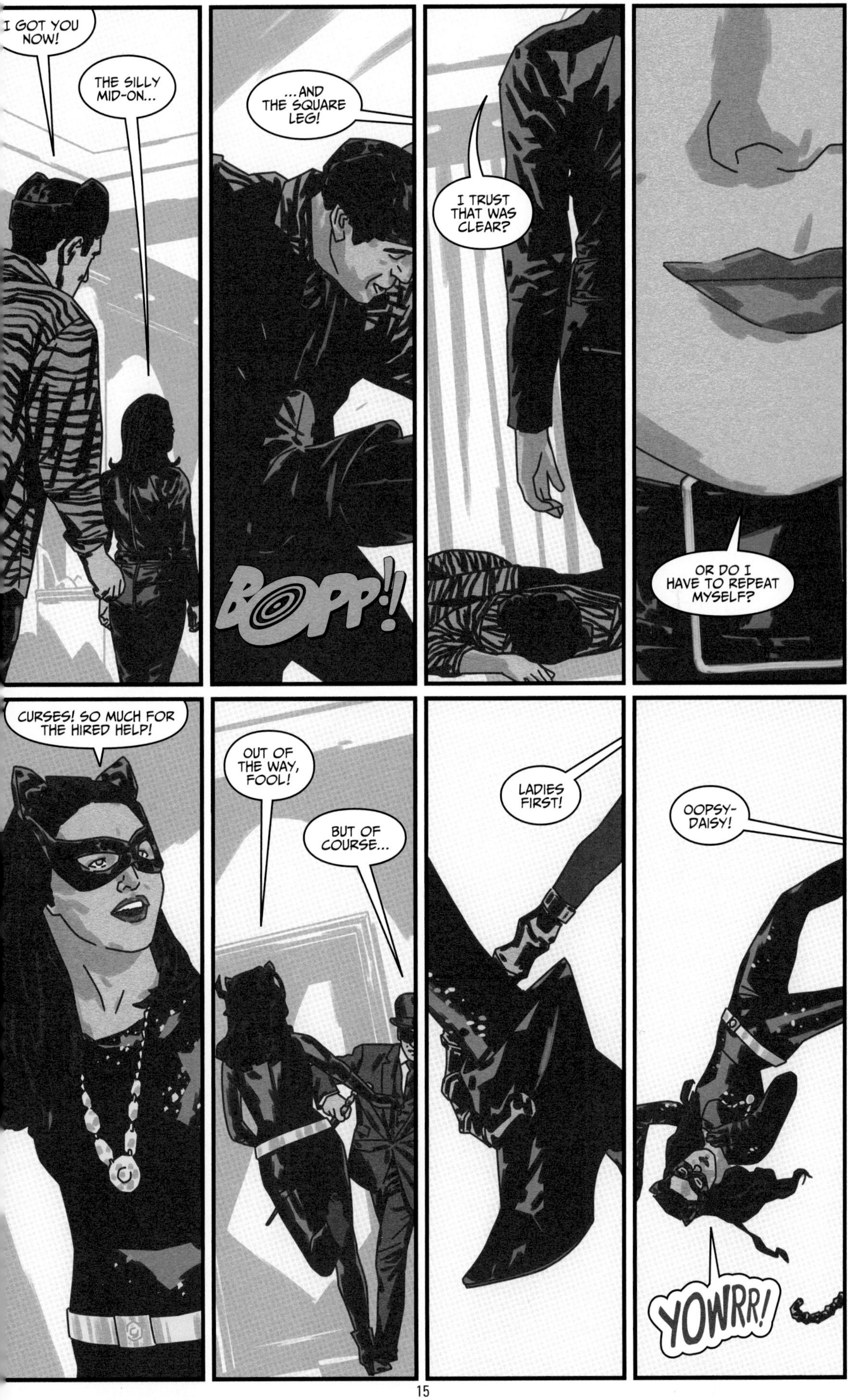
I GOT YOU NOW!
THE SILLY MID-ON...
...AND THE SQUARE LEG!
BOPP!!
I TRUST THAT WAS CLEAR?
OR DO I HAVE TO REPEAT MYSELF?
CURSES! SO MUCH FOR THE HIRED HELP!
OUT OF THE WAY, FOOL!
BUT OF COURSE...
LADIES FIRST!
OOPSY-DAISY!
YOWRR!

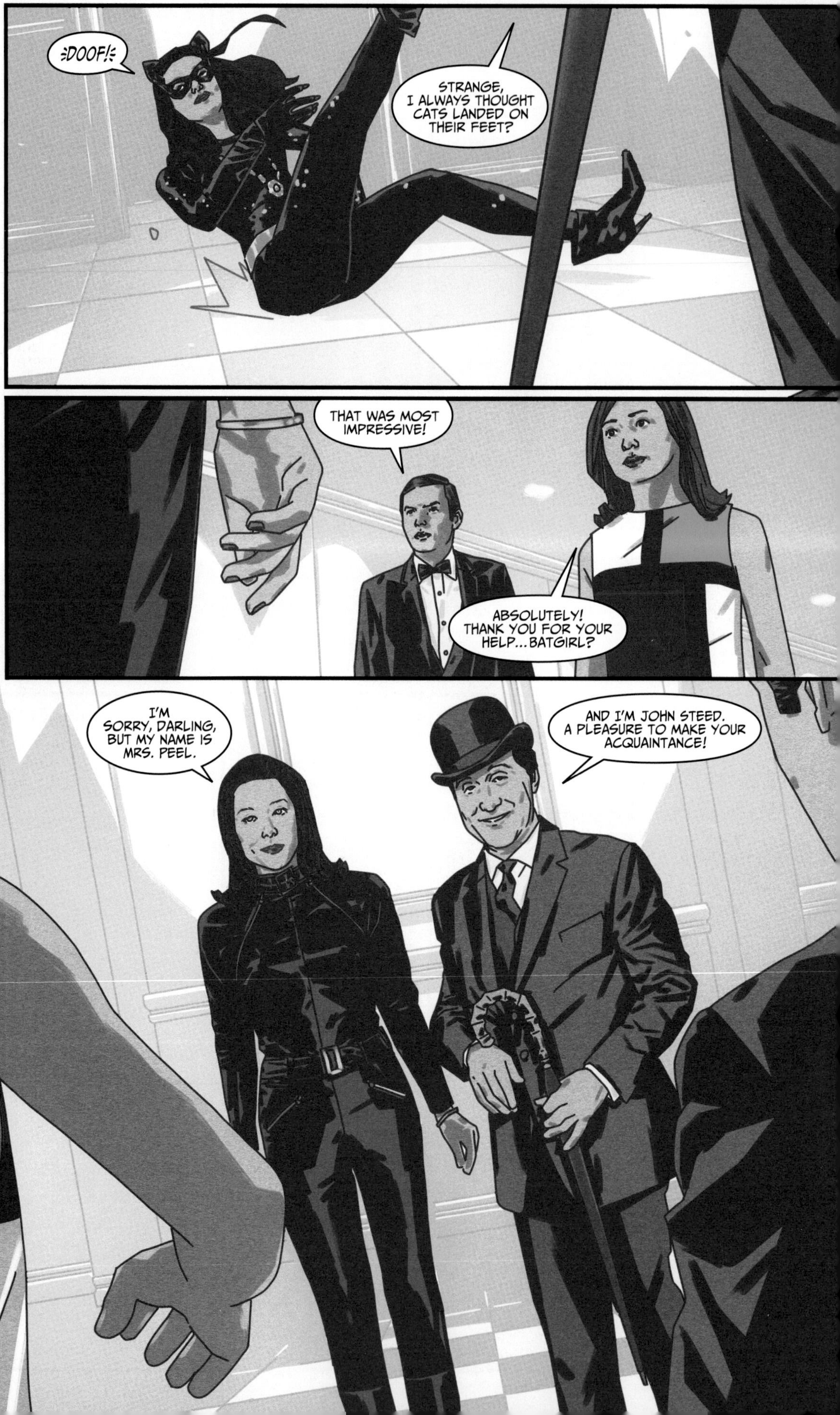
DOOF!
STRANGE, I ALWAYS THOUGHT CATS LANDED ON THEIR FEET?
THAT WAS MOST IMPRESSIVE!
ABSOLUTELY! THANK YOU FOR YOUR HELP... BATGIRL?
I'M SORRY, DARLING, BUT MY NAME IS MRS. PEEL.
AND I'M JOHN STEED. A PLEASURE TO MAKE YOUR ACQUAINTANCE!

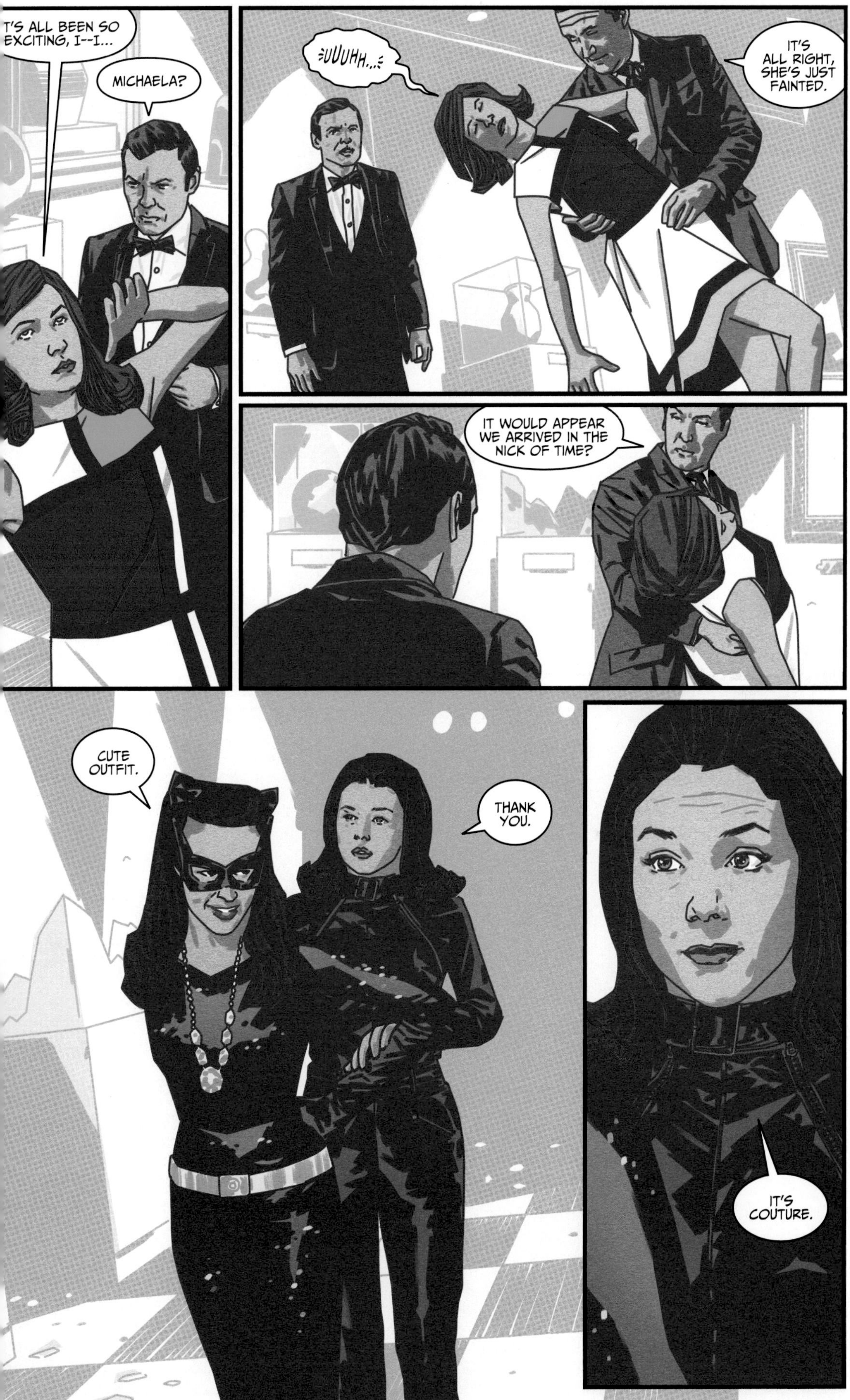

T'S ALL BEEN SO EXCITING, I--I...
MICHAELA?
UUUHH...
IT'S ALL RIGHT, SHE'S JUST FAINTED.
IT WOULD APPEAR WE ARRIVED IN THE NICK OF TIME?
CUTE OUTFIT.
THANK YOU.
IT'S COUTURE.

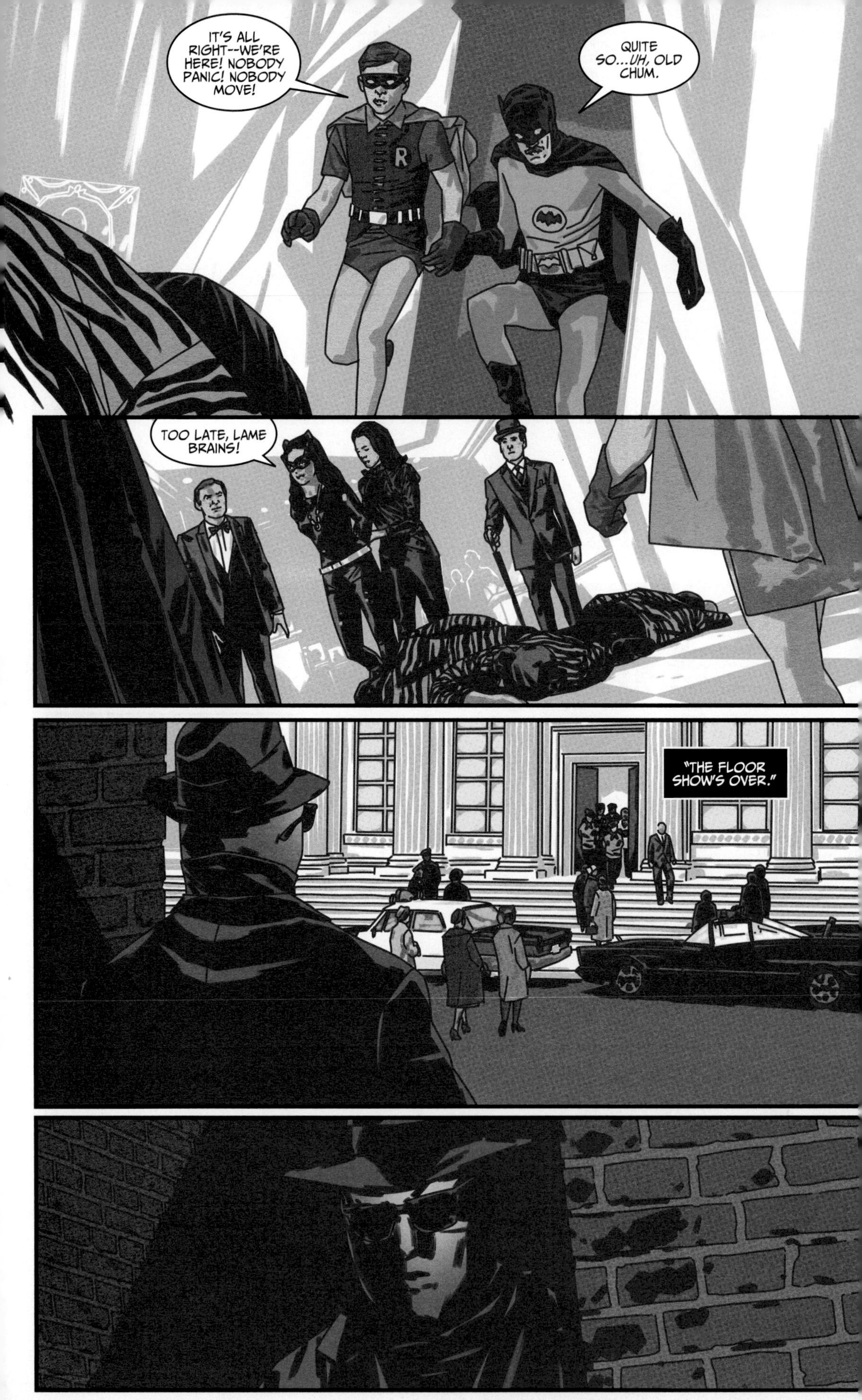

IT'S ALL RIGHT--WE'RE HERE! NOBODY PANIC! NOBODY MOVE!
QUITE SO...UH, OLD CHUM.
TOO LATE, LAME BRAINS!
"THE FLOOR SHOW'S OVER."

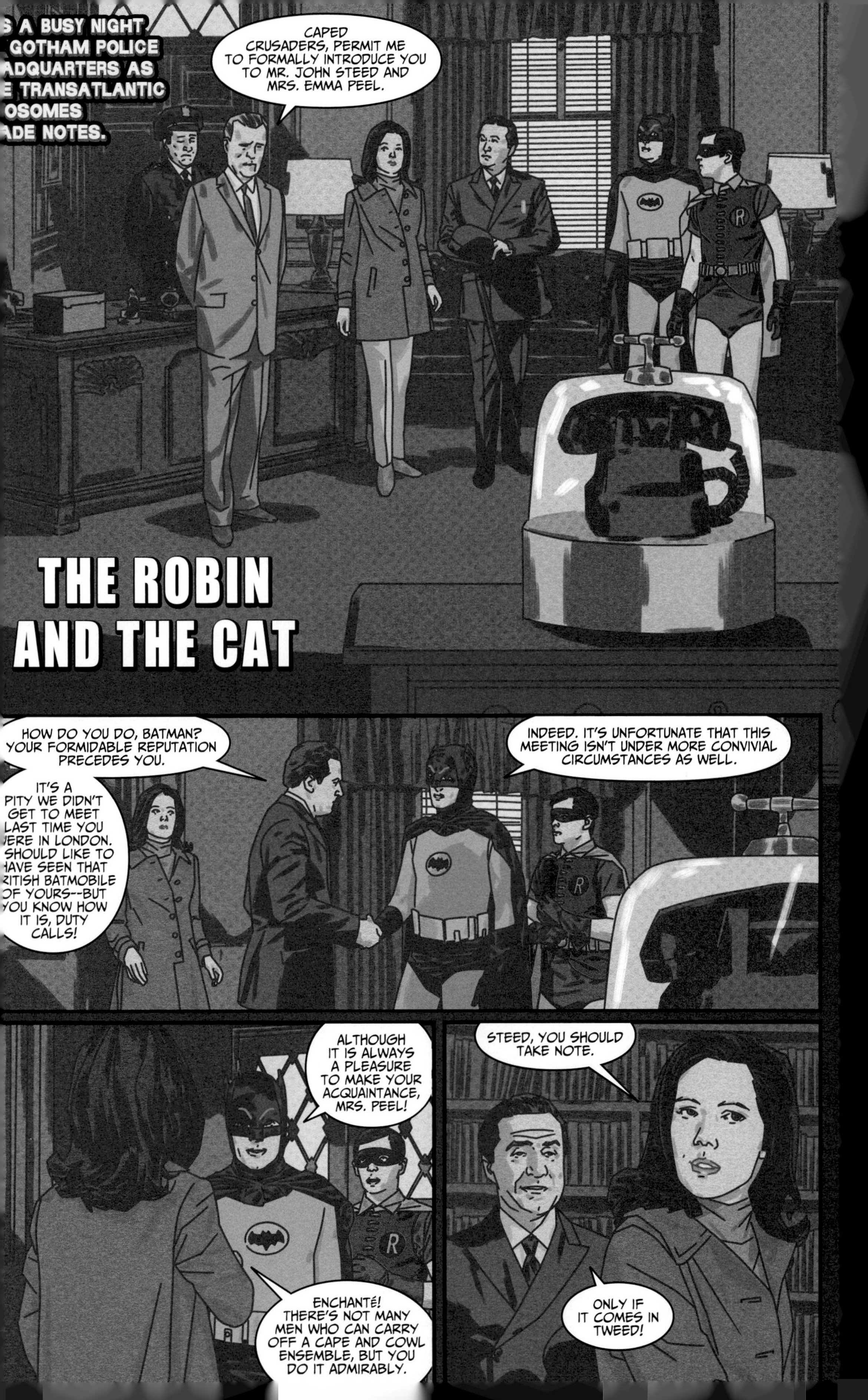
S A BUSY NIGHT
GOTHAM POLICE
ADQUARTERS AS
E TRANSATLANTIC
OSOMES
ADE NOTES.
CAPED CRUSADERS, PERMIT ME TO FORMALLY INTRODUCE YOU TO MR. JOHN STEED AND MRS. EMMA PEEL.
THE ROBIN AND THE CAT
HOW DO YOU DO, BATMAN? YOUR FORMIDABLE REPUTATION PRECEDES YOU.
IT'S A PITY WE DIDN'T GET TO MEET LAST TIME YOU ERE IN LONDON. SHOULD LIKE TO AVE SEEN THAT RITISH BATMOBILE OF YOURS--BUT YOU KNOW HOW IT IS, DUTY CALLS!
INDEED. IT'S UNFORTUNATE THAT THIS MEETING ISN'T UNDER MORE CONVIVIAL CIRCUMSTANCES AS WELL.
ALTHOUGH IT IS ALWAYS A PLEASURE TO MAKE YOUR ACQUAINTANCE, MRS. PEEL!
ENCHANTÉ! THERE'S NOT MANY MEN WHO CAN CARRY OFF A CAPE AND COWL ENSEMBLE, BUT YOU DO IT ADMIRABLY.
STEED, YOU SHOULD TAKE NOTE.
ONLY IF IT COMES IN TWEED!

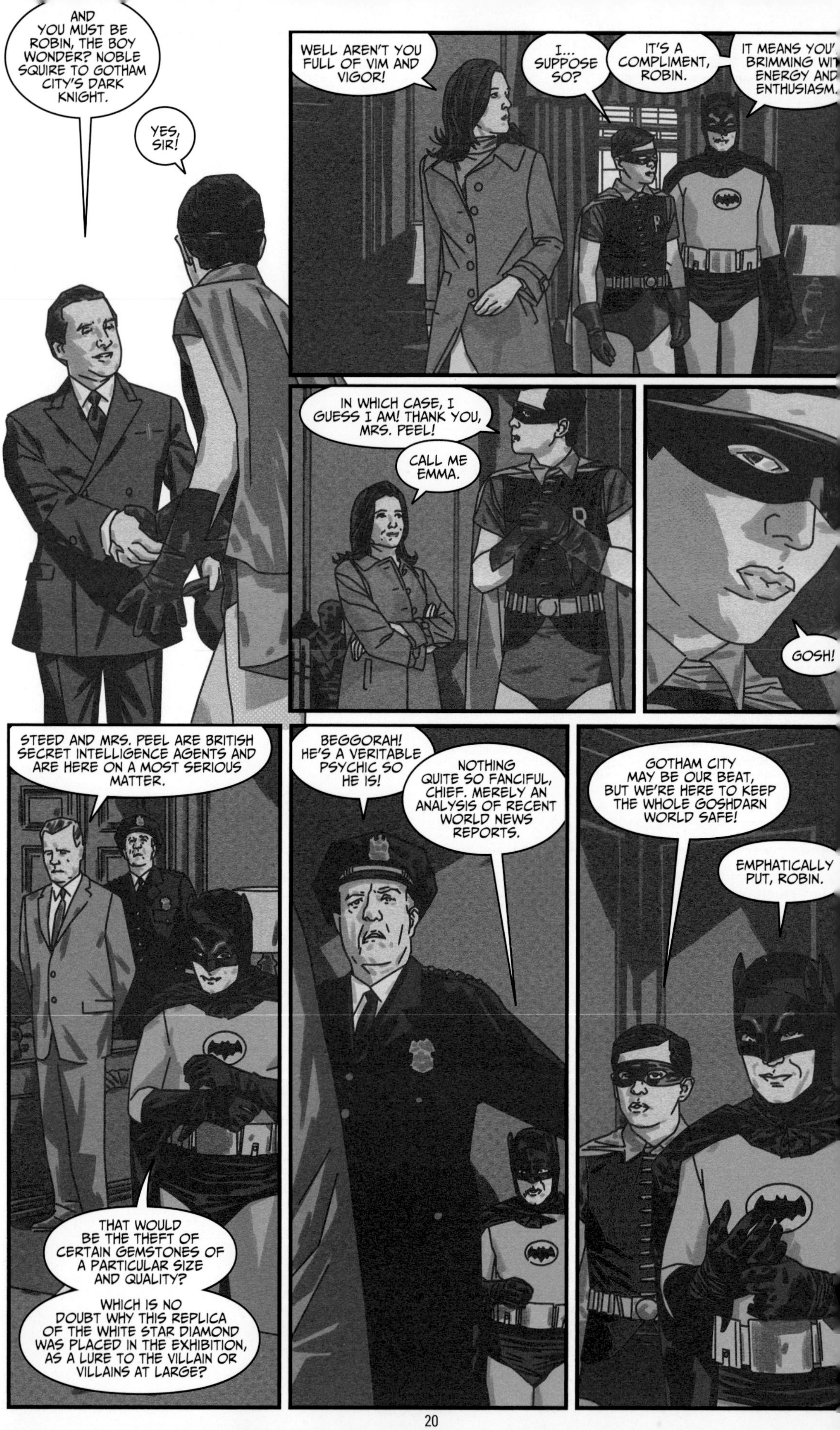
AND YOU MUST BE ROBIN, THE BOY WONDER? NOBLE SQUIRE TO GOTHAM CITY'S DARK KNIGHT.
YES, SIR!
WELL AREN'T YOU FULL OF VIM AND VIGOR!
I... SUPPOSE SO?
IT'S A COMPLIMENT, ROBIN.
IT MEANS YOU' BRIMMING WIT ENERGY AND ENTHUSIASM.
IN WHICH CASE, I GUESS I AM! THANK YOU, MRS. PEEL!
CALL ME EMMA.
GOSH!
STEED AND MRS. PEEL ARE BRITISH SECRET INTELLIGENCE AGENTS AND ARE HERE ON A MOST SERIOUS MATTER.
THAT WOULD BE THE THEFT OF CERTAIN GEMSTONES OF A PARTICULAR SIZE AND QUALITY?
WHICH IS NO DOUBT WHY THIS REPLICA OF THE WHITE STAR DIAMOND WAS PLACED IN THE EXHIBITION, AS A LURE TO THE VILLAIN OR VILLAINS AT LARGE?
BEGGORAH! HE'S A VERITABLE PSYCHIC SO HE IS!
NOTHING QUITE SO FANCIFUL, CHIEF. MERELY AN ANALYSIS OF RECENT WORLD NEWS REPORTS.
GOTHAM CITY MAY BE OUR BEAT, BUT WE'RE HERE TO KEEP THE WHOLE GOSHDARN WORLD SAFE!
EMPHATICALLY PUT, ROBIN.

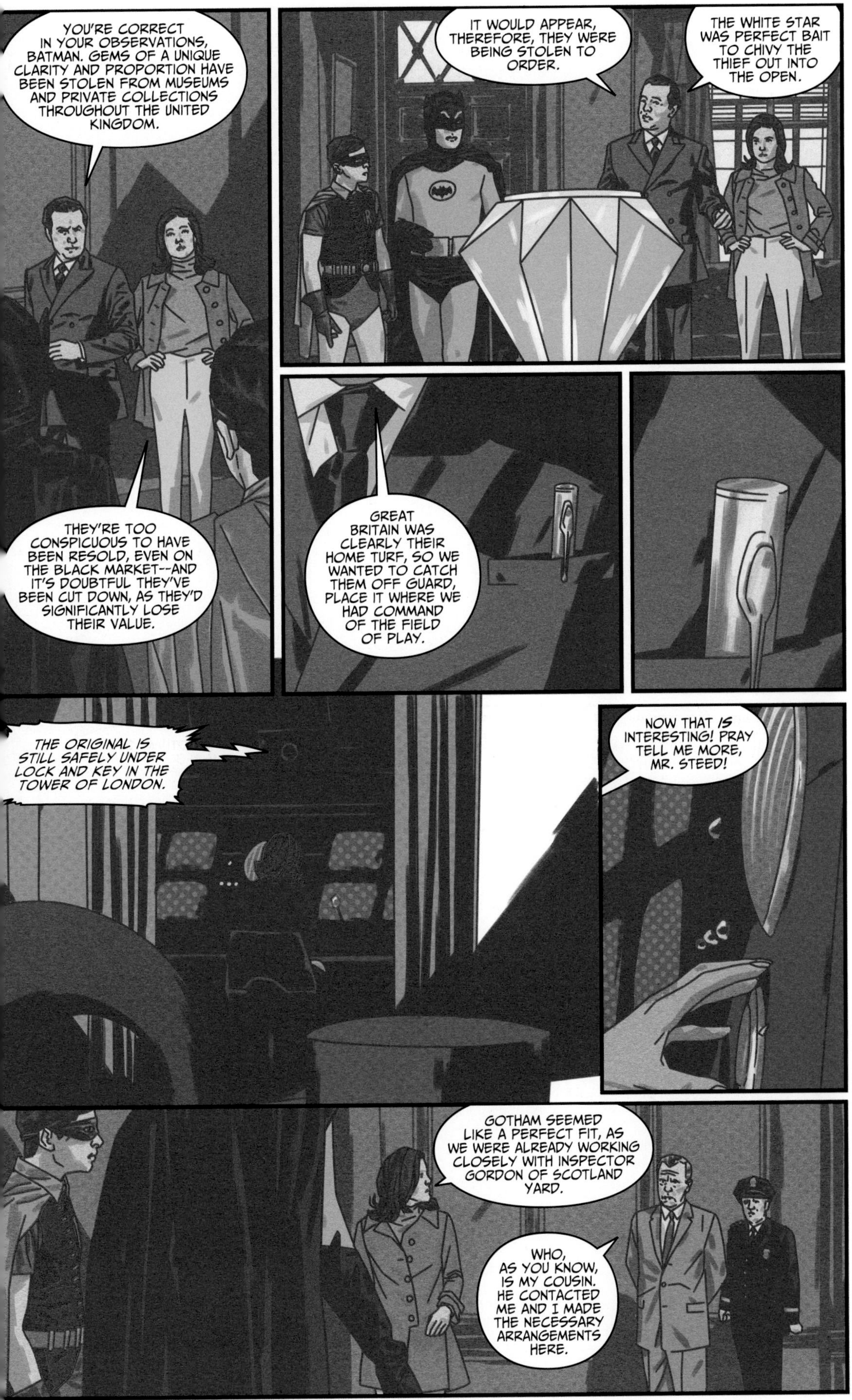
YOU'RE CORRECT IN YOUR OBSERVATIONS, BATMAN. GEMS OF A UNIQUE CLARITY AND PROPORTION HAVE BEEN STOLEN FROM MUSEUMS AND PRIVATE COLLECTIONS THROUGHOUT THE UNITED KINGDOM.
THEY'RE TOO CONSPICUOUS TO HAVE BEEN RESOLD, EVEN ON THE BLACK MARKET--AND IT'S DOUBTFUL THEY'VE BEEN CUT DOWN, AS THEY'D SIGNIFICANTLY LOSE THEIR VALUE.
IT WOULD APPEAR, THEREFORE, THEY WERE BEING STOLEN TO ORDER.
THE WHITE STAR WAS PERFECT BAIT TO CHIVY THE THIEF OUT INTO THE OPEN.
GREAT BRITAIN WAS CLEARLY THEIR HOME TURF, SO WE WANTED TO CATCH THEM OFF GUARD, PLACE IT WHERE WE HAD COMMAND OF THE FIELD OF PLAY.
THE ORIGINAL IS STILL SAFELY UNDER LOCK AND KEY IN THE TOWER OF LONDON.
NOW THAT IS INTERESTING! PRAY TELL ME MORE, MR. STEED!
GOTHAM SEEMED LIKE A PERFECT FIT, AS WE WERE ALREADY WORKING CLOSELY WITH INSPECTOR GORDON OF SCOTLAND YARD.
WHO, AS YOU KNOW, IS MY COUSIN. HE CONTACTED ME AND I MADE THE NECESSARY ARRANGEMENTS HERE.

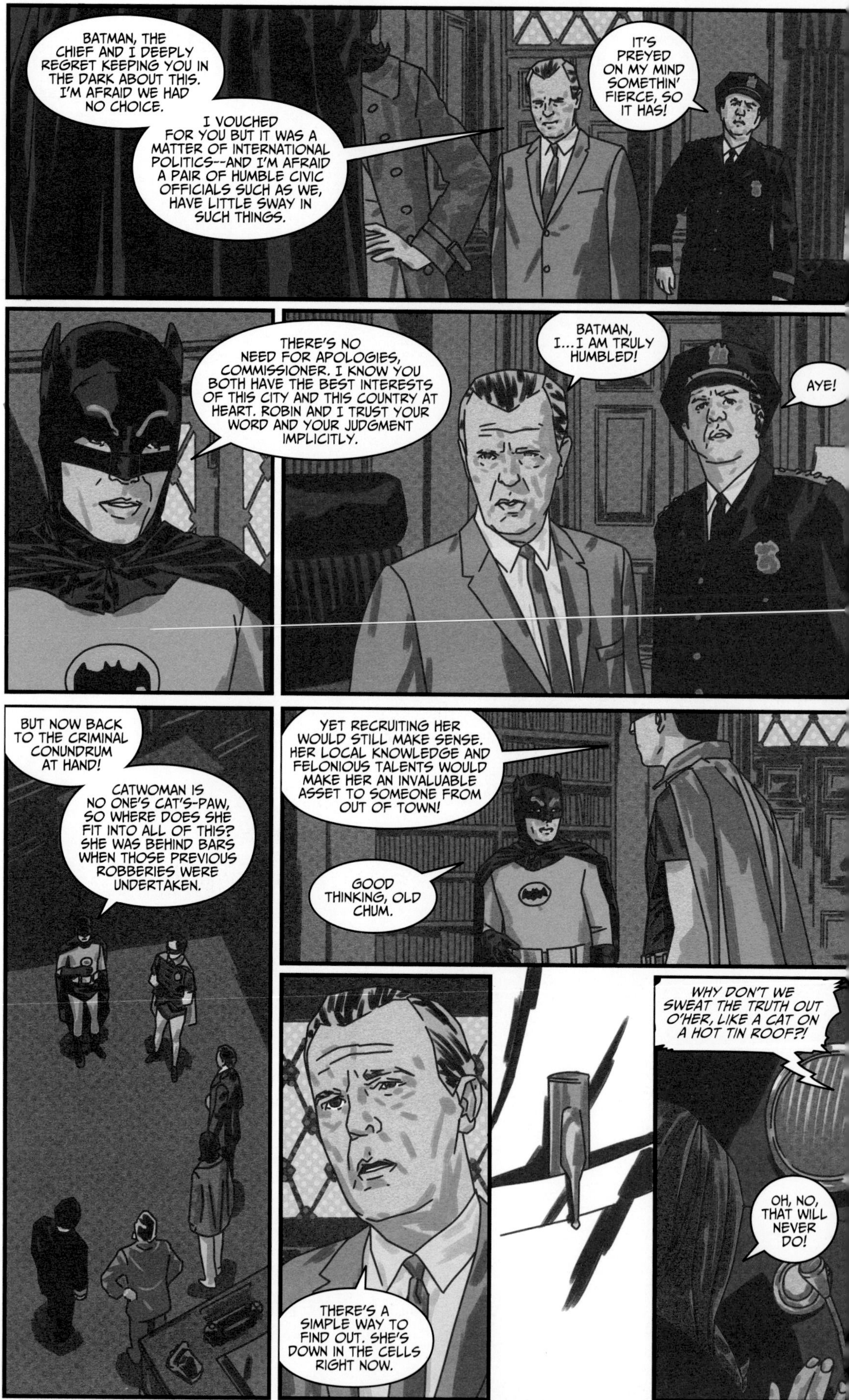
BATMAN, THE CHIEF AND I DEEPLY REGRET KEEPING YOU IN THE DARK ABOUT THIS. I'M AFRAID WE HAD NO CHOICE.
I VOUCHED FOR YOU BUT IT WAS A MATTER OF INTERNATIONAL POLITICS--AND I'M AFRAID A PAIR OF HUMBLE CIVIC OFFICIALS SUCH AS WE, HAVE LITTLE SWAY IN SUCH THINGS.
IT'S PREYED ON MY MIND SOMETHIN' FIERCE, SO IT HAS!
THERE'S NO NEED FOR APOLOGIES, COMMISSIONER. I KNOW YOU BOTH HAVE THE BEST INTERESTS OF THIS CITY AND THIS COUNTRY AT HEART. ROBIN AND I TRUST YOUR WORD AND YOUR JUDGMENT IMPLICITLY.
BATMAN, I...I AM TRULY HUMBLED!
AYE!
BUT NOW BACK TO THE CRIMINAL CONUNDRUM AT HAND!
CATWOMAN IS NO ONE'S CAT'S-PAW, SO WHERE DOES SHE FIT INTO ALL OF THIS? SHE WAS BEHIND BARS WHEN THOSE PREVIOUS ROBBERIES WERE UNDERTAKEN.
YET RECRUITING HER WOULD STILL MAKE SENSE. HER LOCAL KNOWLEDGE AND FELONIOUS TALENTS WOULD MAKE HER AN INVALUABLE ASSET TO SOMEONE FROM OUT OF TOWN!
GOOD THINKING, OLD CHUM.
THERE'S A SIMPLE WAY TO FIND OUT. SHE'S DOWN IN THE CELLS RIGHT NOW.
WHY DON'T WE SWEAT THE TRUTH OUT O'HER, LIKE A CAT ON A HOT TIN ROOF?!
OH, NO, THAT WILL NEVER DO!

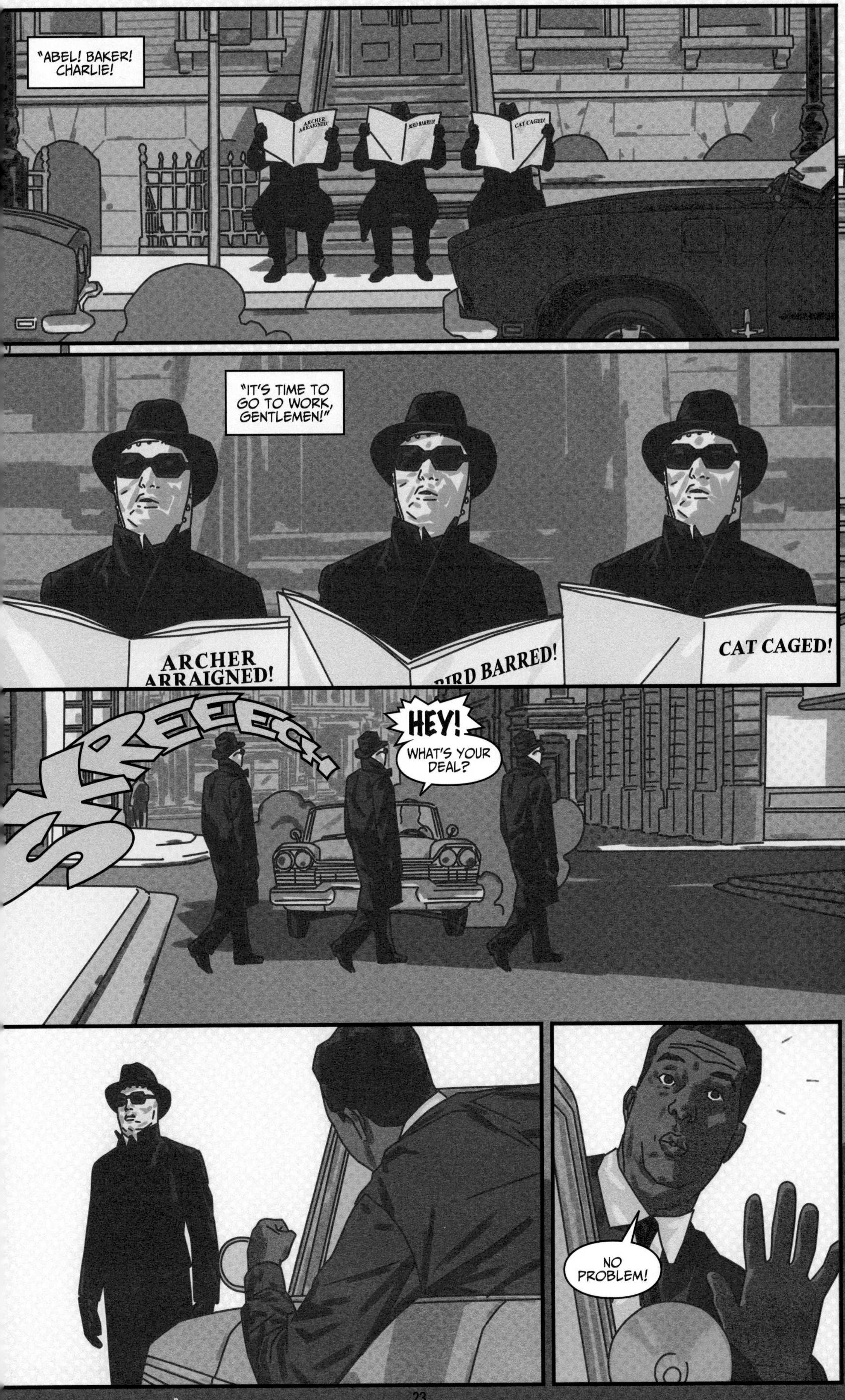
"ABEL! BAKER! CHARLIE!
ARCHER ARRAIGNED!
BIRD BARRED!
CAT CAGED!
"IT'S TIME TO GO TO WORK, GENTLEMEN!"
ARCHER ARRAIGNED!
BIRD BARRED!
CAT CAGED!
SKREEECH!
HEY! WHAT'S YOUR DEAL?
NO PROBLEM!

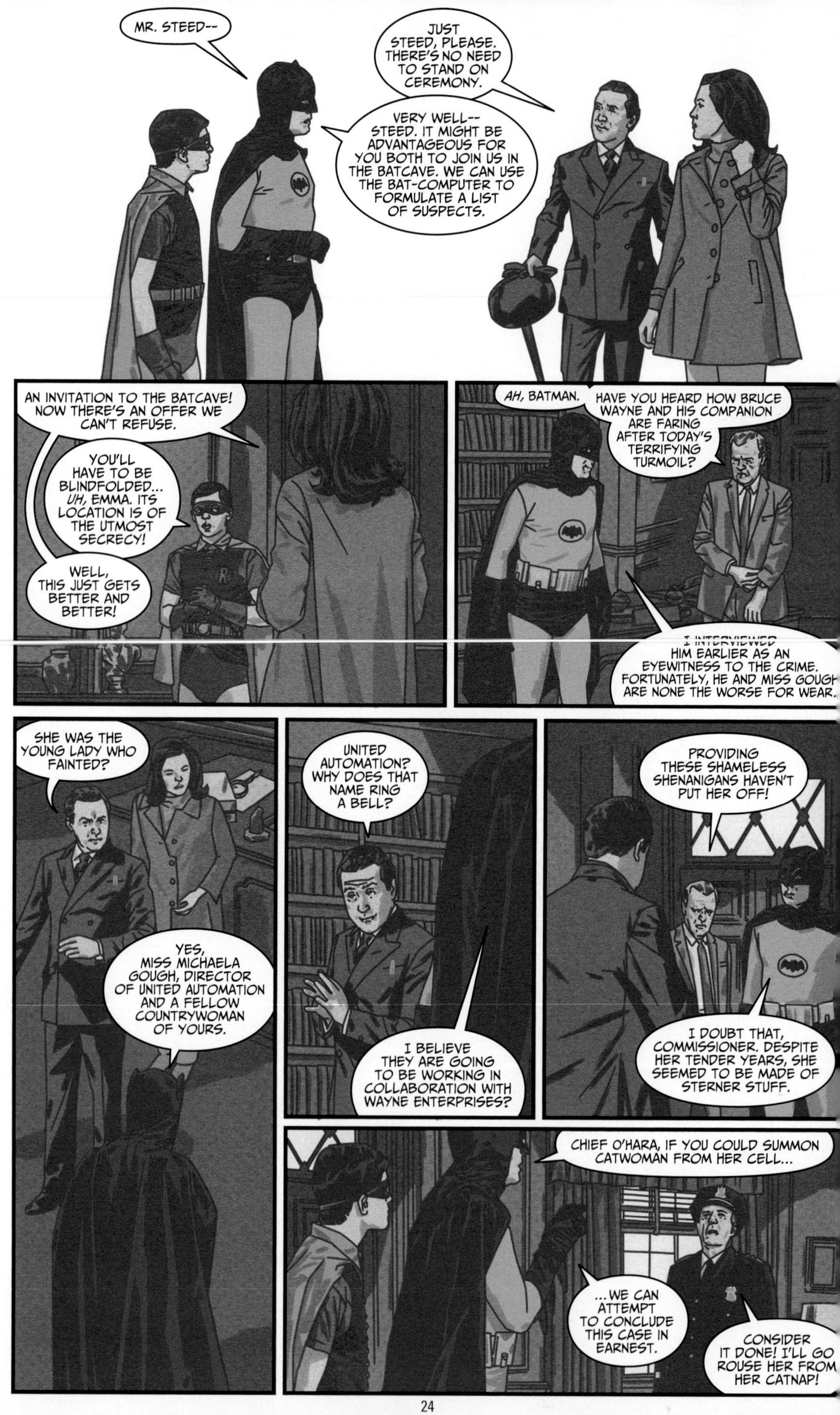

MR. STEED--
JUST STEED, PLEASE. THERE'S NO NEED TO STAND ON CEREMONY.
VERY WELL-- STEED. IT MIGHT BE ADVANTAGEOUS FOR YOU BOTH TO JOIN US IN THE BATCAVE. WE CAN USE THE BAT-COMPUTER TO FORMULATE A LIST OF SUSPECTS.
AN INVITATION TO THE BATCAVE! NOW THERE'S AN OFFER WE CAN'T REFUSE.
YOU'LL HAVE TO BE BLINDFOLDED... *UH,* EMMA. ITS LOCATION IS OF THE UTMOST SECRECY!
WELL, THIS JUST GETS BETTER AND BETTER!
AH, BATMAN.
HAVE YOU HEARD HOW BRUCE WAYNE AND HIS COMPANION ARE FARING AFTER TODAY'S TERRIFYING TURMOIL?
I INTERVIEWED HIM EARLIER AS AN EYEWITNESS TO THE CRIME. FORTUNATELY, HE AND MISS GOUGH ARE NONE THE WORSE FOR WEAR.
SHE WAS THE YOUNG LADY WHO FAINTED?
YES, MISS MICHAELA GOUGH, DIRECTOR OF UNITED AUTOMATION AND A FELLOW COUNTRYWOMAN OF YOURS.
UNITED AUTOMATION? WHY DOES THAT NAME RING A BELL?
I BELIEVE THEY ARE GOING TO BE WORKING IN COLLABORATION WITH WAYNE ENTERPRISES?
PROVIDING THESE SHAMELESS SHENANIGANS HAVEN'T PUT HER OFF!
I DOUBT THAT, COMMISSIONER. DESPITE HER TENDER YEARS, SHE SEEMED TO BE MADE OF STERNER STUFF.
CHIEF O'HARA, IF YOU COULD SUMMON CATWOMAN FROM HER CELL...
...WE CAN ATTEMPT TO CONCLUDE THIS CASE IN EARNEST.
CONSIDER IT DONE! I'LL GO ROUSE HER FROM HER CATNAP!

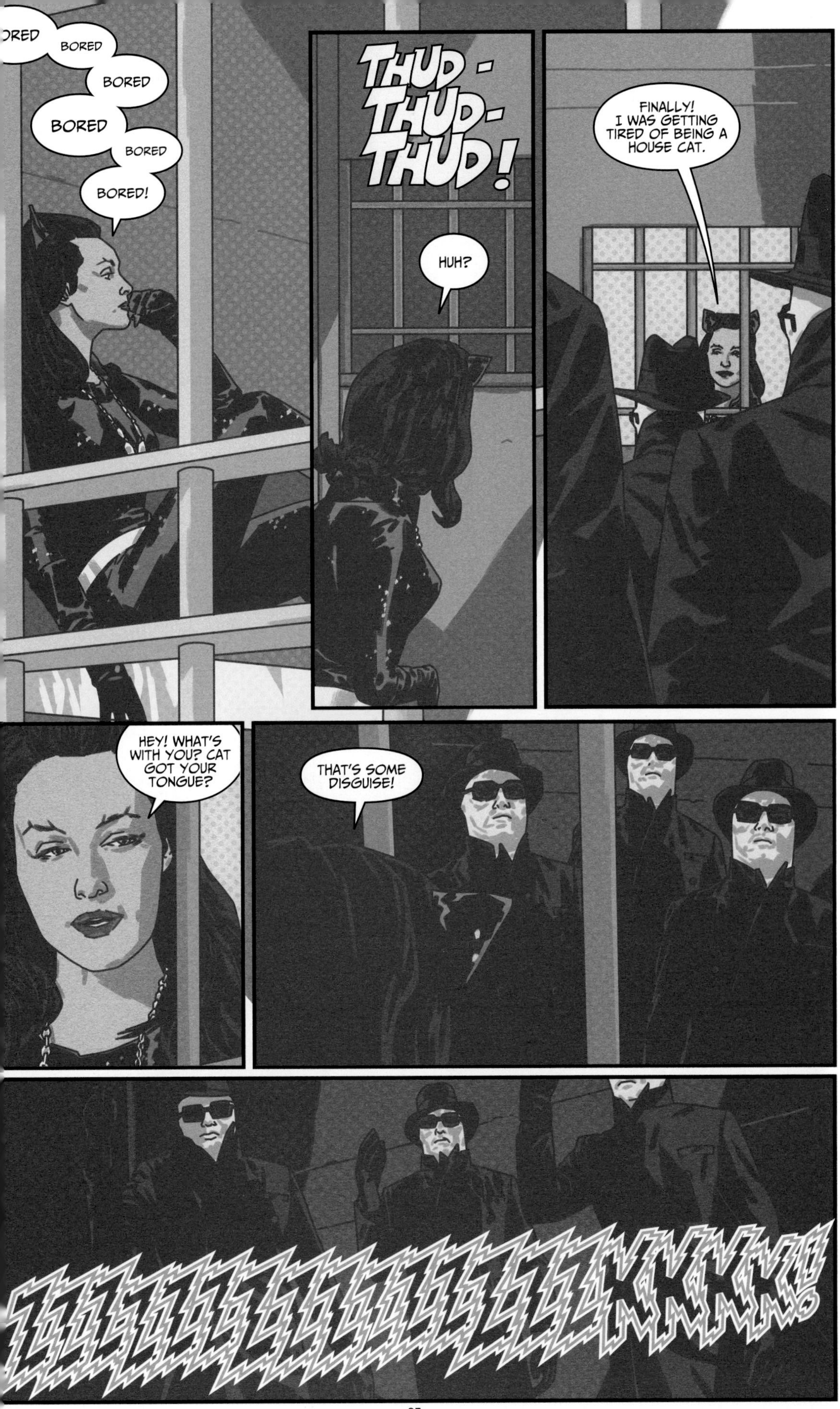

BORED
BORED
BORED
BORED
BORED
BORED!
THUD-THUD-THUD!
HUH?
FINALLY! I WAS GETTING TIRED OF BEING A HOUSE CAT.
HEY! WHAT'S WITH YOU? CAT GOT YOUR TONGUE?
THAT'S SOME DISGUISE!
ZZZZZZZZZZZZZKKK!

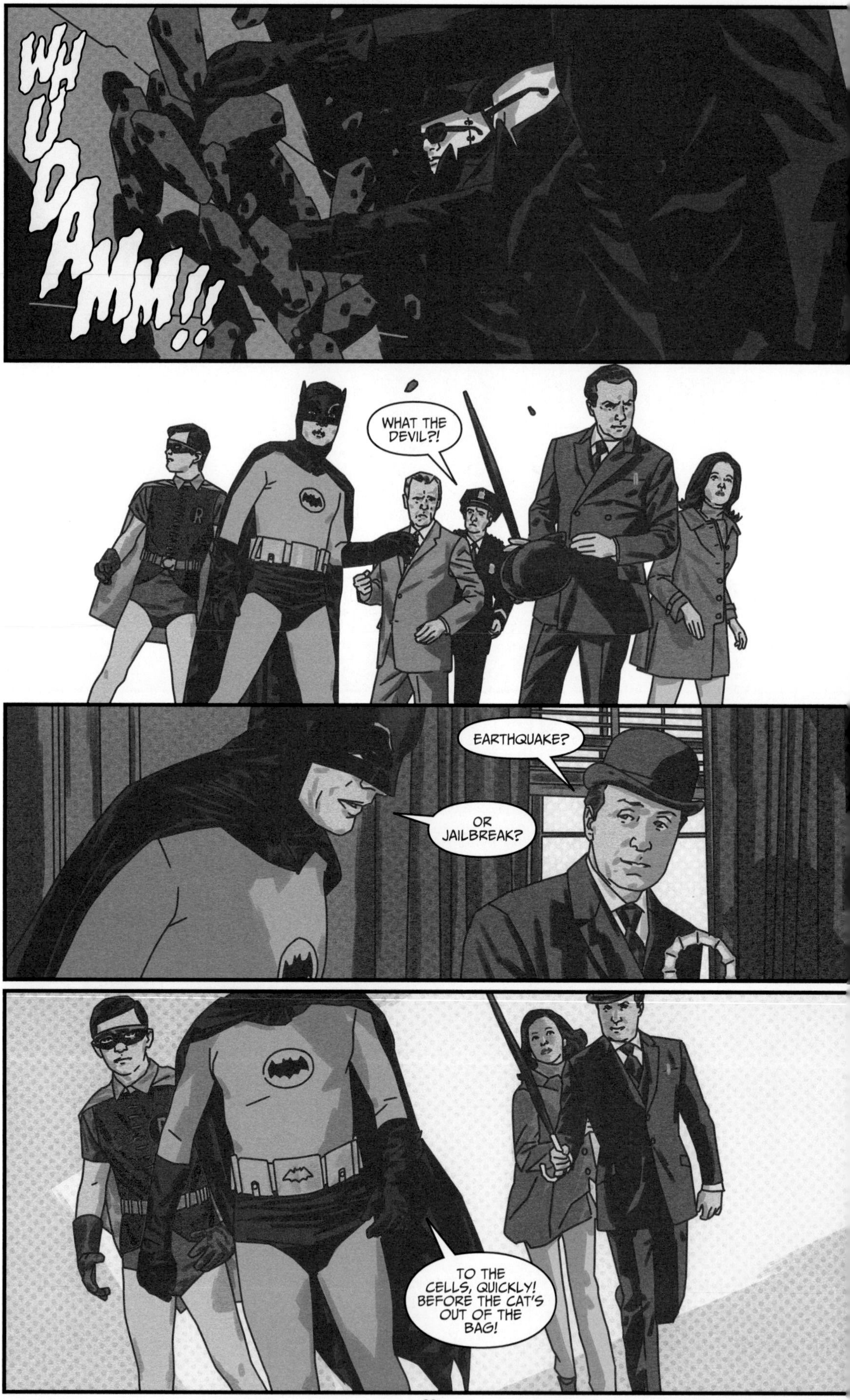
WHUDAMM!!!
WHAT THE DEVIL?!
EARTHQUAKE?
OR JAILBREAK?
TO THE CELLS, QUICKLY! BEFORE THE CAT'S OUT OF THE BAG!

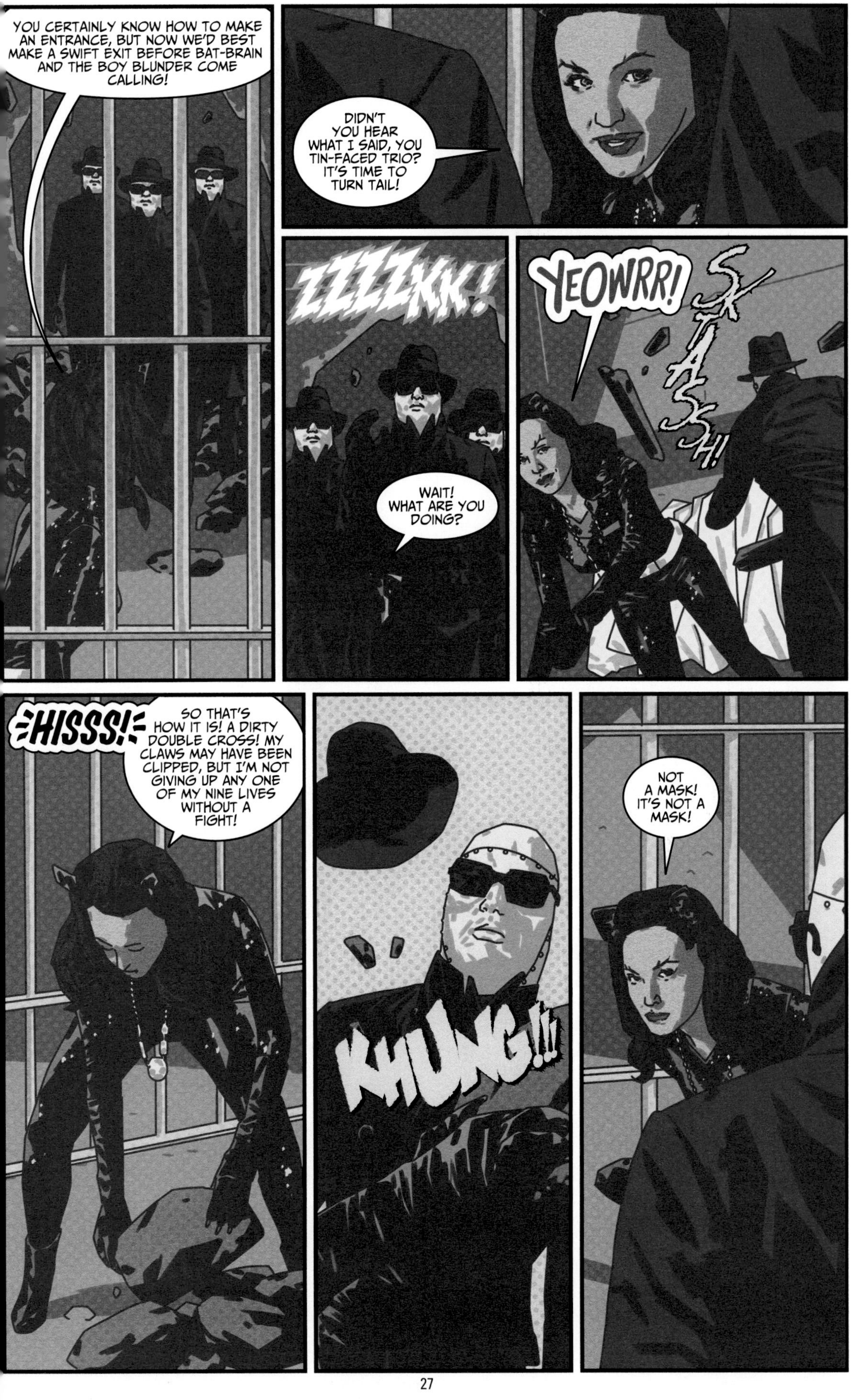
YOU CERTAINLY KNOW HOW TO MAKE AN ENTRANCE, BUT NOW WE'D BEST MAKE A SWIFT EXIT BEFORE BAT-BRAIN AND THE BOY BLUNDER COME CALLING!
DIDN'T YOU HEAR WHAT I SAID, YOU TIN-FACED TRIO? IT'S TIME TO TURN TAIL!
ZZZZKK!
WAIT! WHAT ARE YOU DOING?
YEOWRR!
SKLASSH!
HISSS!
SO THAT'S HOW IT IS! A DIRTY DOUBLE CROSS! MY CLAWS MAY HAVE BEEN CLIPPED, BUT I'M NOT GIVING UP ANY ONE OF MY NINE LIVES WITHOUT A FIGHT!
KHUNG!!!
NOT A MASK! IT'S NOT A MASK!

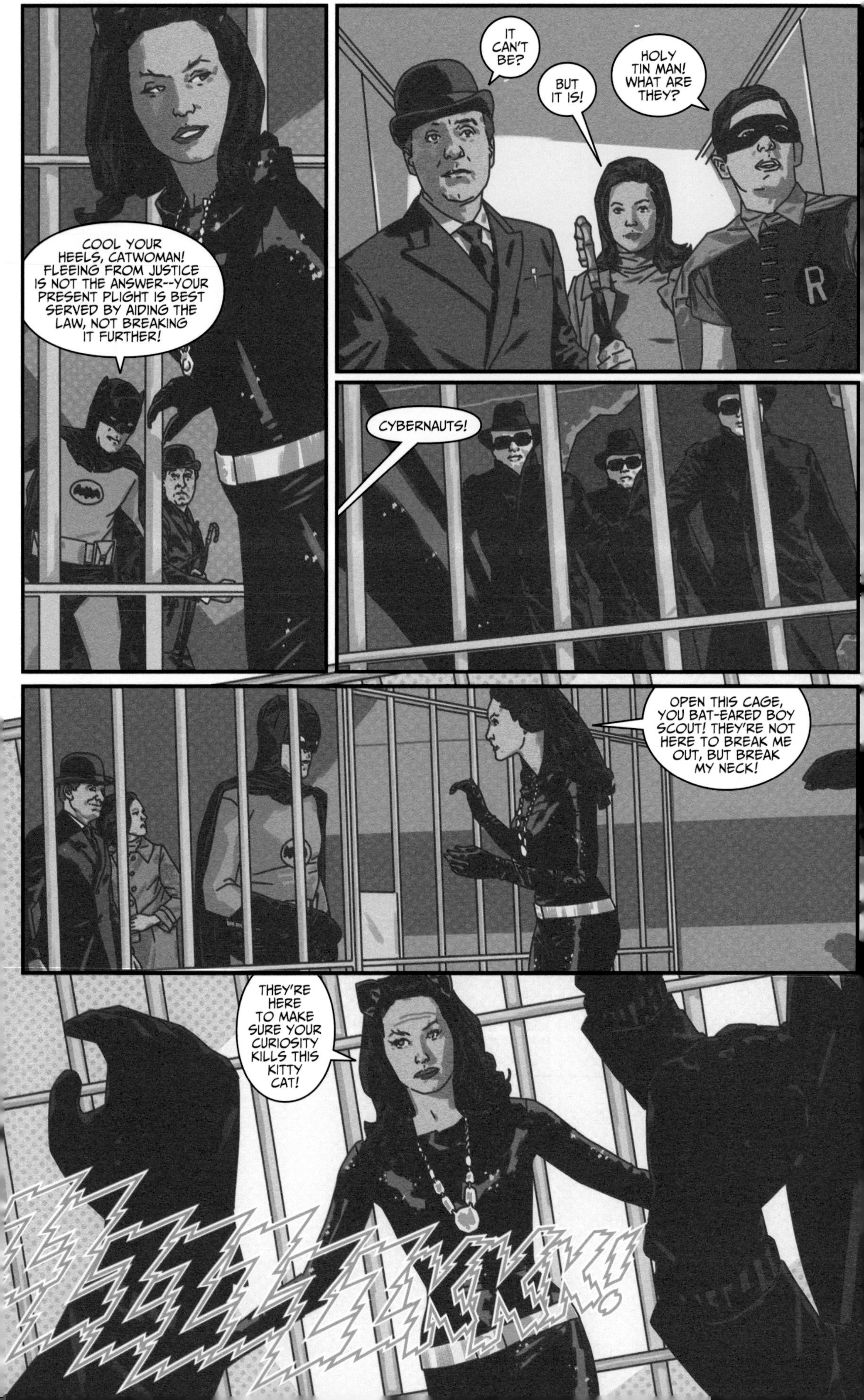
COOL YOUR HEELS, CATWOMAN! FLEEING FROM JUSTICE IS NOT THE ANSWER--YOUR PRESENT PLIGHT IS BEST SERVED BY AIDING THE LAW, NOT BREAKING IT FURTHER!
IT CAN'T BE?
BUT IT IS!
HOLY TIN MAN! WHAT ARE THEY?
CYBERNAUTS!
OPEN THIS CAGE, YOU BAT-EARED BOY SCOUT! THEY'RE NOT HERE TO BREAK ME OUT, BUT BREAK MY NECK!
THEY'RE HERE TO MAKE SURE YOUR CURIOSITY KILLS THIS KITTY CAT!
ZZZZAKKK!

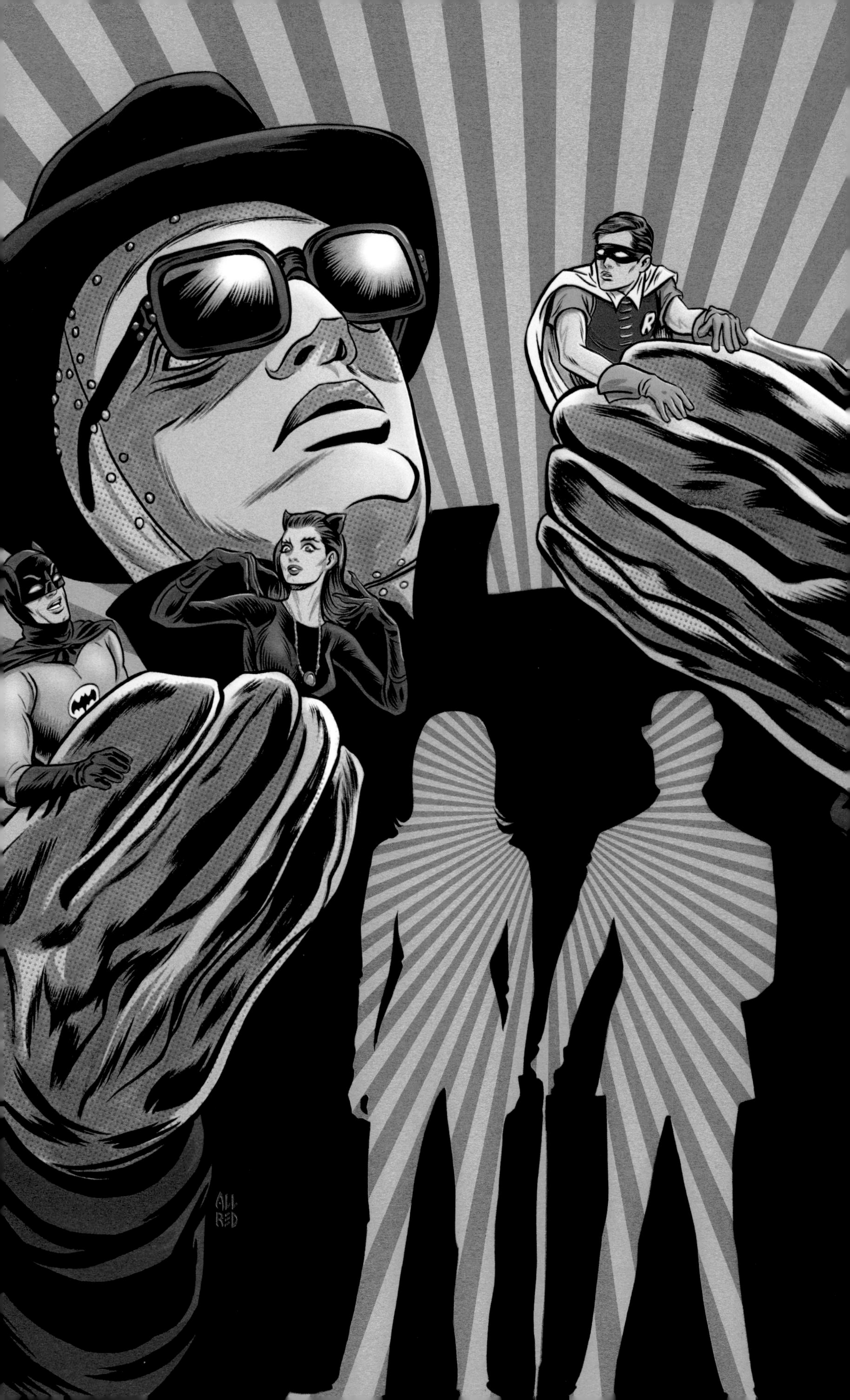
ALL
RED

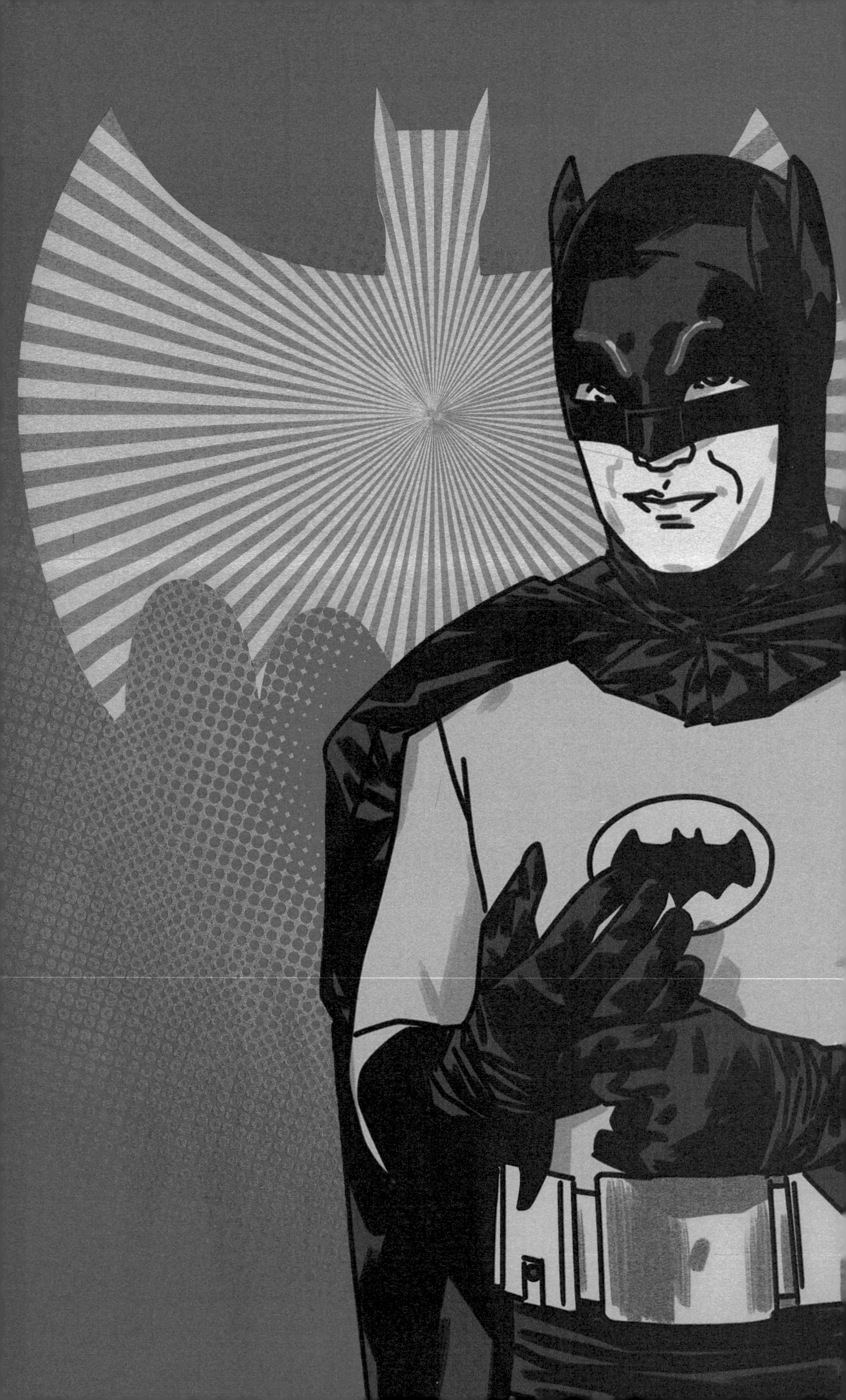

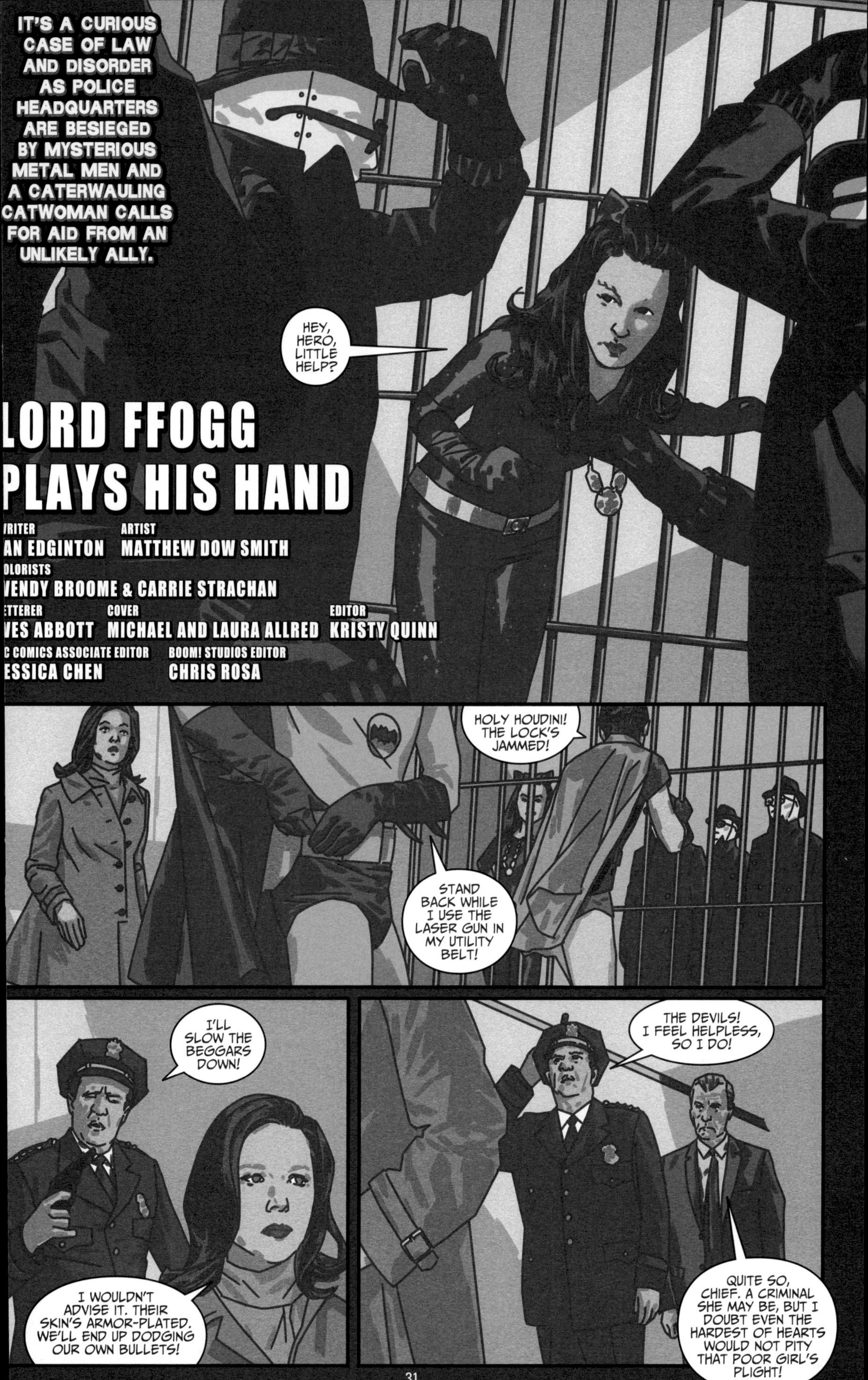
IT'S A CURIOUS CASE OF LAW AND DISORDER AS POLICE HEADQUARTERS ARE BESIEGED BY MYSTERIOUS METAL MEN AND A CATERWAULING CATWOMAN CALLS FOR AID FROM AN UNLIKELY ALLY.
HEY, HERO, LITTLE HELP?
LORD FFOGG PLAYS HIS HAND
RITER AN EDGINTON
ARTIST MATTHEW DOW SMITH
OLORISTS VENDY BROOME & CARRIE STRACHAN
ETTERER VES ABBOTT
COVER MICHAEL AND LAURA ALLRED
EDITOR KRISTY QUINN
C COMICS ASSOCIATE EDITOR ESSICA CHEN
BOOM! STUDIOS EDITOR CHRIS ROSA
HOLY HOUDINI! THE LOCK'S JAMMED!
STAND BACK WHILE I USE THE LASER GUN IN MY UTILITY BELT!
I'LL SLOW THE BEGGARS DOWN!
I WOULDN'T ADVISE IT. THEIR SKIN'S ARMOR-PLATED. WE'LL END UP DODGING OUR OWN BULLETS!
THE DEVILS! I FEEL HELPLESS, SO I DO!
QUITE SO, CHIEF. A CRIMINAL SHE MAY BE, BUT I DOUBT EVEN THE HARDEST OF HEARTS WOULD NOT PITY THAT POOR GIRL'S PLIGHT!

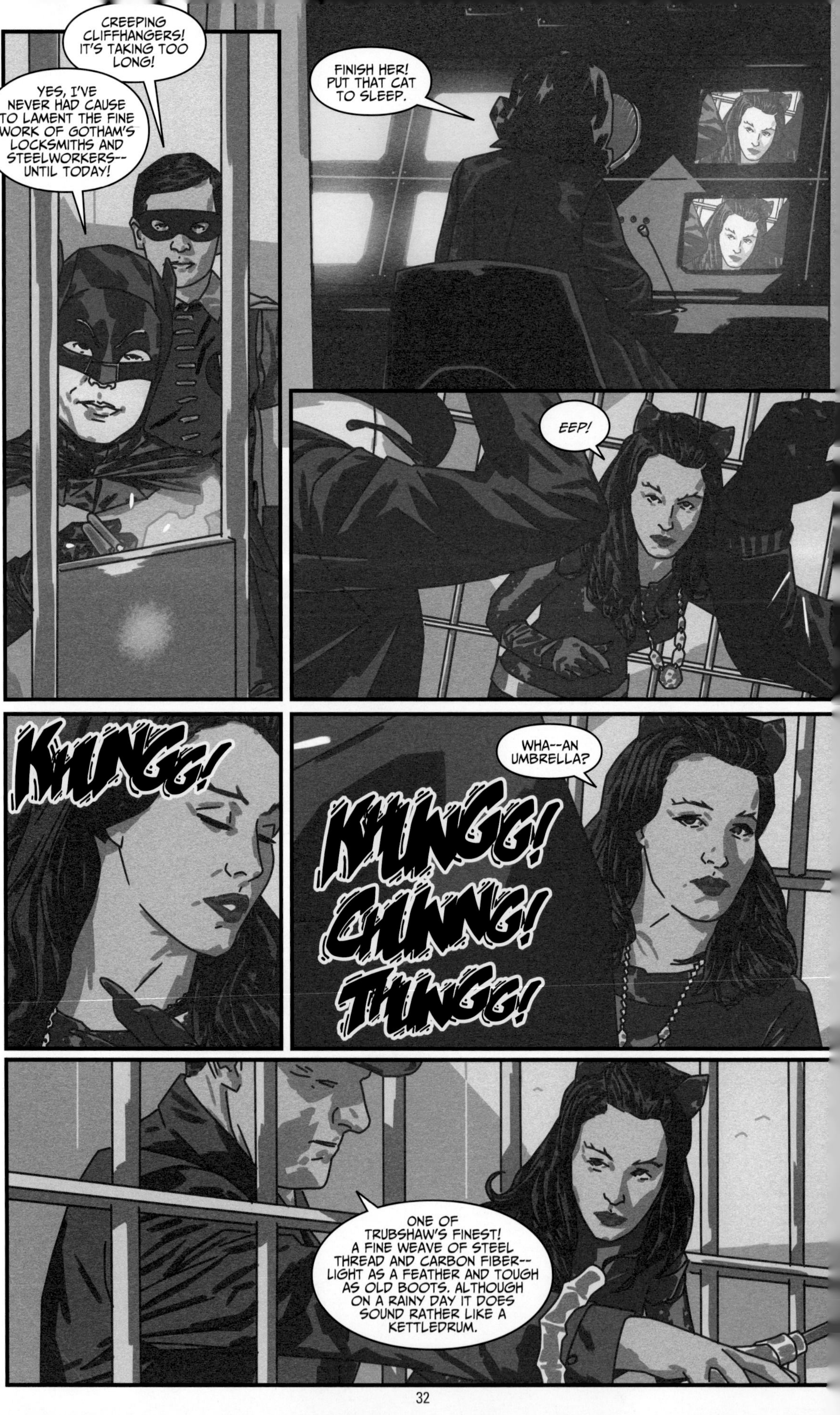
CREEPING CLIFFHANGERS! IT'S TAKING TOO LONG!
YES, I'VE NEVER HAD CAUSE TO LAMENT THE FINE WORK OF GOTHAM'S LOCKSMITHS AND STEELWORKERS-- UNTIL TODAY!
FINISH HER! PUT THAT CAT TO SLEEP.
EEP!
KHUNGG!
WHA--AN UMBRELLA?
KHUNGG! CHUNNG! THUNGG!
ONE OF TRUBSHAW'S FINEST! A FINE WEAVE OF STEEL THREAD AND CARBON FIBER-- LIGHT AS A FEATHER AND TOUGH AS OLD BOOTS. ALTHOUGH ON A RAINY DAY IT DOES SOUND RATHER LIKE A KETTLEDRUM.

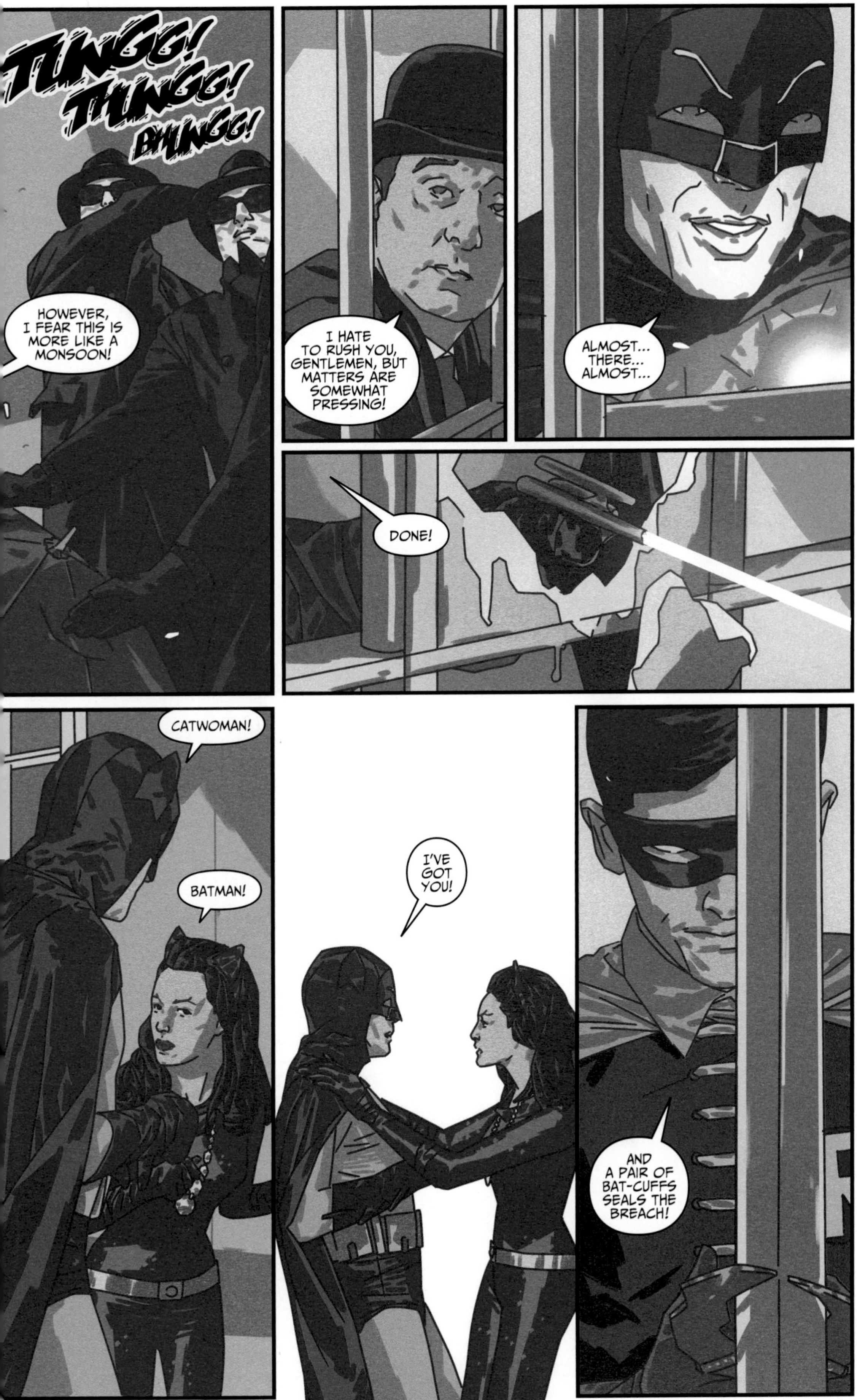
TUNGG! THUNGG! BHUNGG!
HOWEVER, I FEAR THIS IS MORE LIKE A MONSOON!
I HATE TO RUSH YOU, GENTLEMEN, BUT MATTERS ARE SOMEWHAT PRESSING!
ALMOST... THERE... ALMOST...
DONE!
CATWOMAN!
BATMAN!
I'VE GOT YOU!
AND A PAIR OF BAT-CUFFS SEALS THE BREACH!

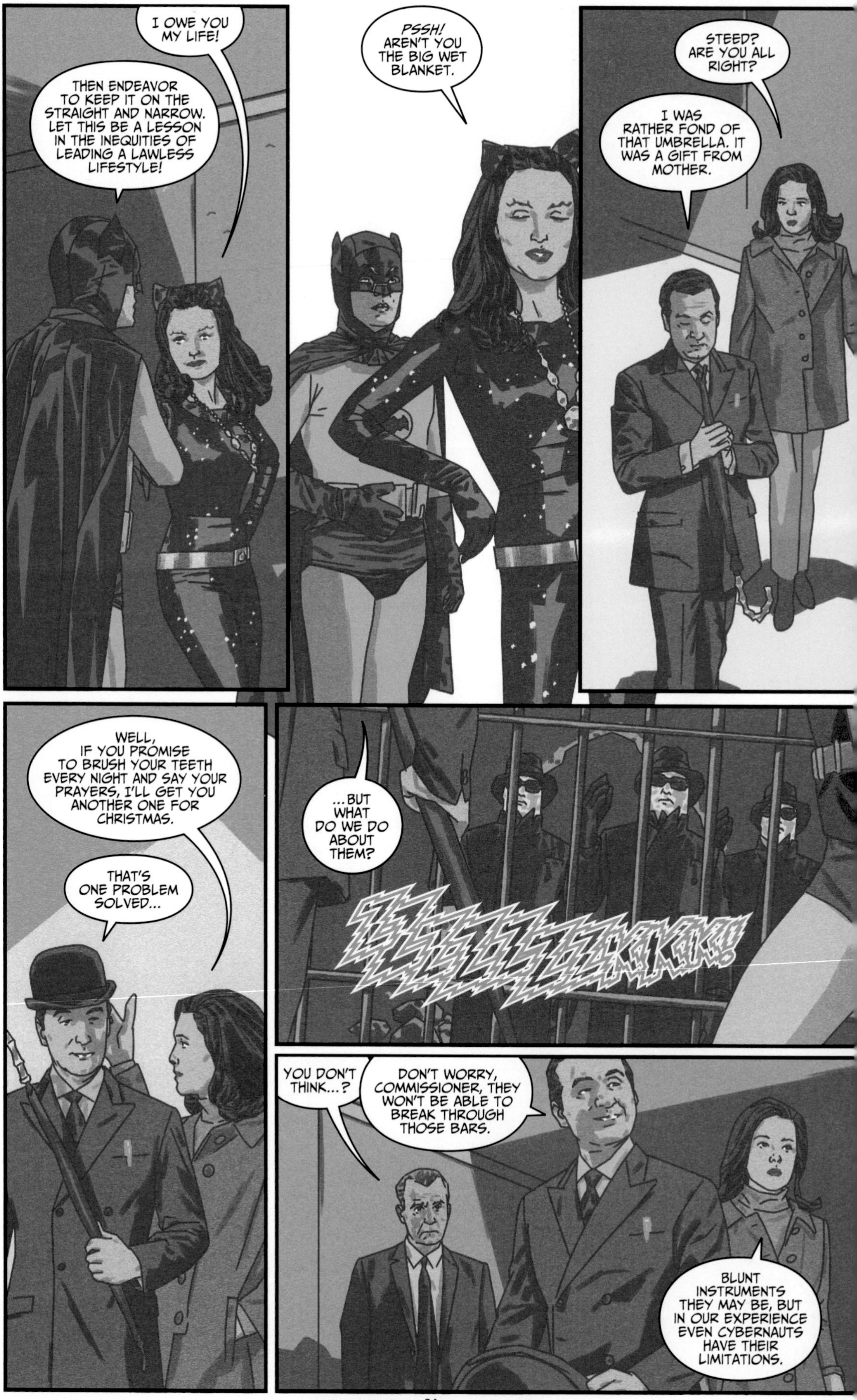
I OWE YOU MY LIFE!
THEN ENDEAVOR TO KEEP IT ON THE STRAIGHT AND NARROW. LET THIS BE A LESSON IN THE INEQUITIES OF LEADING A LAWLESS LIFESTYLE!
PSSH! AREN'T YOU THE BIG WET BLANKET.
STEED? ARE YOU ALL RIGHT?
I WAS RATHER FOND OF THAT UMBRELLA. IT WAS A GIFT FROM MOTHER.
WELL, IF YOU PROMISE TO BRUSH YOUR TEETH EVERY NIGHT AND SAY YOUR PRAYERS, I'LL GET YOU ANOTHER ONE FOR CHRISTMAS.
THAT'S ONE PROBLEM SOLVED...
...BUT WHAT DO WE DO ABOUT THEM?
YOU DON'T THINK...?
DON'T WORRY, COMMISSIONER, THEY WON'T BE ABLE TO BREAK THROUGH THOSE BARS.
BLUNT INSTRUMENTS THEY MAY BE, BUT IN OUR EXPERIENCE EVEN CYBERNAUTS HAVE THEIR LIMITATIONS.

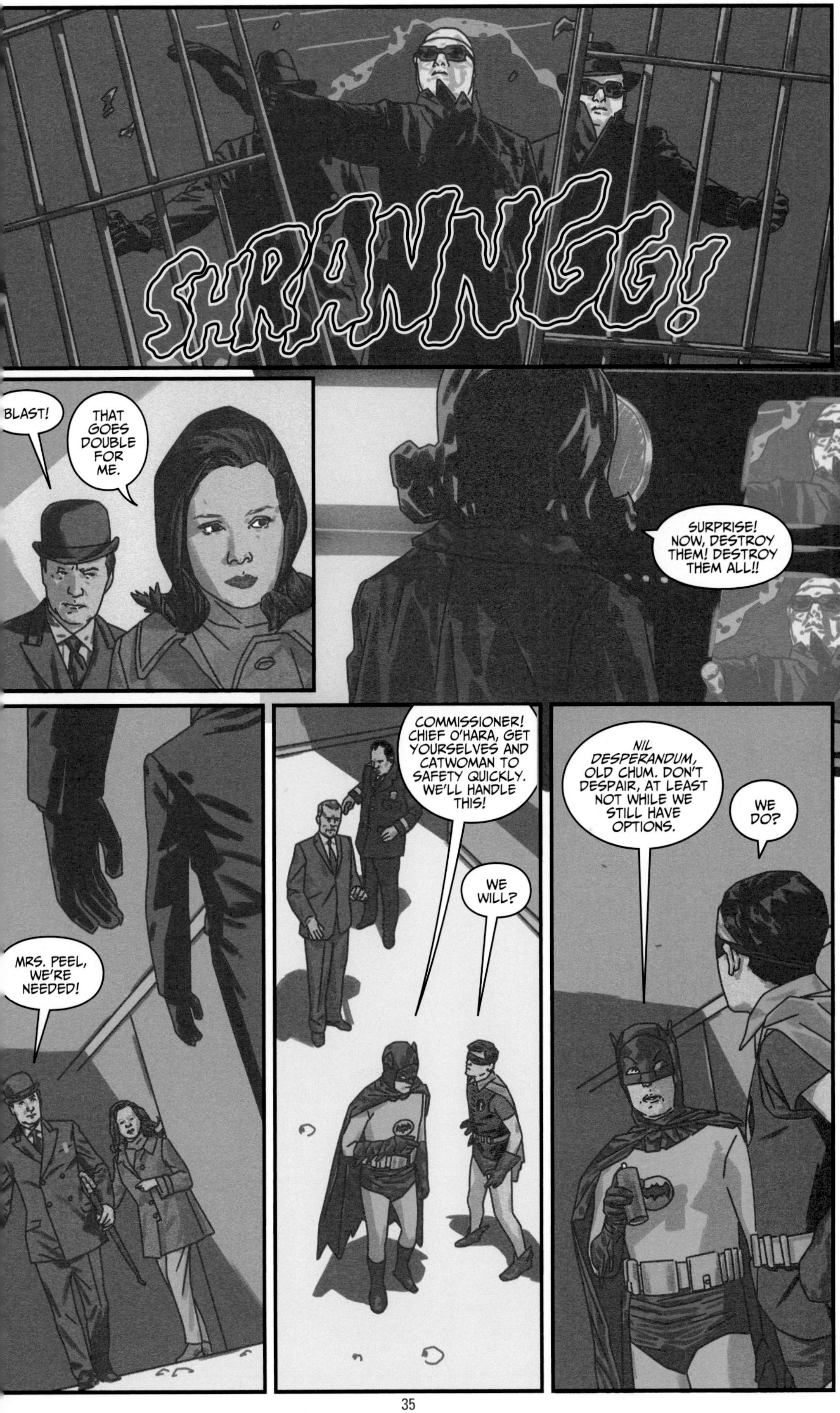
SHRANNGG!
BLAST!
THAT GOES DOUBLE FOR ME.
SURPRISE! NOW, DESTROY THEM! DESTROY THEM ALL!!
MRS. PEEL, WE'RE NEEDED!
COMMISSIONER! CHIEF O'HARA, GET YOURSELVES AND CATWOMAN TO SAFETY QUICKLY. WE'LL HANDLE THIS!
WE WILL?
NIL DESPERANDUM, OLD CHUM. DON'T DESPAIR, AT LEAST NOT WHILE WE STILL HAVE OPTIONS.
WE DO?

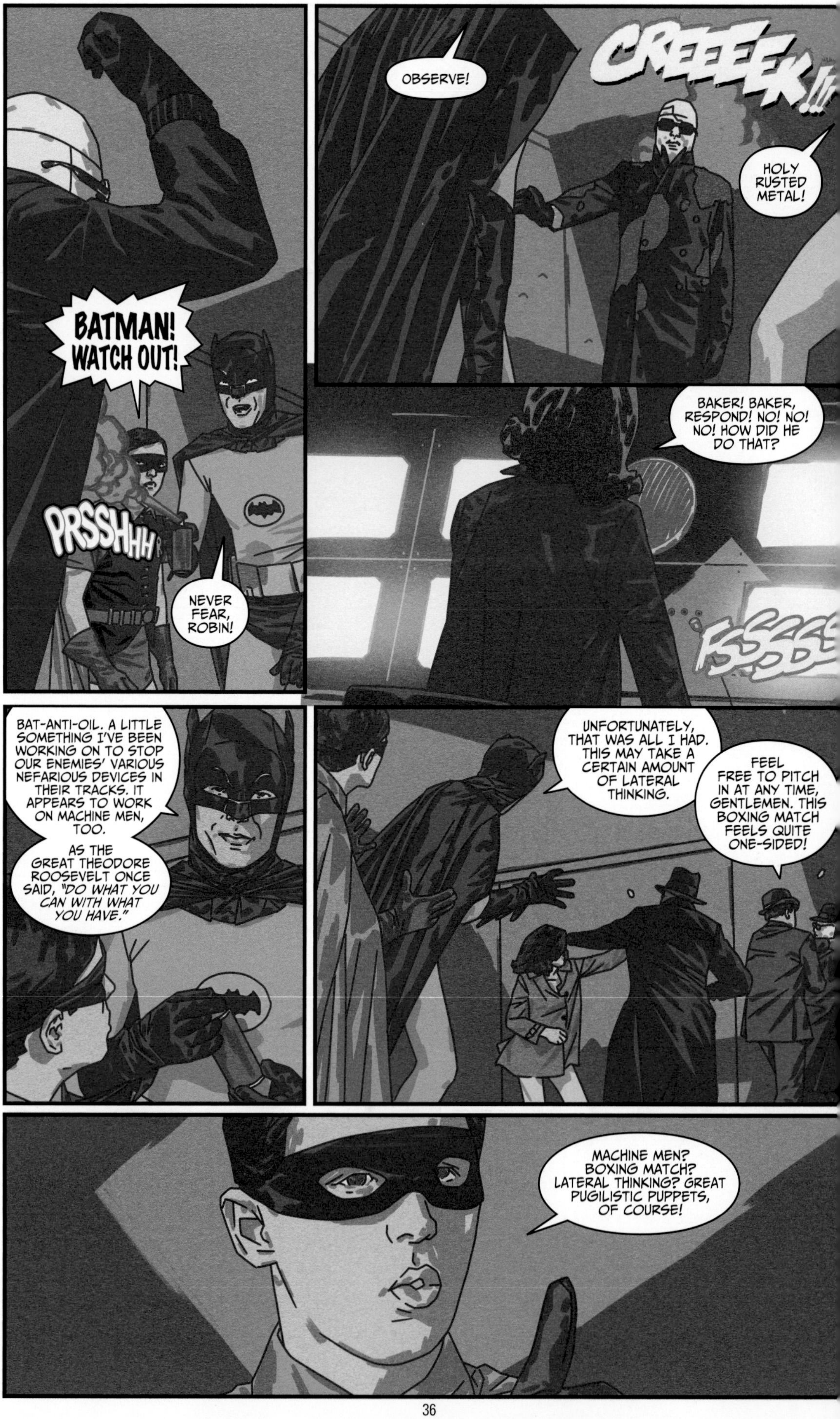
BATMAN! WATCH OUT!
PRSSHHH
NEVER FEAR, ROBIN!
OBSERVE!
CREEEEK!!!
HOLY RUSTED METAL!
BAKER! BAKER, RESPOND! NO! NO! NO! HOW DID HE DO THAT?
FSSSSS
BAT-ANTI-OIL. A LITTLE SOMETHING I'VE BEEN WORKING ON TO STOP OUR ENEMIES' VARIOUS NEFARIOUS DEVICES IN THEIR TRACKS. IT APPEARS TO WORK ON MACHINE MEN, TOO.
AS THE GREAT THEODORE ROOSEVELT ONCE SAID, "DO WHAT YOU CAN WITH WHAT YOU HAVE."
UNFORTUNATELY, THAT WAS ALL I HAD. THIS MAY TAKE A CERTAIN AMOUNT OF LATERAL THINKING.
FEEL FREE TO PITCH IN AT ANY TIME, GENTLEMEN. THIS BOXING MATCH FEELS QUITE ONE-SIDED!
MACHINE MEN? BOXING MATCH? LATERAL THINKING? GREAT PUGILISTIC PUPPETS, OF COURSE!

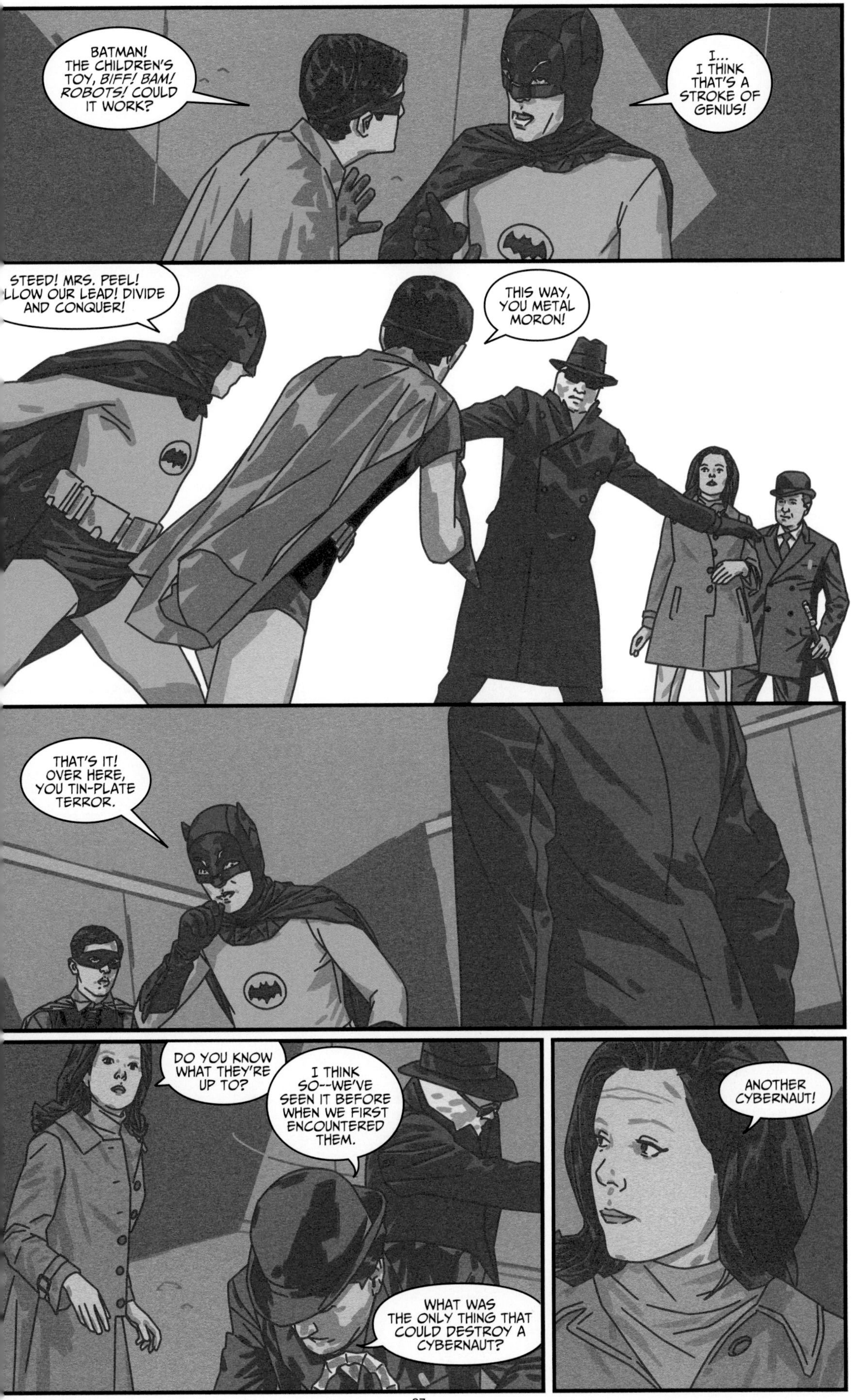
BATMAN! THE CHILDREN'S TOY, BIFF! BAM! ROBOTS! COULD IT WORK?
I... I THINK THAT'S A STROKE OF GENIUS!
STEED! MRS. PEEL! LLOW OUR LEAD! DIVIDE AND CONQUER!
THIS WAY, YOU METAL MORON!
THAT'S IT! OVER HERE, YOU TIN-PLATE TERROR.
DO YOU KNOW WHAT THEY'RE UP TO?
I THINK SO--WE'VE SEEN IT BEFORE WHEN WE FIRST ENCOUNTERED THEM.
WHAT WAS THE ONLY THING THAT COULD DESTROY A CYBERNAUT?
ANOTHER CYBERNAUT!

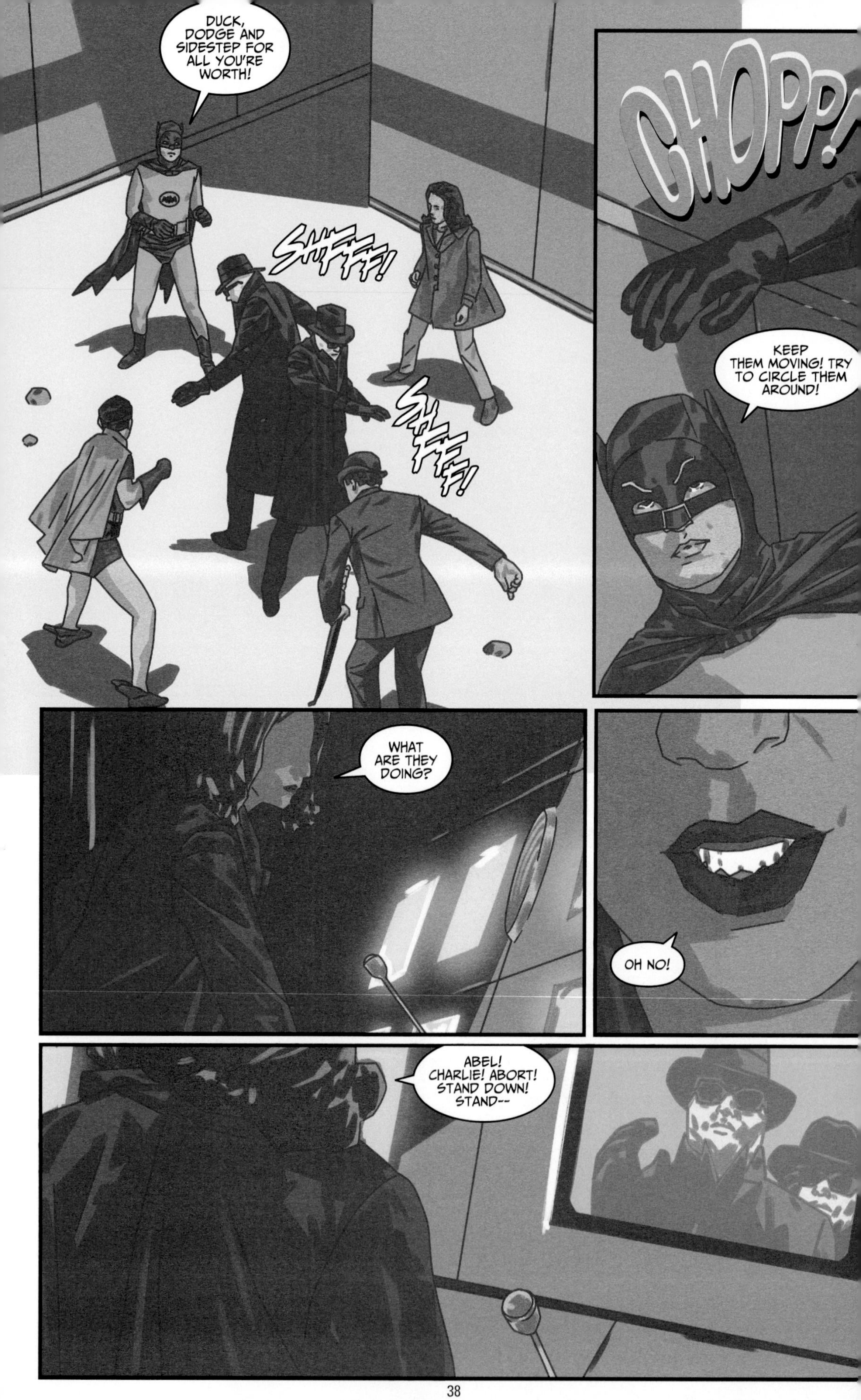
DUCK, DODGE AND SIDESTEP FOR ALL YOU'RE WORTH!
SHFFFF!
SHFFFF!
CHOPP!
KEEP THEM MOVING! TRY TO CIRCLE THEM AROUND!
WHAT ARE THEY DOING?
OH NO!
ABEL! CHARLIE! ABORT! STAND DOWN! STAND--

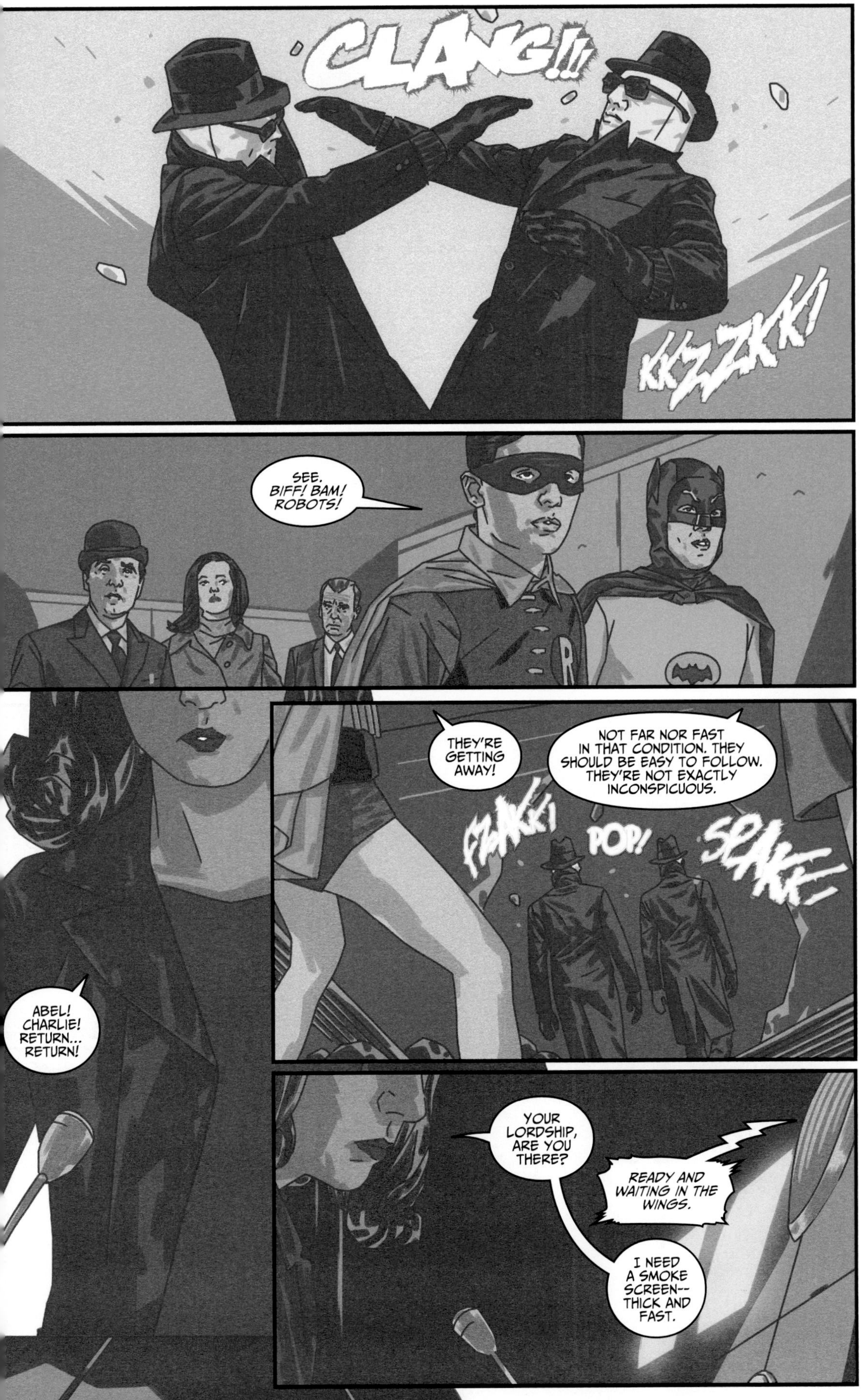
CLANG!!!
KKZZKK!
SEE. BIFF! BAM! ROBOTS!
THEY'RE GETTING AWAY!
NOT FAR NOR FAST IN THAT CONDITION. THEY SHOULD BE EASY TO FOLLOW. THEY'RE NOT EXACTLY INCONSPICUOUS.
POP!
ABEL! CHARLIE! RETURN... RETURN!
YOUR LORDSHIP, ARE YOU THERE?
READY AND WAITING IN THE WINGS.
I NEED A SMOKE SCREEN-- THICK AND FAST.

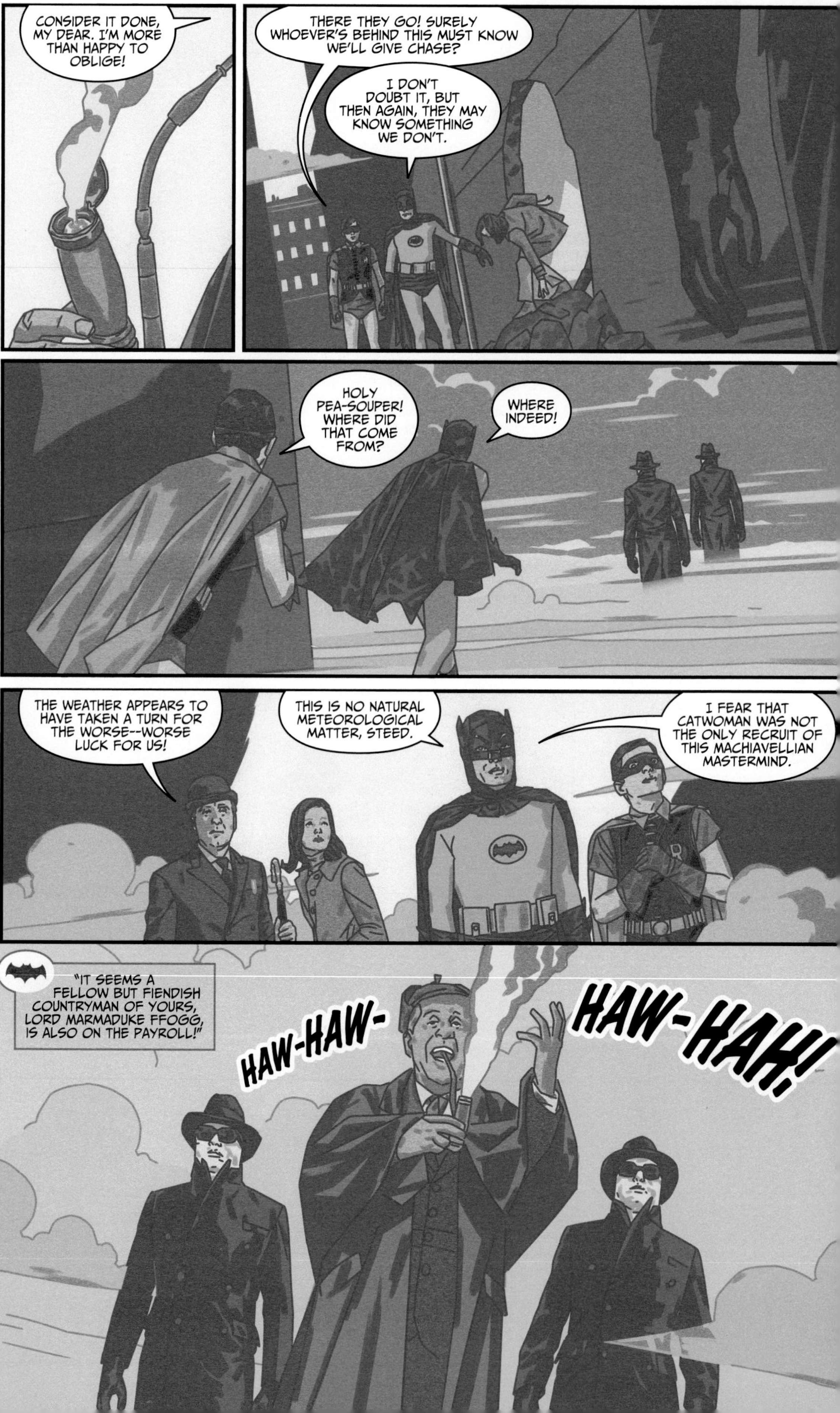
CONSIDER IT DONE, MY DEAR. I'M MORE THAN HAPPY TO OBLIGE!
THERE THEY GO! SURELY WHOEVER'S BEHIND THIS MUST KNOW WE'LL GIVE CHASE?
I DON'T DOUBT IT, BUT THEN AGAIN, THEY MAY KNOW SOMETHING WE DON'T.
HOLY PEA-SOUPER! WHERE DID THAT COME FROM?
WHERE INDEED!
THE WEATHER APPEARS TO HAVE TAKEN A TURN FOR THE WORSE--WORSE LUCK FOR US!
THIS IS NO NATURAL METEOROLOGICAL MATTER, STEED.
I FEAR THAT CATWOMAN WAS NOT THE ONLY RECRUIT OF THIS MACHIAVELLIAN MASTERMIND.
"IT SEEMS A FELLOW BUT FIENDISH COUNTRYMAN OF YOURS, LORD MARMADUKE FFOGG, IS ALSO ON THE PAYROLL!"
HAW-HAW-
HAW-HAH!

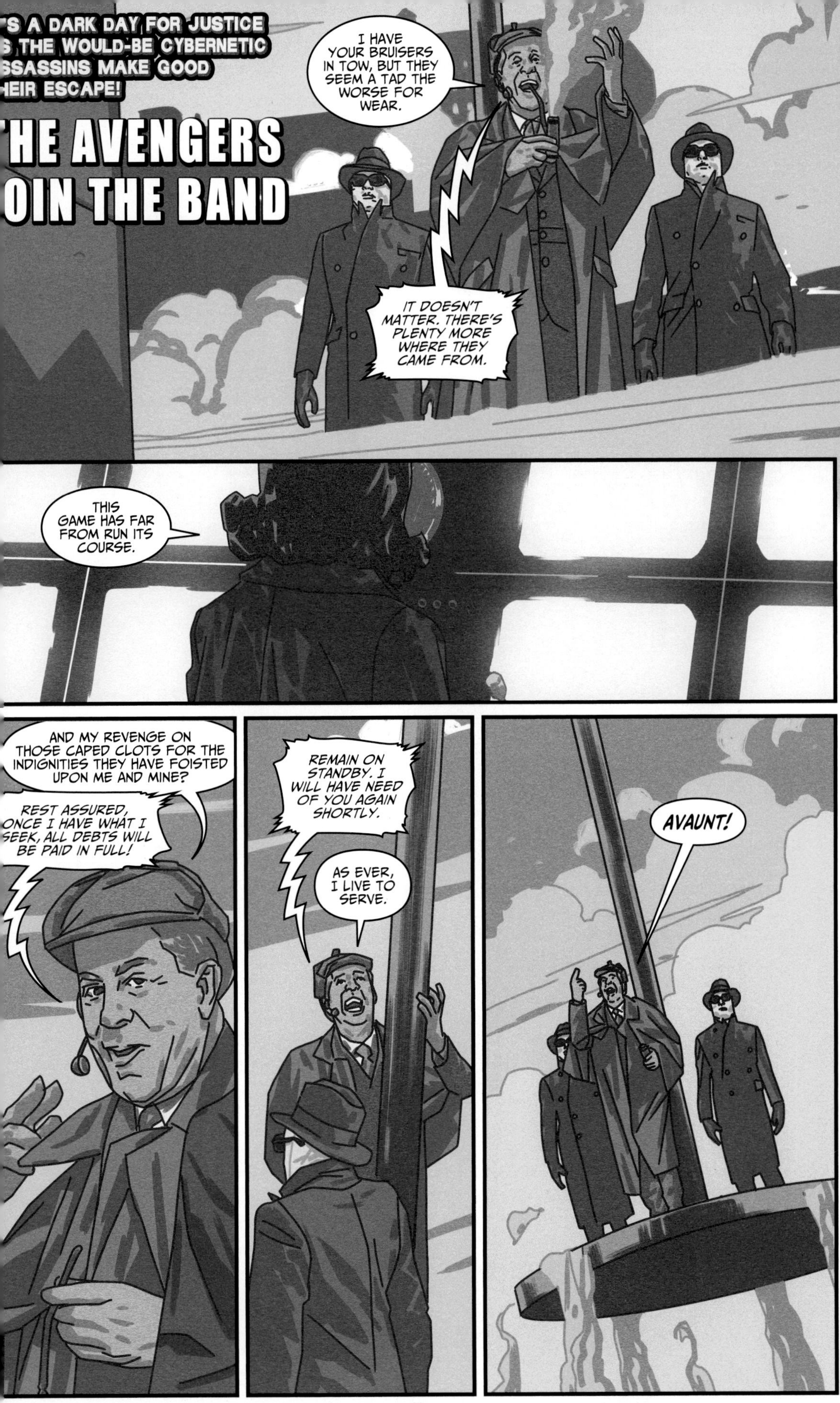
'S A DARK DAY FOR JUSTICE S THE WOULD-BE CYBERNETIC SSASSINS MAKE GOOD HEIR ESCAPE!
'HE AVENGERS OIN THE BAND
I HAVE YOUR BRUISERS IN TOW, BUT THEY SEEM A TAD THE WORSE FOR WEAR.
IT DOESN'T MATTER. THERE'S PLENTY MORE WHERE THEY CAME FROM.
THIS GAME HAS FAR FROM RUN ITS COURSE.
AND MY REVENGE ON THOSE CAPED CLOTS FOR THE INDIGNITIES THEY HAVE FOISTED UPON ME AND MINE?
REST ASSURED, ONCE I HAVE WHAT I SEEK, ALL DEBTS WILL BE PAID IN FULL!
REMAIN ON STANDBY. I WILL HAVE NEED OF YOU AGAIN SHORTLY.
AS EVER, I LIVE TO SERVE.
AVAUNT!

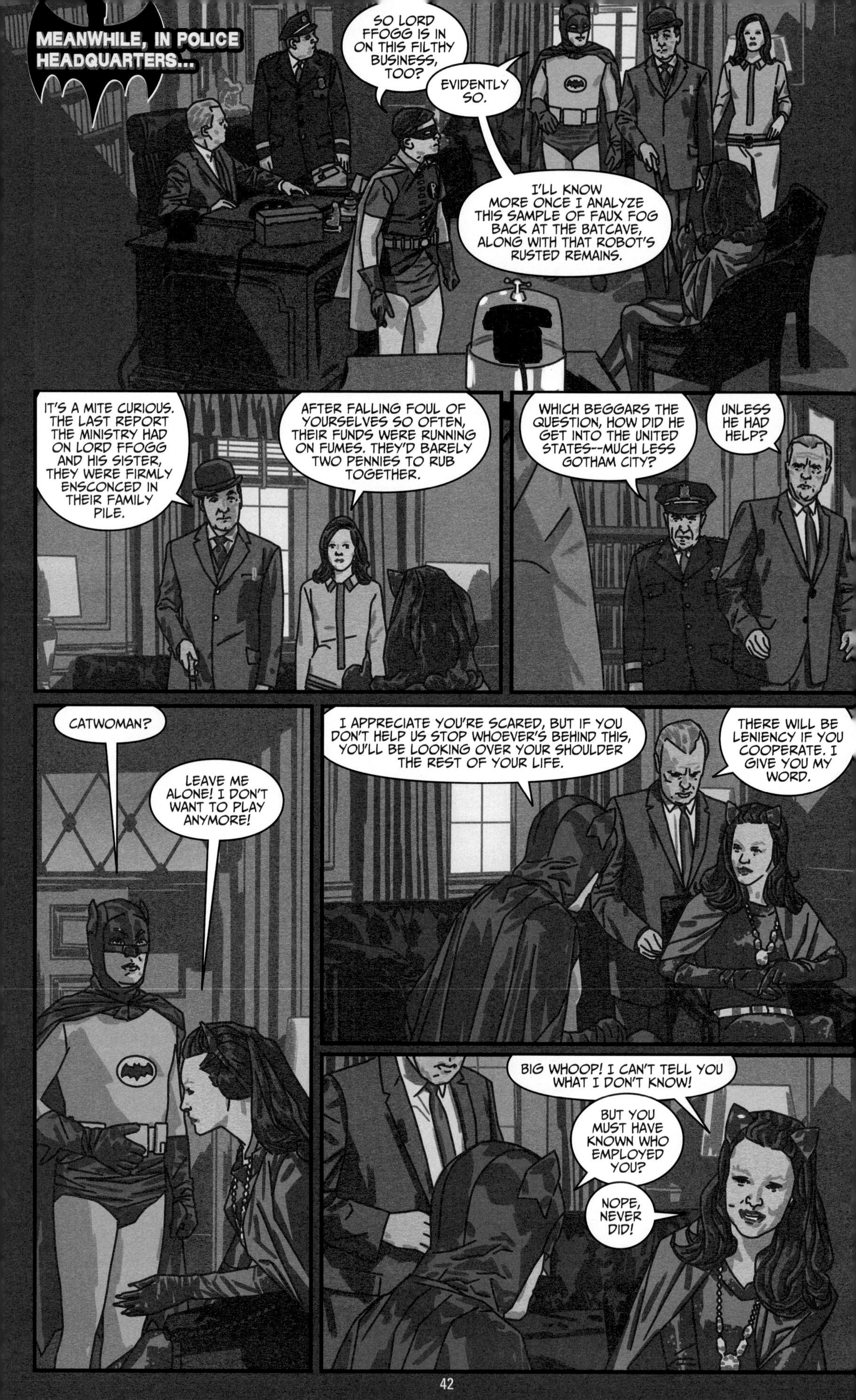
MEANWHILE, IN POLICE HEADQUARTERS...
SO LORD FFOGG IS IN ON THIS FILTHY BUSINESS, TOO?
EVIDENTLY SO.
I'LL KNOW MORE ONCE I ANALYZE THIS SAMPLE OF FAUX FOG BACK AT THE BATCAVE, ALONG WITH THAT ROBOT'S RUSTED REMAINS.
IT'S A MITE CURIOUS. THE LAST REPORT THE MINISTRY HAD ON LORD FFOGG AND HIS SISTER, THEY WERE FIRMLY ENSCONCED IN THEIR FAMILY PILE.
AFTER FALLING FOUL OF YOURSELVES SO OFTEN, THEIR FUNDS WERE RUNNING ON FUMES. THEY'D BARELY TWO PENNIES TO RUB TOGETHER.
WHICH BEGGARS THE QUESTION, HOW DID HE GET INTO THE UNITED STATES--MUCH LESS GOTHAM CITY?
UNLESS HE HAD HELP?
CATWOMAN?
LEAVE ME ALONE! I DON'T WANT TO PLAY ANYMORE!
I APPRECIATE YOU'RE SCARED, BUT IF YOU DON'T HELP US STOP WHOEVER'S BEHIND THIS, YOU'LL BE LOOKING OVER YOUR SHOULDER THE REST OF YOUR LIFE.
THERE WILL BE LENIENCY IF YOU COOPERATE. I GIVE YOU MY WORD.
BIG WHOOP! I CAN'T TELL YOU WHAT I DON'T KNOW!
BUT YOU MUST HAVE KNOWN WHO EMPLOYED YOU?
NOPE, NEVER DID!

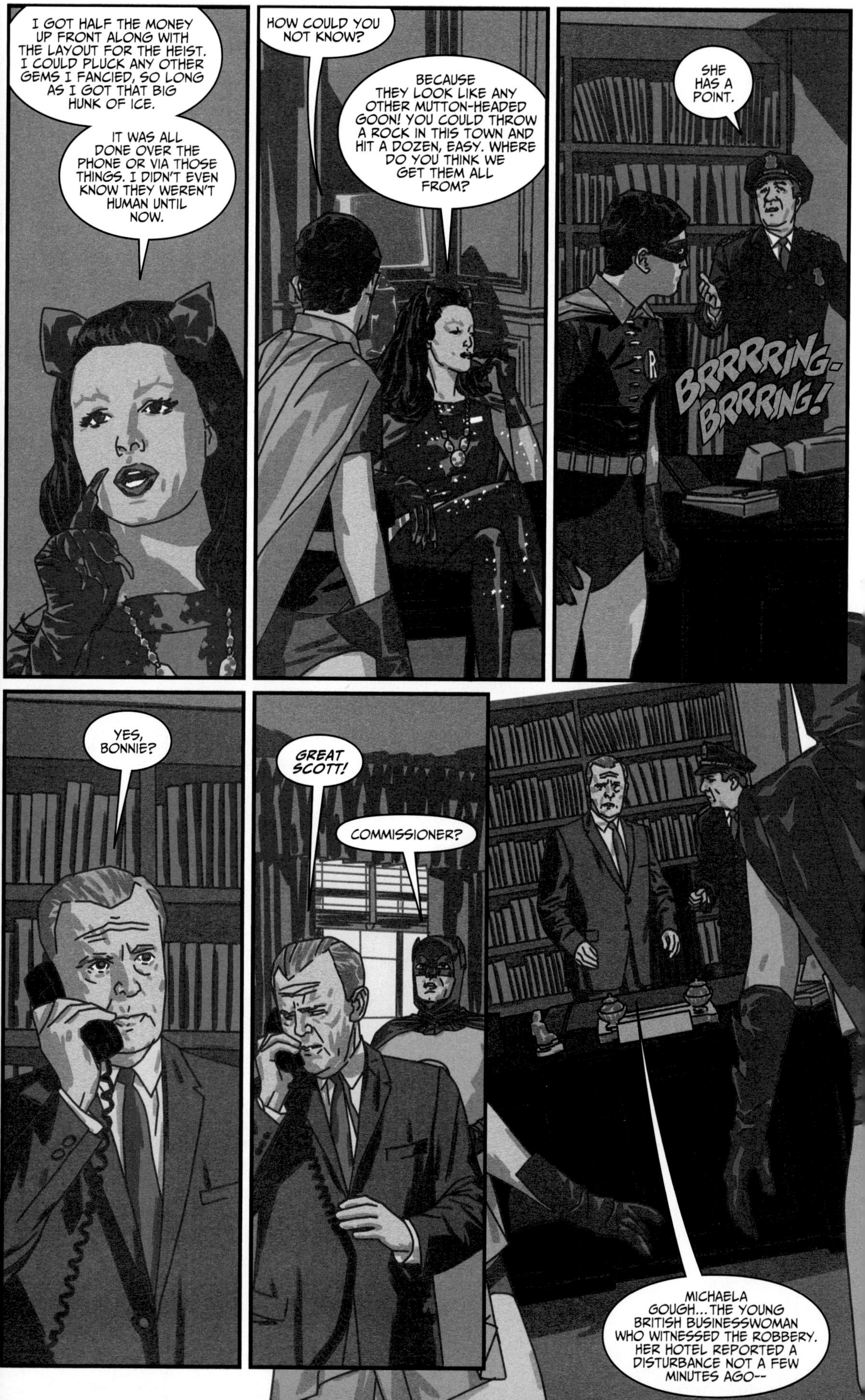
I GOT HALF THE MONEY UP FRONT ALONG WITH THE LAYOUT FOR THE HEIST. I COULD PLUCK ANY OTHER GEMS I FANCIED, SO LONG AS I GOT THAT BIG HUNK OF ICE.
IT WAS ALL DONE OVER THE PHONE OR VIA THOSE THINGS. I DIDN'T EVEN KNOW THEY WEREN'T HUMAN UNTIL NOW.
HOW COULD YOU NOT KNOW?
BECAUSE THEY LOOK LIKE ANY OTHER MUTTON-HEADED GOON! YOU COULD THROW A ROCK IN THIS TOWN AND HIT A DOZEN, EASY. WHERE DO YOU THINK WE GET THEM ALL FROM?
SHE HAS A POINT.
BRRRRING-BRRRING!
YES, BONNIE?
GREAT SCOTT!
COMMISSIONER?
MICHAELA GOUGH... THE YOUNG BRITISH BUSINESSWOMAN WHO WITNESSED THE ROBBERY. HER HOTEL REPORTED A DISTURBANCE NOT A FEW MINUTES AGO--

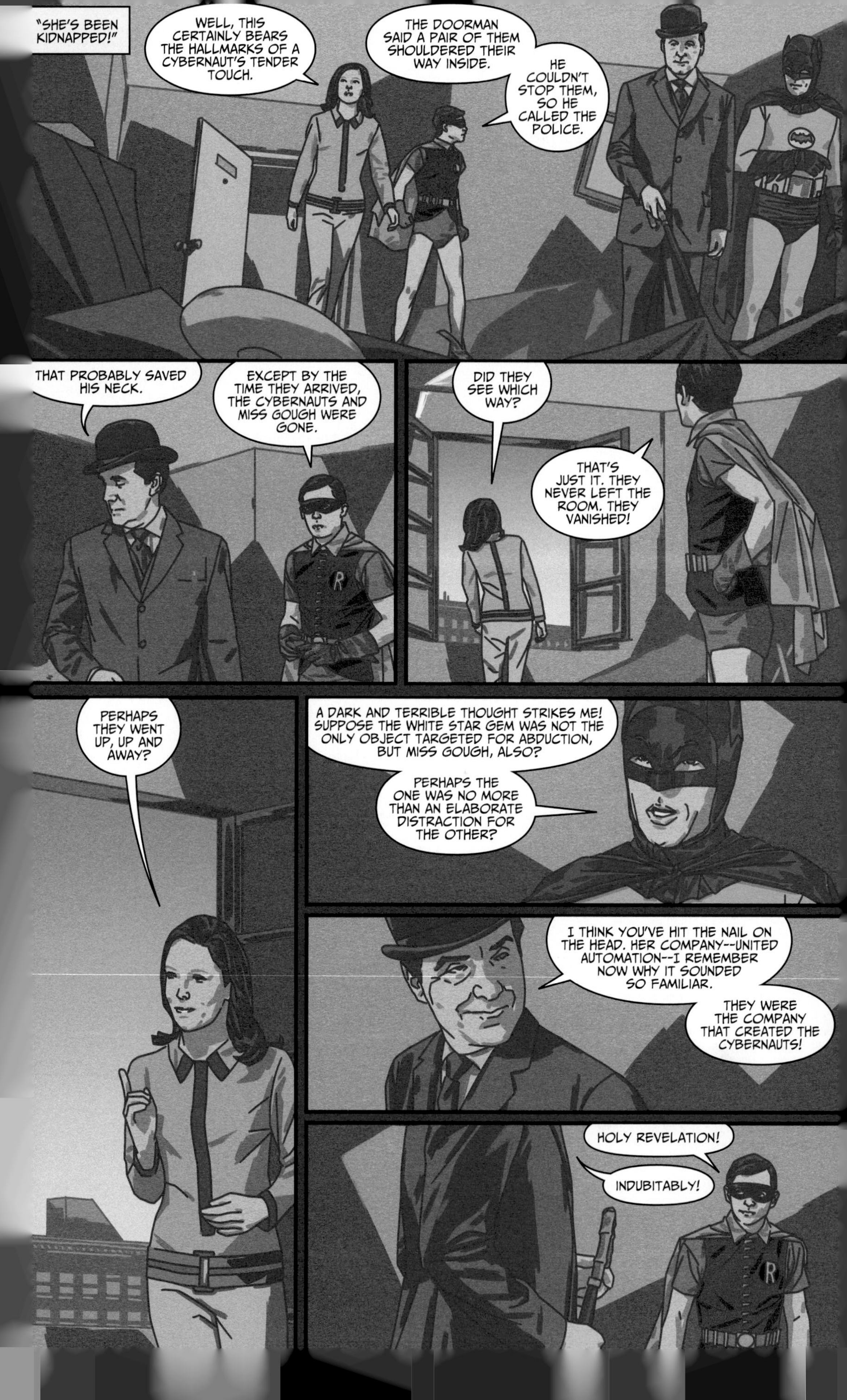
"SHE'S BEEN KIDNAPPED!"
WELL, THIS CERTAINLY BEARS THE HALLMARKS OF A CYBERNAUT'S TENDER TOUCH.
THE DOORMAN SAID A PAIR OF THEM SHOULDERED THEIR WAY INSIDE.
HE COULDN'T STOP THEM, SO HE CALLED THE POLICE.
THAT PROBABLY SAVED HIS NECK.
EXCEPT BY THE TIME THEY ARRIVED, THE CYBERNAUTS AND MISS GOUGH WERE GONE.
DID THEY SEE WHICH WAY?
THAT'S JUST IT. THEY NEVER LEFT THE ROOM. THEY VANISHED!
PERHAPS THEY WENT UP, UP AND AWAY?
A DARK AND TERRIBLE THOUGHT STRIKES ME! SUPPOSE THE WHITE STAR GEM WAS NOT THE ONLY OBJECT TARGETED FOR ABDUCTION, BUT MISS GOUGH, ALSO?
PERHAPS THE ONE WAS NO MORE THAN AN ELABORATE DISTRACTION FOR THE OTHER?
I THINK YOU'VE HIT THE NAIL ON THE HEAD. HER COMPANY--UNITED AUTOMATION--I REMEMBER NOW WHY IT SOUNDED SO FAMILIAR.
THEY WERE THE COMPANY THAT CREATED THE CYBERNAUTS!
HOLY REVELATION!
INDUBITABLY!

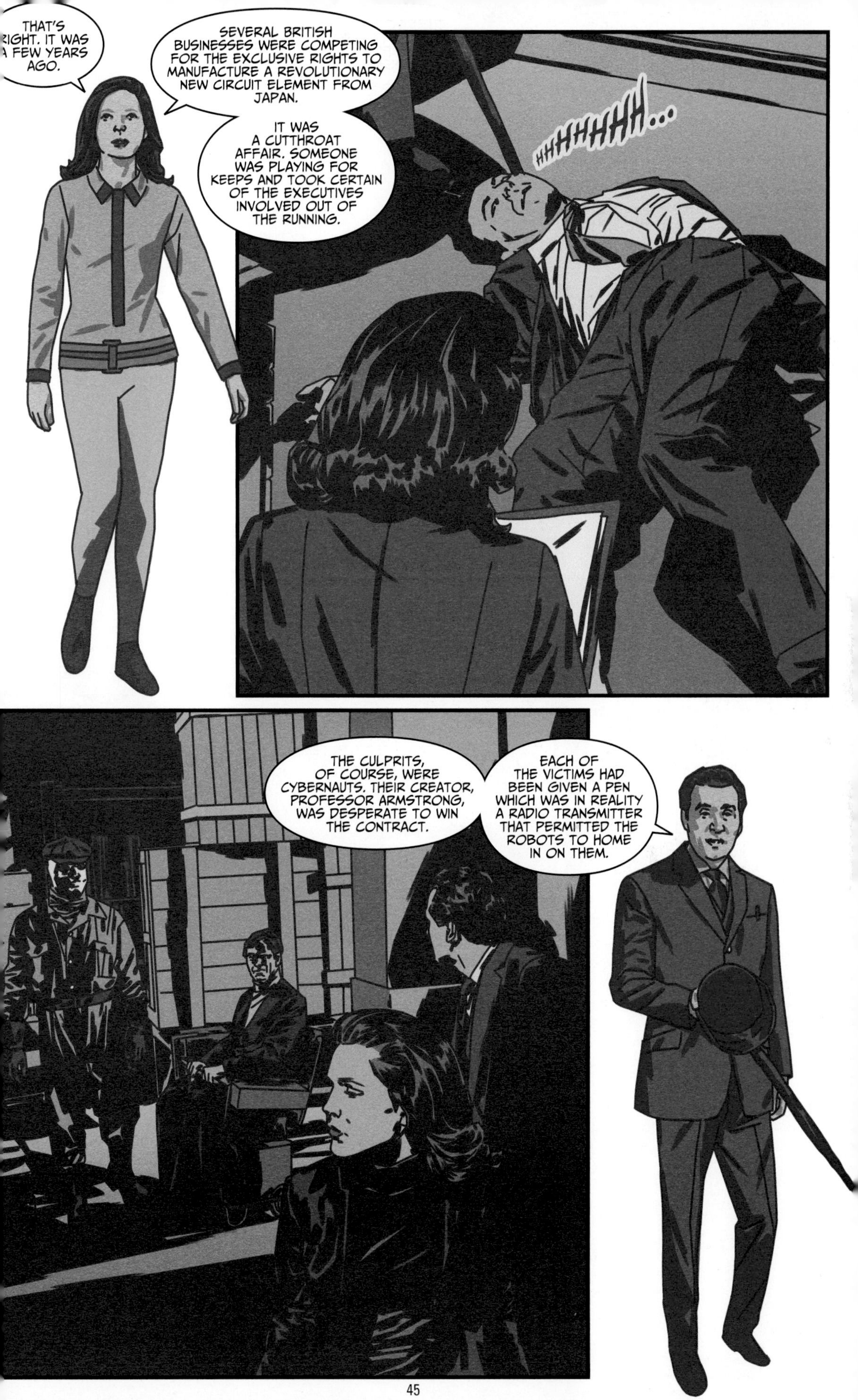
THAT'S RIGHT. IT WAS A FEW YEARS AGO.
SEVERAL BRITISH BUSINESSES WERE COMPETING FOR THE EXCLUSIVE RIGHTS TO MANUFACTURE A REVOLUTIONARY NEW CIRCUIT ELEMENT FROM JAPAN.
IT WAS A CUTTHROAT AFFAIR. SOMEONE WAS PLAYING FOR KEEPS AND TOOK CERTAIN OF THE EXECUTIVES INVOLVED OUT OF THE RUNNING.
HHHHHHH...
THE CULPRITS, OF COURSE, WERE CYBERNAUTS. THEIR CREATOR, PROFESSOR ARMSTRONG, WAS DESPERATE TO WIN THE CONTRACT.
EACH OF THE VICTIMS HAD BEEN GIVEN A PEN WHICH WAS IN REALITY A RADIO TRANSMITTER THAT PERMITTED THE ROBOTS TO HOME IN ON THEM.

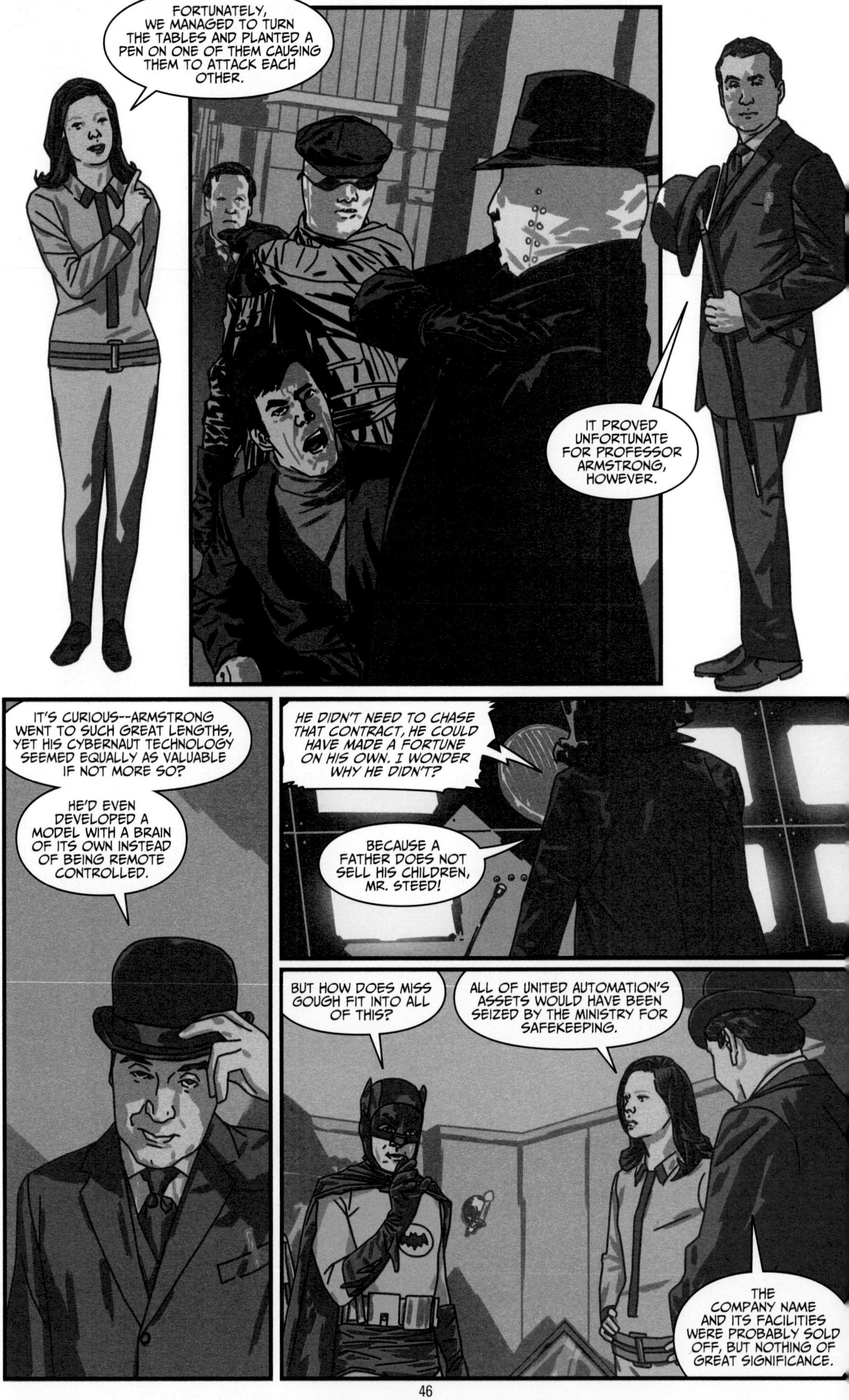
FORTUNATELY, WE MANAGED TO TURN THE TABLES AND PLANTED A PEN ON ONE OF THEM CAUSING THEM TO ATTACK EACH OTHER.
IT PROVED UNFORTUNATE FOR PROFESSOR ARMSTRONG, HOWEVER.
IT'S CURIOUS--ARMSTRONG WENT TO SUCH GREAT LENGTHS, YET HIS CYBERNAUT TECHNOLOGY SEEMED EQUALLY AS VALUABLE IF NOT MORE SO?
HE'D EVEN DEVELOPED A MODEL WITH A BRAIN OF ITS OWN INSTEAD OF BEING REMOTE CONTROLLED.
HE DIDN'T NEED TO CHASE THAT CONTRACT, HE COULD HAVE MADE A FORTUNE ON HIS OWN. I WONDER WHY HE DIDN'T?
BECAUSE A FATHER DOES NOT SELL HIS CHILDREN, MR. STEED!
BUT HOW DOES MISS GOUGH FIT INTO ALL OF THIS?
ALL OF UNITED AUTOMATION'S ASSETS WOULD HAVE BEEN SEIZED BY THE MINISTRY FOR SAFEKEEPING.
THE COMPANY NAME AND ITS FACILITIES WERE PROBABLY SOLD OFF, BUT NOTHING OF GREAT SIGNIFICANCE.

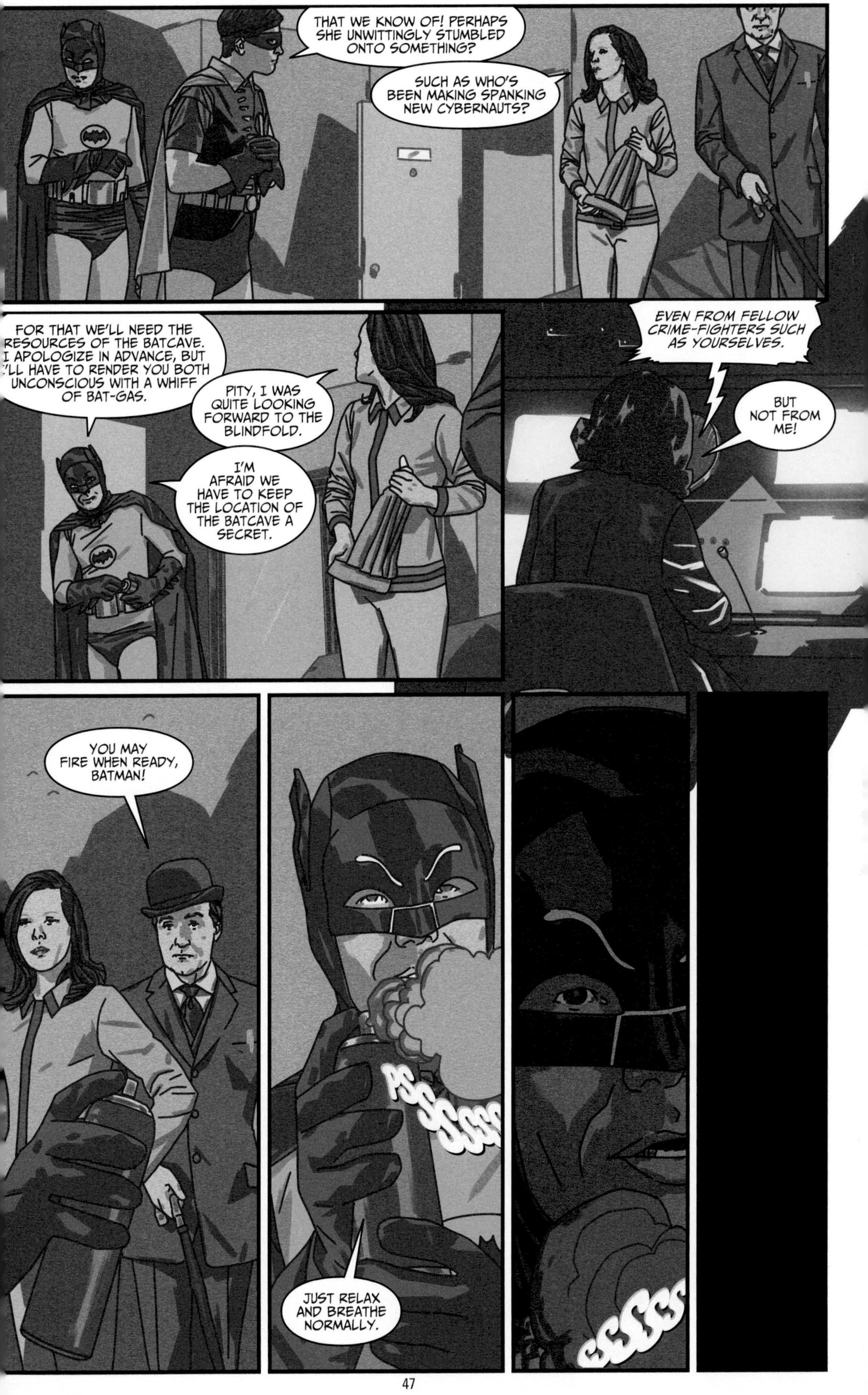

THAT WE KNOW OF! PERHAPS SHE UNWITTINGLY STUMBLED ONTO SOMETHING?
SUCH AS WHO'S BEEN MAKING SPANKING NEW CYBERNAUTS?
FOR THAT WE'LL NEED THE RESOURCES OF THE BATCAVE. I APOLOGIZE IN ADVANCE, BUT I'LL HAVE TO RENDER YOU BOTH UNCONSCIOUS WITH A WHIFF OF BAT-GAS.
PITY, I WAS QUITE LOOKING FORWARD TO THE BLINDFOLD.
I'M AFRAID WE HAVE TO KEEP THE LOCATION OF THE BATCAVE A SECRET.
EVEN FROM FELLOW CRIME-FIGHTERS SUCH AS YOURSELVES.
BUT NOT FROM ME!
YOU MAY FIRE WHEN READY, BATMAN!
PSSSSS
JUST RELAX AND BREATHE NORMALLY.
SSSSS

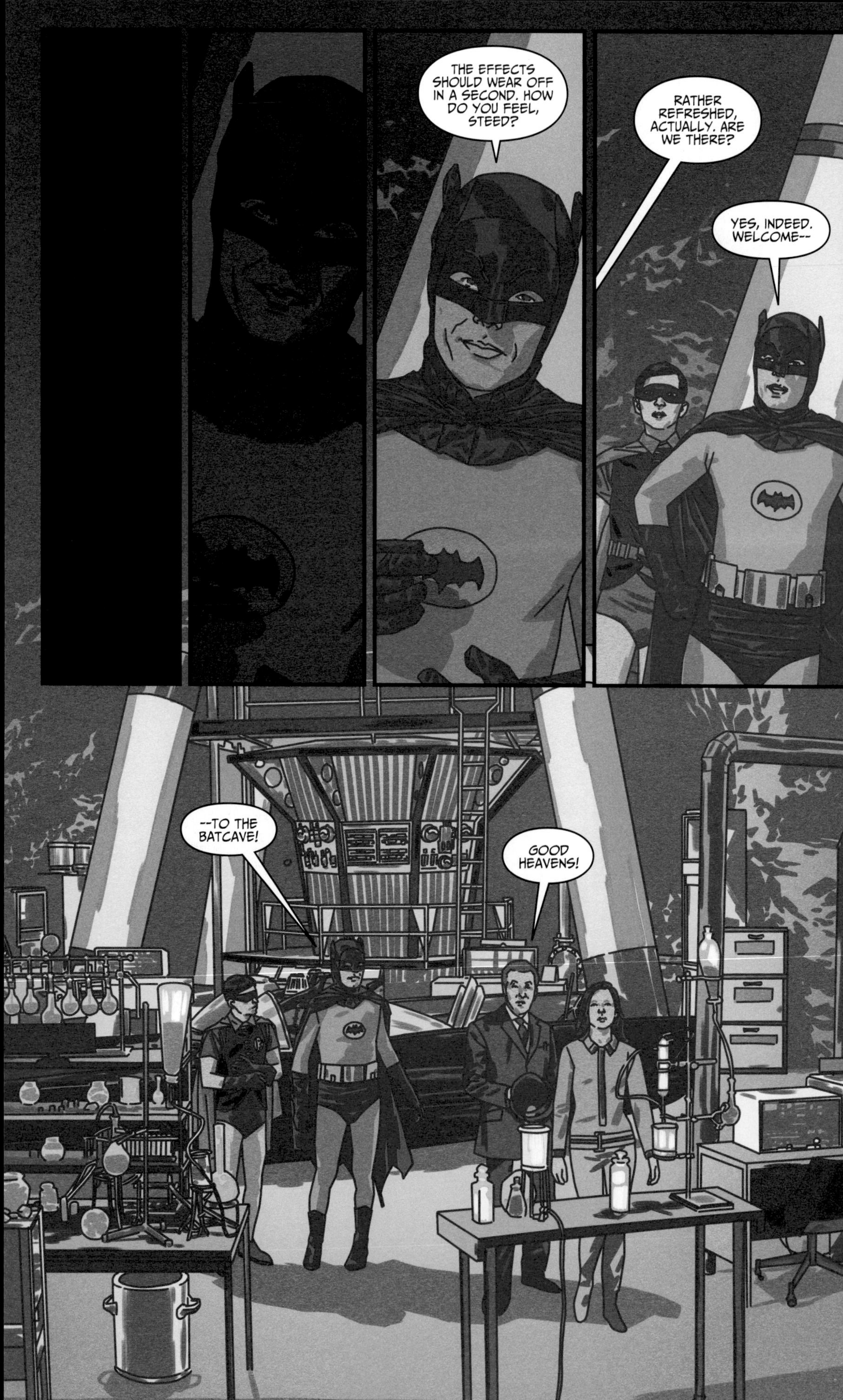

THE EFFECTS SHOULD WEAR OFF IN A SECOND. HOW DO YOU FEEL, STEED?
RATHER REFRESHED, ACTUALLY. ARE WE THERE?
YES, INDEED. WELCOME--
--TO THE BATCAVE!
GOOD HEAVENS!

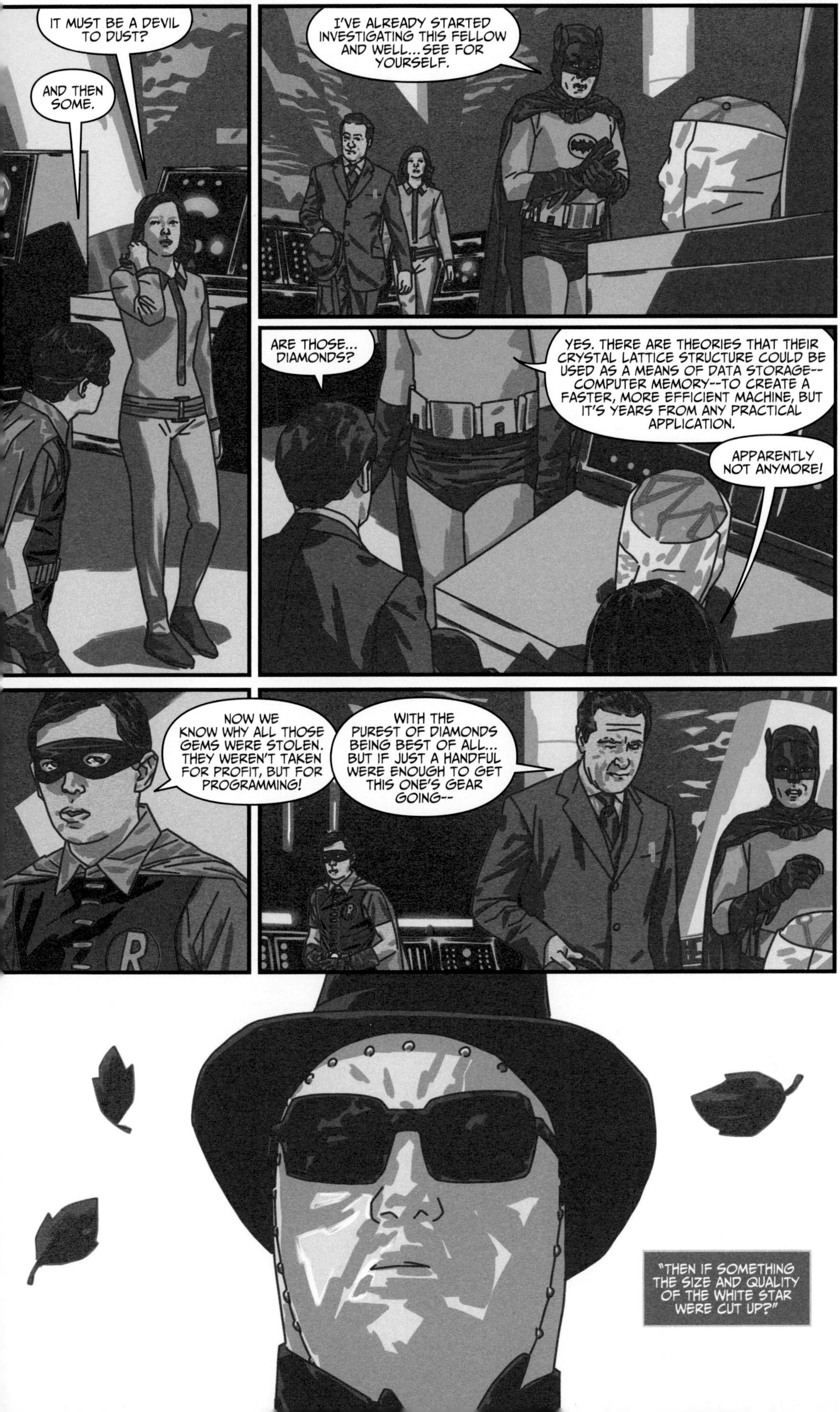
IT MUST BE A DEVIL TO DUST?
AND THEN SOME.
I'VE ALREADY STARTED INVESTIGATING THIS FELLOW AND WELL...SEE FOR YOURSELF.
ARE THOSE... DIAMONDS?
YES. THERE ARE THEORIES THAT THEIR CRYSTAL LATTICE STRUCTURE COULD BE USED AS A MEANS OF DATA STORAGE--COMPUTER MEMORY--TO CREATE A FASTER, MORE EFFICIENT MACHINE, BUT IT'S YEARS FROM ANY PRACTICAL APPLICATION.
APPARENTLY NOT ANYMORE!
NOW WE KNOW WHY ALL THOSE GEMS WERE STOLEN. THEY WEREN'T TAKEN FOR PROFIT, BUT FOR PROGRAMMING!
WITH THE PUREST OF DIAMONDS BEING BEST OF ALL... BUT IF JUST A HANDFUL WERE ENOUGH TO GET THIS ONE'S GEAR GOING--
"THEN IF SOMETHING THE SIZE AND QUALITY OF THE WHITE STAR WERE CUT UP?"

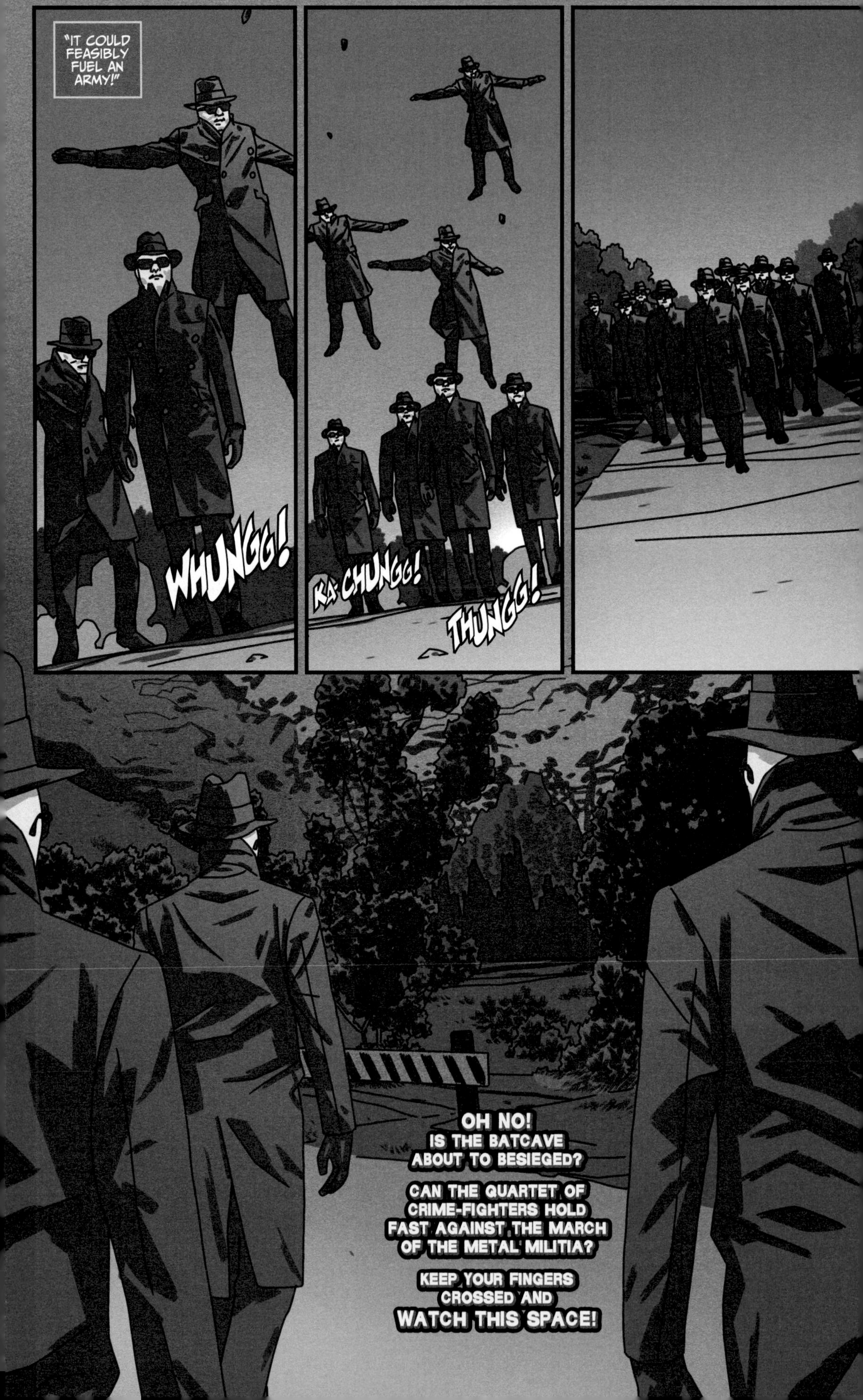
"IT COULD FEASIBLY FUEL AN ARMY!"
WHUNGG!
KA-CHUNGG!
THUNGG!
OH NO!
IS THE BATCAVE ABOUT TO BESIEGED?
CAN THE QUARTET OF CRIME-FIGHTERS HOLD FAST AGAINST THE MARCH OF THE METAL MILITIA?
KEEP YOUR FINGERS CROSSED AND
WATCH THIS SPACE!

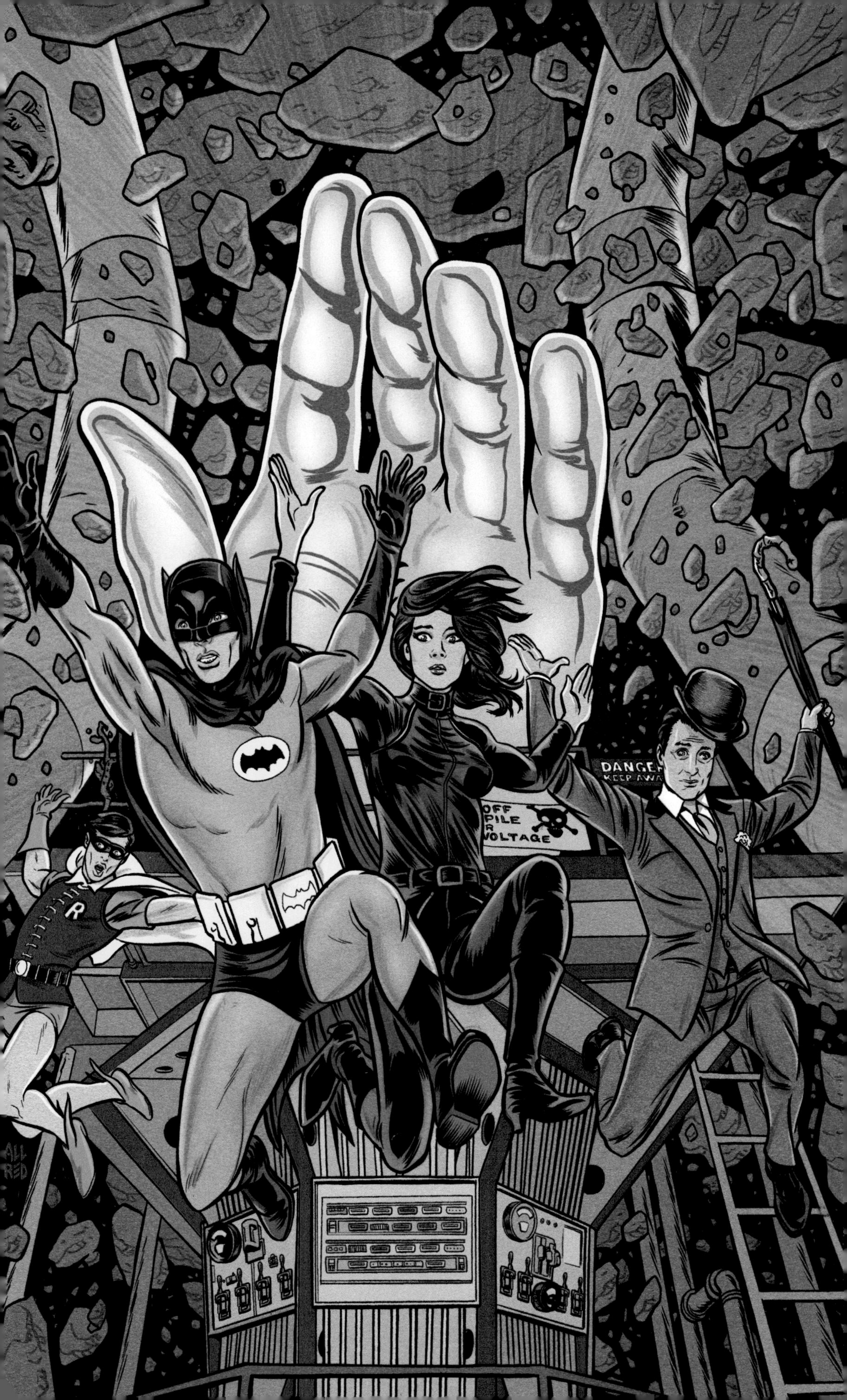
DANGE
KEEP AWA
OFF
PILE
R
VOLTAGE
ALL
RED

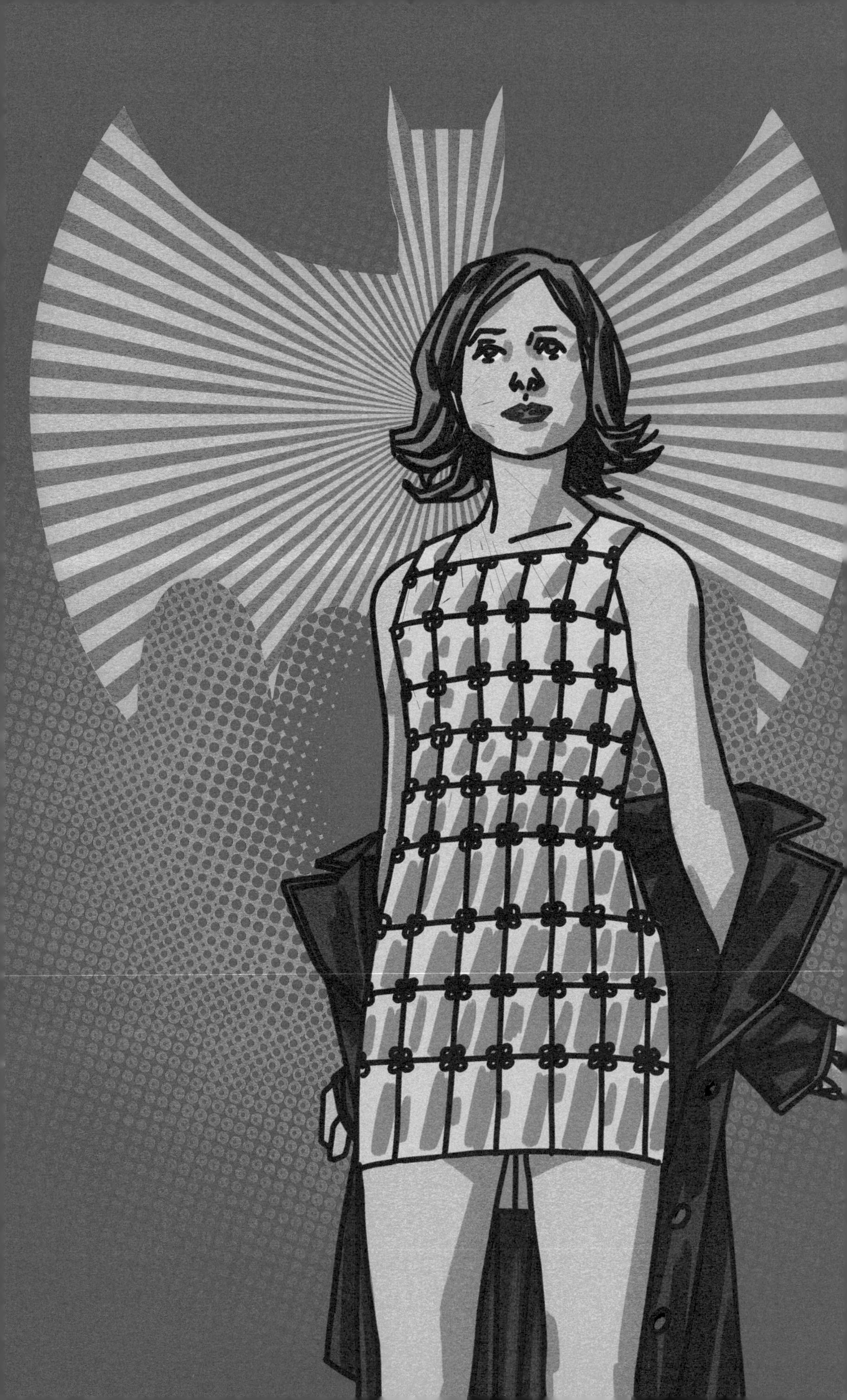

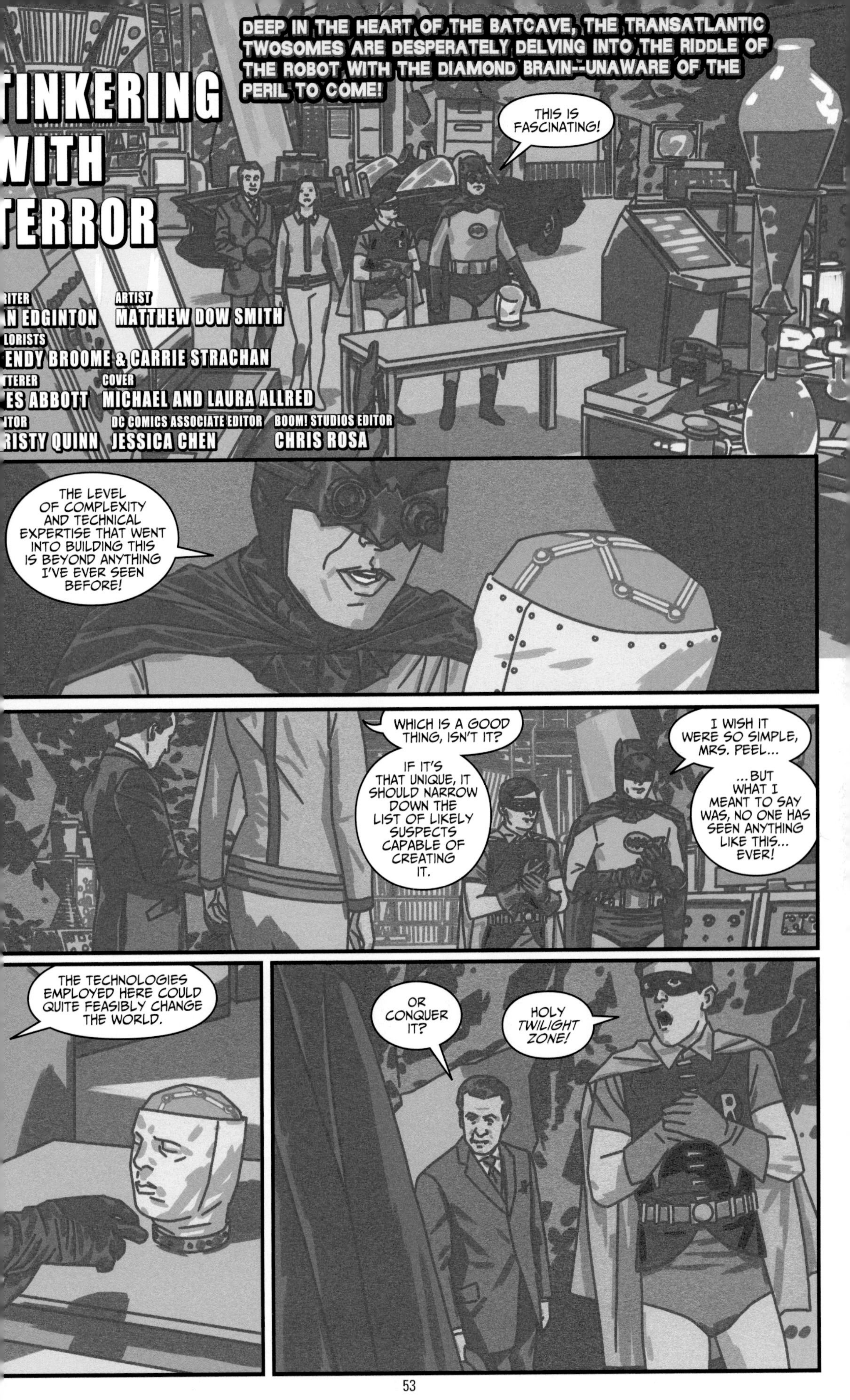

DEEP IN THE HEART OF THE BATCAVE, THE TRANSATLANTIC TWOSOMES ARE DESPERATELY DELVING INTO THE RIDDLE OF THE ROBOT WITH THE DIAMOND BRAIN--UNAWARE OF THE PERIL TO COME!
TINKERING WITH TERROR
RITER N EDGINTON
ARTIST MATTHEW DOW SMITH
LORISTS ENDY BROOME & CARRIE STRACHAN
TTERER ES ABBOTT
COVER MICHAEL AND LAURA ALLRED
ITOR RISTY QUINN
DC COMICS ASSOCIATE EDITOR JESSICA CHEN
BOOM! STUDIOS EDITOR CHRIS ROSA
THIS IS FASCINATING!
THE LEVEL OF COMPLEXITY AND TECHNICAL EXPERTISE THAT WENT INTO BUILDING THIS IS BEYOND ANYTHING I'VE EVER SEEN BEFORE!
WHICH IS A GOOD THING, ISN'T IT?
IF IT'S THAT UNIQUE, IT SHOULD NARROW DOWN THE LIST OF LIKELY SUSPECTS CAPABLE OF CREATING IT.
I WISH IT WERE SO SIMPLE, MRS. PEEL...
...BUT WHAT I MEANT TO SAY WAS, NO ONE HAS SEEN ANYTHING LIKE THIS... EVER!
THE TECHNOLOGIES EMPLOYED HERE COULD QUITE FEASIBLY CHANGE THE WORLD.
OR CONQUER IT?
HOLY TWILIGHT ZONE!

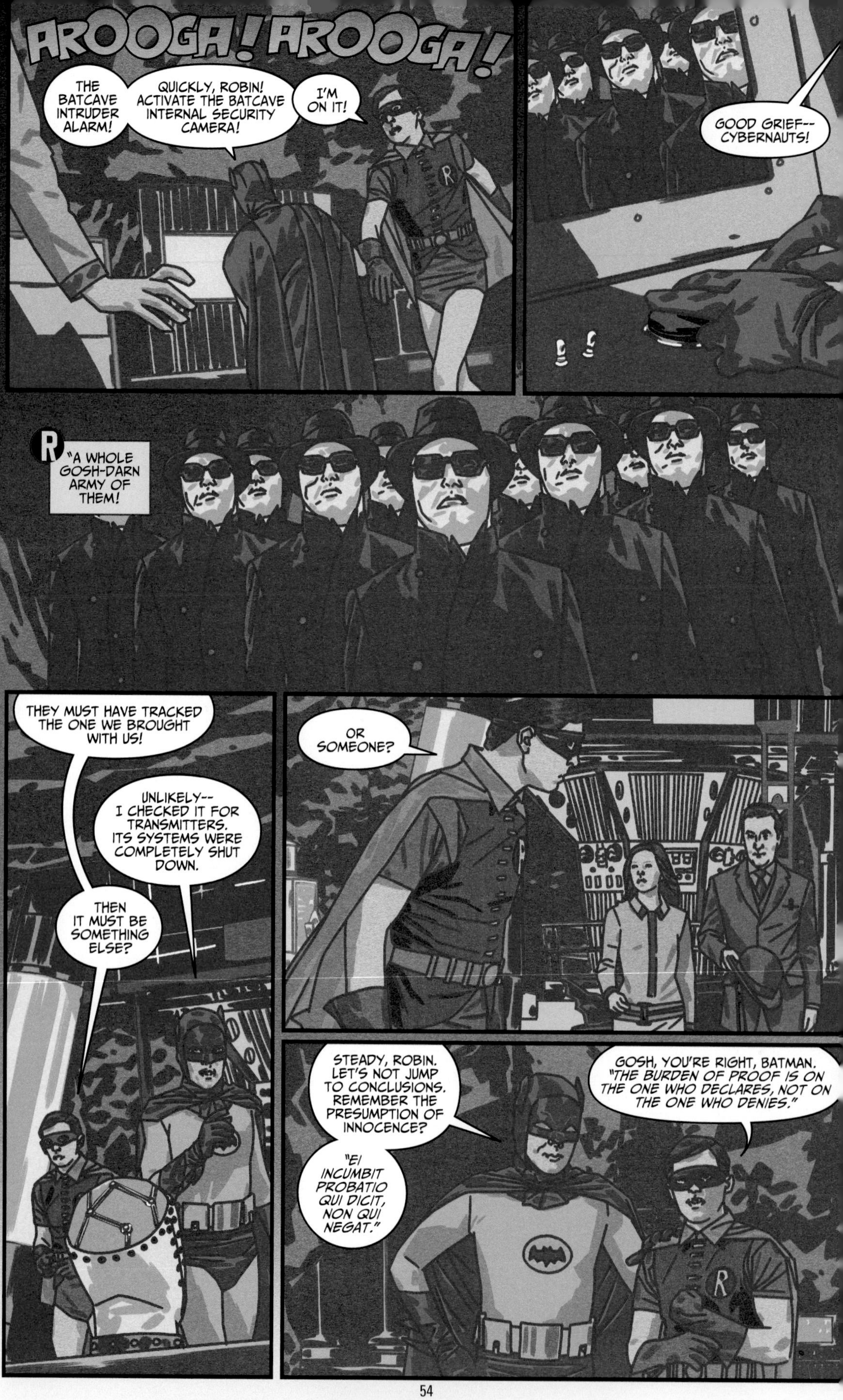
AROOGA! AROOGA!
THE BATCAVE INTRUDER ALARM!
QUICKLY, ROBIN! ACTIVATE THE BATCAVE INTERNAL SECURITY CAMERA!
I'M ON IT!
GOOD GRIEF-- CYBERNAUTS!
"A WHOLE GOSH-DARN ARMY OF THEM!
THEY MUST HAVE TRACKED THE ONE WE BROUGHT WITH US!
UNLIKELY-- I CHECKED IT FOR TRANSMITTERS. ITS SYSTEMS WERE COMPLETELY SHUT DOWN.
THEN IT MUST BE SOMETHING ELSE?
OR SOMEONE?
STEADY, ROBIN. LET'S NOT JUMP TO CONCLUSIONS. REMEMBER THE PRESUMPTION OF INNOCENCE?
"EI INCUMBIT PROBATIO QUI DICIT, NON QUI NEGAT."
GOSH, YOU'RE RIGHT, BATMAN. "THE BURDEN OF PROOF IS ON THE ONE WHO DECLARES, NOT ON THE ONE WHO DENIES."

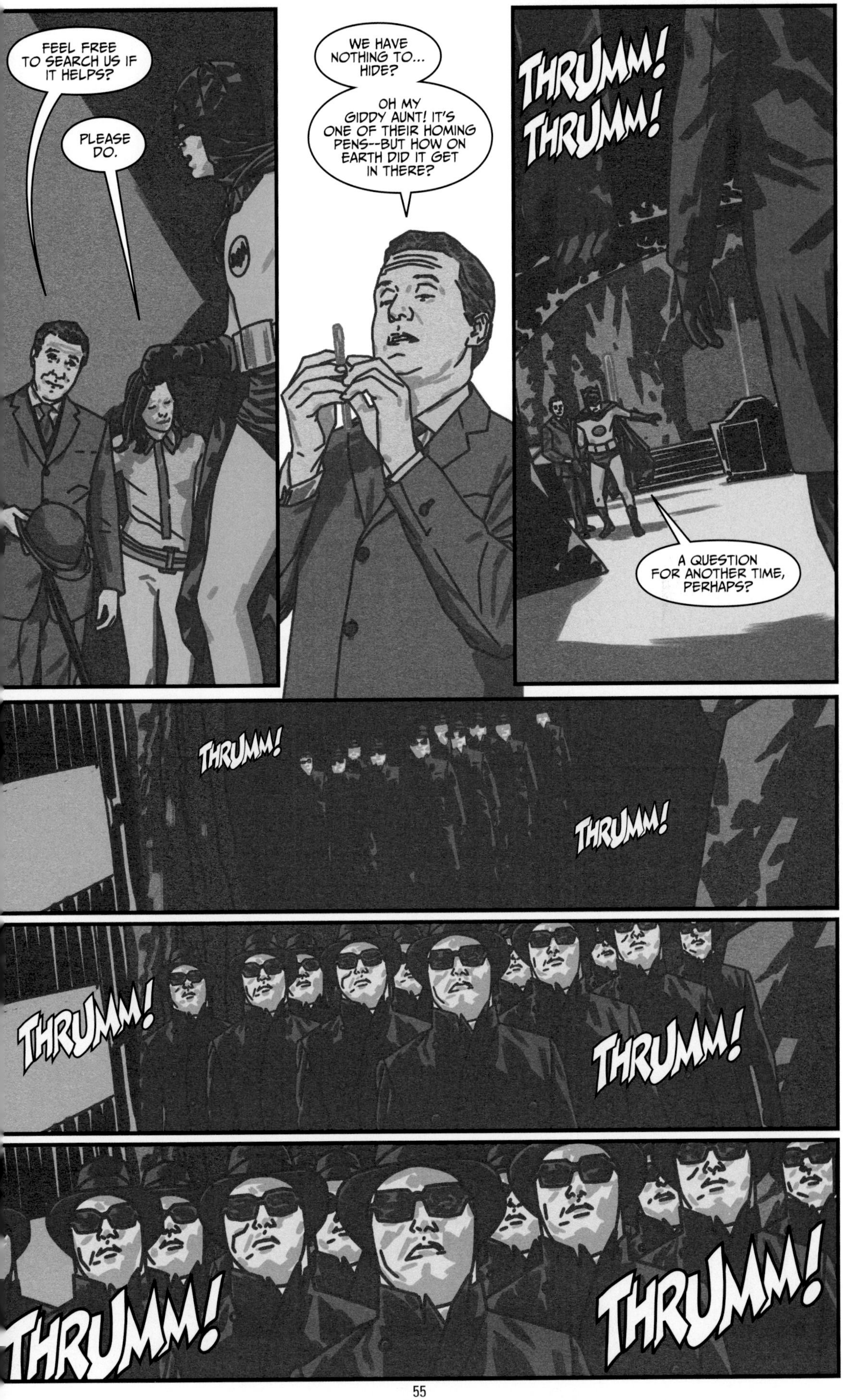
FEEL FREE TO SEARCH US IF IT HELPS?
PLEASE DO.
WE HAVE NOTHING TO... HIDE?
OH MY GIDDY AUNT! IT'S ONE OF THEIR HOMING PENS--BUT HOW ON EARTH DID IT GET IN THERE?
THRUMM! THRUMM!
A QUESTION FOR ANOTHER TIME, PERHAPS?
THRUMM!
THRUMM!
THRUMM!
THRUMM!
THRUMM!
THRUMM!

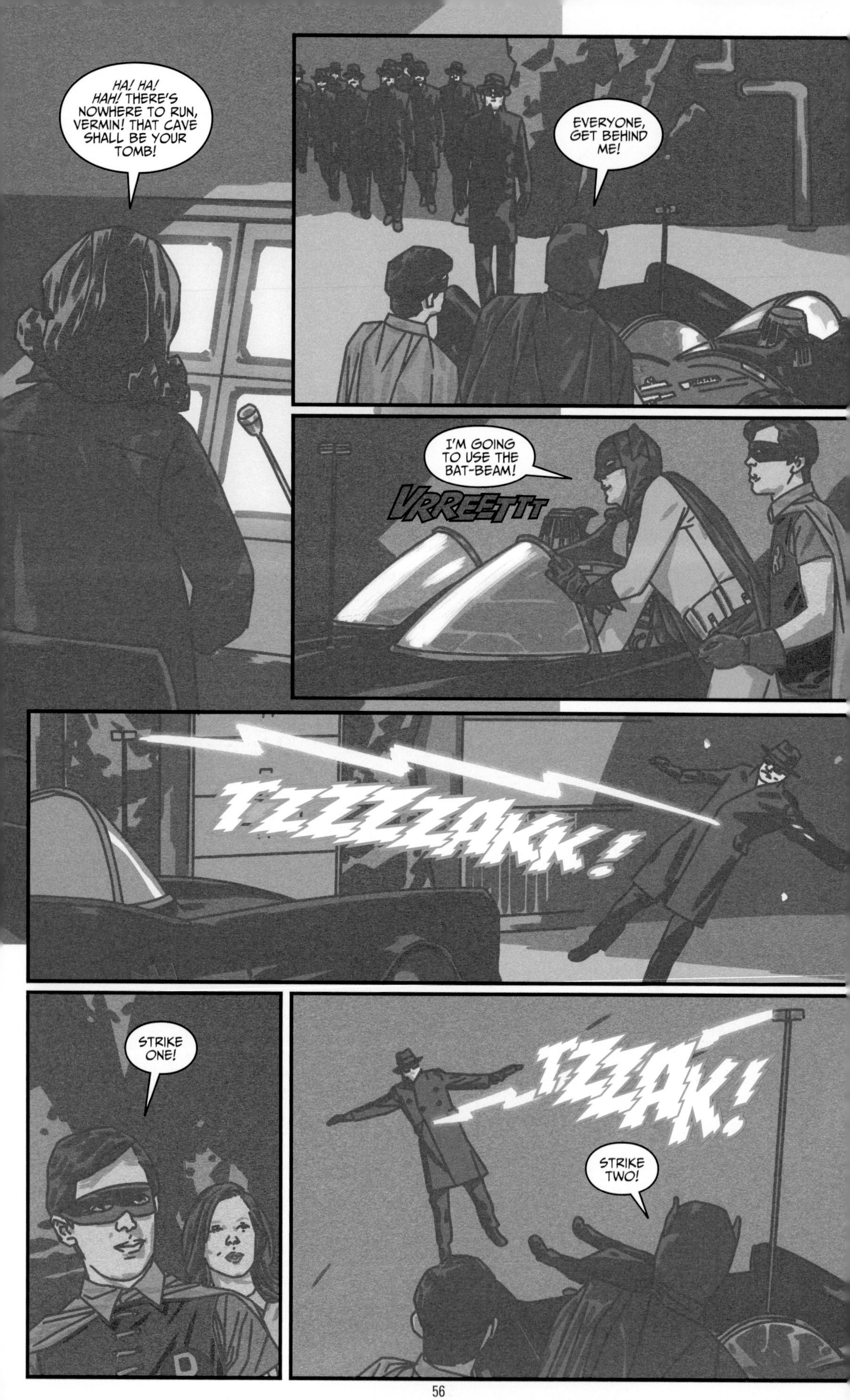

HA! HA! HAH! THERE'S NOWHERE TO RUN, VERMIN! THAT CAVE SHALL BE YOUR TOMB!
EVERYONE, GET BEHIND ME!
I'M GOING TO USE THE BAT-BEAM!
VRREETTT
TZZZZAKK!
STRIKE ONE!
TZZZAK!
STRIKE TWO!

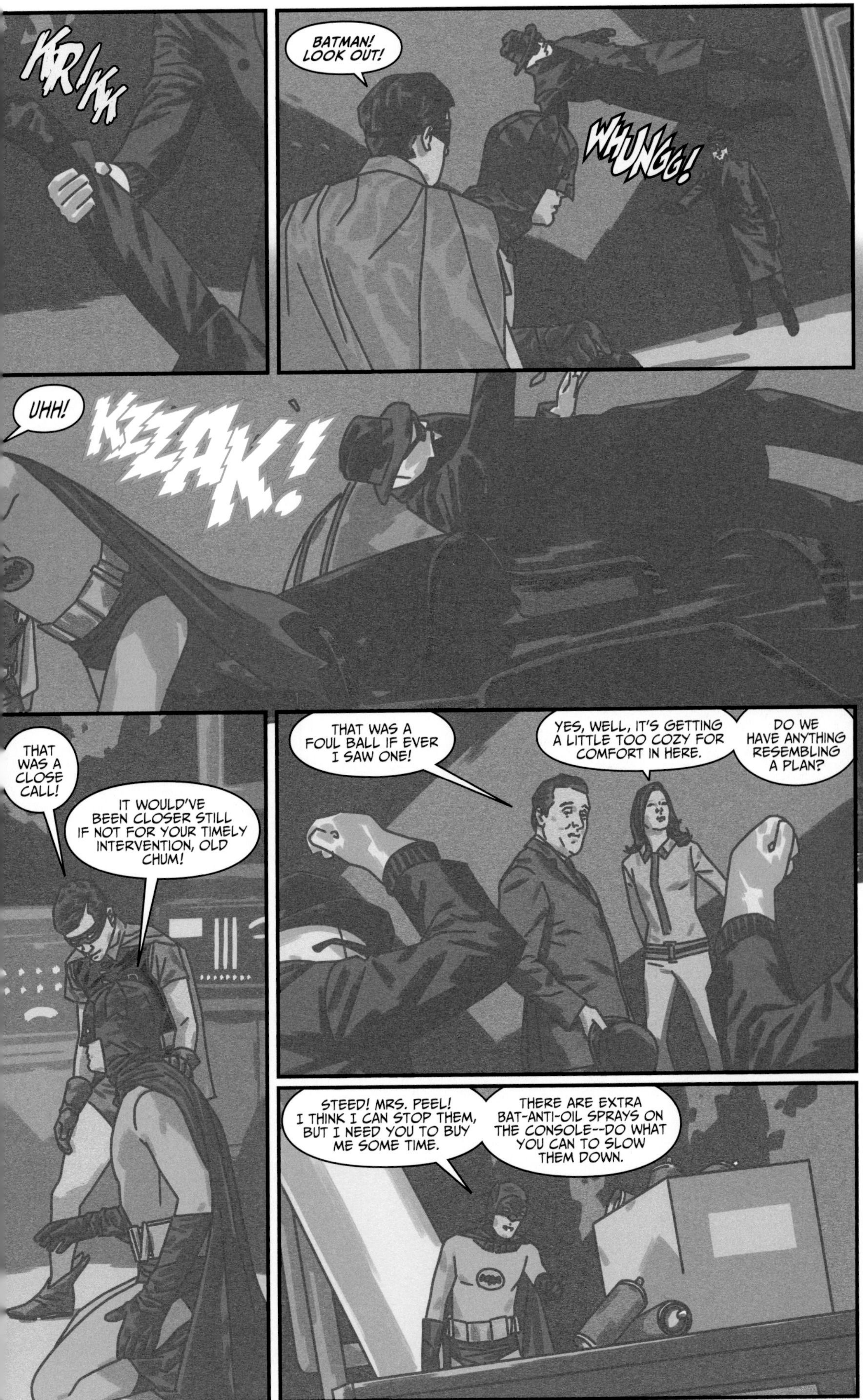
KRIKK
BATMAN! LOOK OUT!
WHUNGG!
UHH!
KRZAK!
THAT WAS A CLOSE CALL!
IT WOULD'VE BEEN CLOSER STILL IF NOT FOR YOUR TIMELY INTERVENTION, OLD CHUM!
THAT WAS A FOUL BALL IF EVER I SAW ONE!
YES, WELL, IT'S GETTING A LITTLE TOO COZY FOR COMFORT IN HERE.
DO WE HAVE ANYTHING RESEMBLING A PLAN?
STEED! MRS. PEEL! I THINK I CAN STOP THEM, BUT I NEED YOU TO BUY ME SOME TIME.
THERE ARE EXTRA BAT-ANTI-OIL SPRAYS ON THE CONSOLE--DO WHAT YOU CAN TO SLOW THEM DOWN.

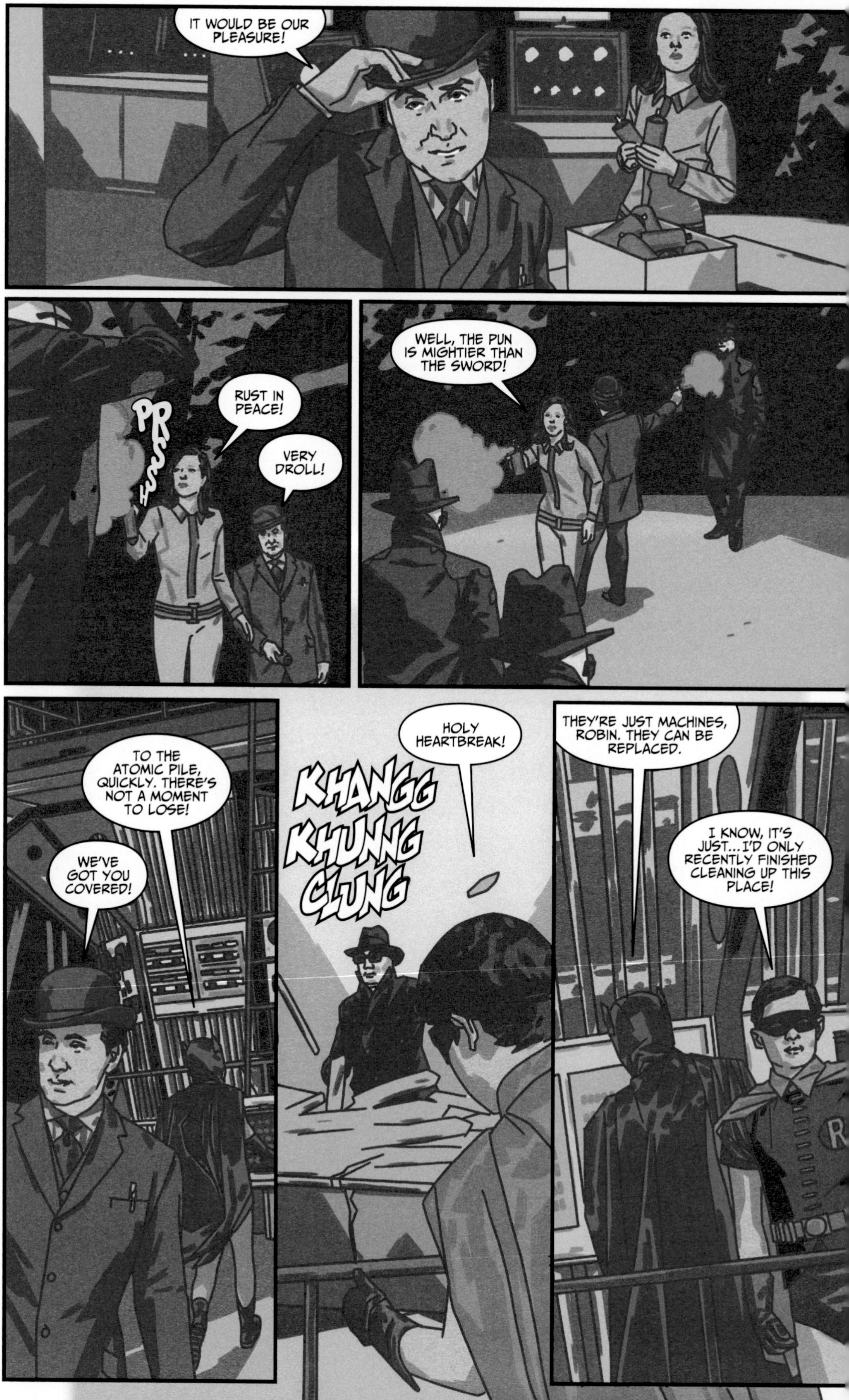
IT WOULD BE OUR PLEASURE!
PRSSSS
RUST IN PEACE!
VERY DROLL!
WELL, THE PUN IS MIGHTIER THAN THE SWORD!
TO THE ATOMIC PILE, QUICKLY. THERE'S NOT A MOMENT TO LOSE!
WE'VE GOT YOU COVERED!
KHANGG KHUNNG CLUNG
HOLY HEARTBREAK!
THEY'RE JUST MACHINES, ROBIN. THEY CAN BE REPLACED.
I KNOW, IT'S JUST...I'D ONLY RECENTLY FINISHED CLEANING UP THIS PLACE!

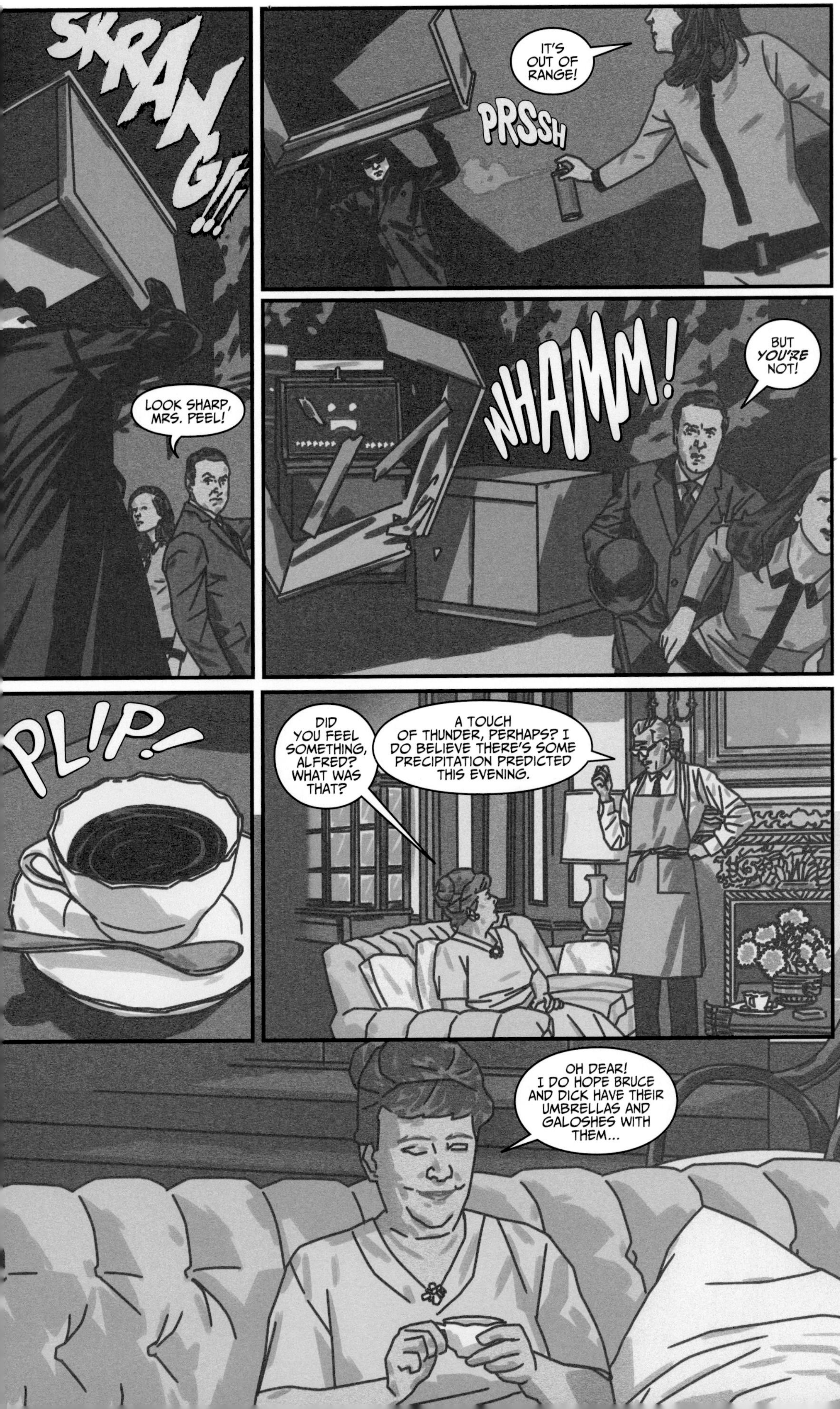
SKRANG!!!
LOOK SHARP, MRS. PEEL!
IT'S OUT OF RANGE!
PRSSH
WHAMM!
BUT YOU'RE NOT!
PLIP!
DID YOU FEEL SOMETHING, ALFRED? WHAT WAS THAT?
A TOUCH OF THUNDER, PERHAPS? I DO BELIEVE THERE'S SOME PRECIPITATION PREDICTED THIS EVENING.
OH DEAR! I DO HOPE BRUCE AND DICK HAVE THEIR UMBRELLAS AND GALOSHES WITH THEM...

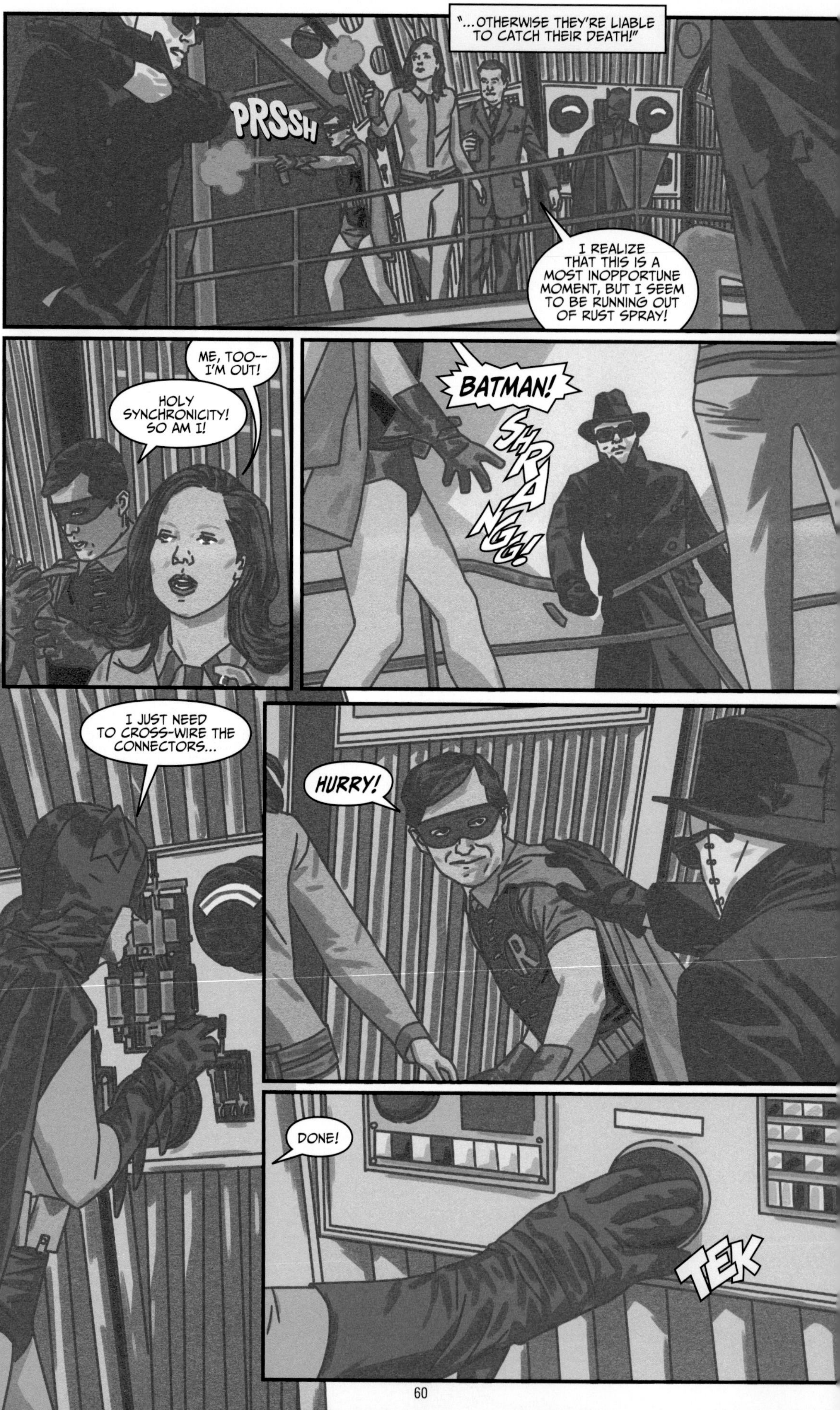
"...OTHERWISE THEY'RE LIABLE TO CATCH THEIR DEATH!"
PRSSH
I REALIZE THAT THIS IS A MOST INOPPORTUNE MOMENT, BUT I SEEM TO BE RUNNING OUT OF RUST SPRAY!
HOLY SYNCHRONICITY! SO AM I!
ME, TOO-- I'M OUT!
BATMAN!
SHRANGG!
I JUST NEED TO CROSS-WIRE THE CONNECTORS...
HURRY!
DONE!
TEK

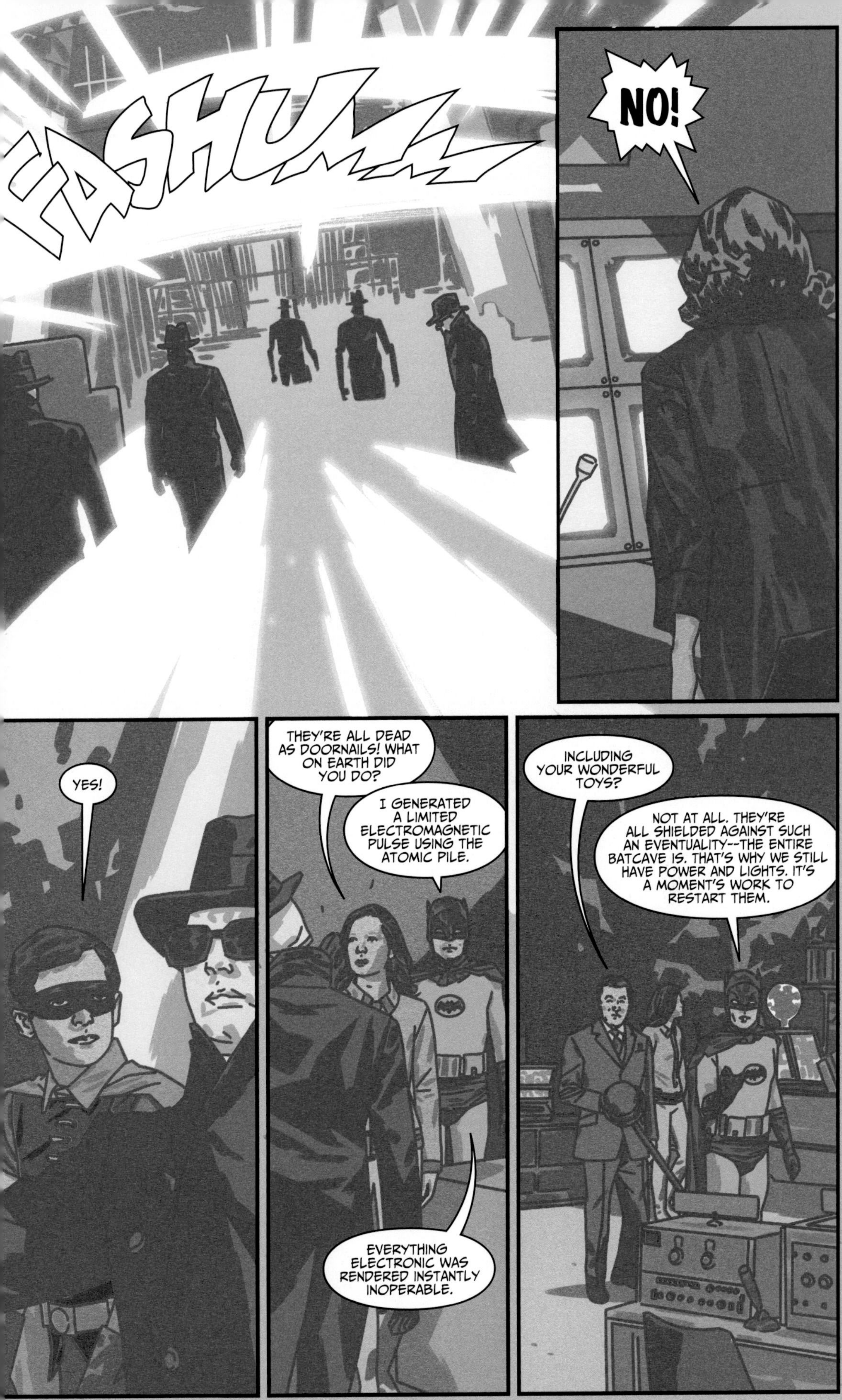
FASHUM
NO!
YES!
THEY'RE ALL DEAD AS DOORNAILS! WHAT ON EARTH DID YOU DO?
I GENERATED A LIMITED ELECTROMAGNETIC PULSE USING THE ATOMIC PILE.
EVERYTHING ELECTRONIC WAS RENDERED INSTANTLY INOPERABLE.
INCLUDING YOUR WONDERFUL TOYS?
NOT AT ALL. THEY'RE ALL SHIELDED AGAINST SUCH AN EVENTUALITY--THE ENTIRE BATCAVE IS. THAT'S WHY WE STILL HAVE POWER AND LIGHTS. IT'S A MOMENT'S WORK TO RESTART THEM.

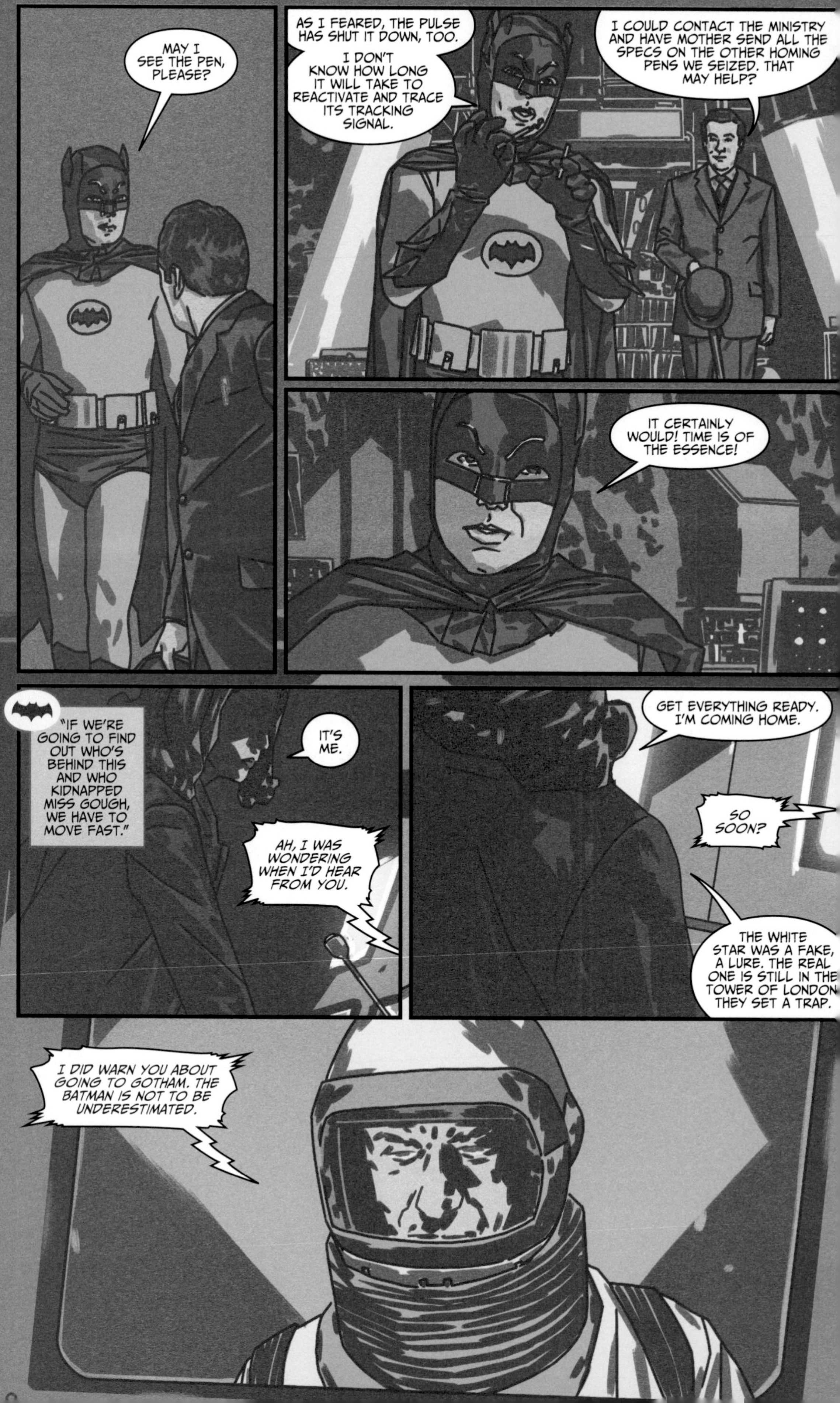
MAY I SEE THE PEN, PLEASE?
AS I FEARED, THE PULSE HAS SHUT IT DOWN, TOO.
I DON'T KNOW HOW LONG IT WILL TAKE TO REACTIVATE AND TRACE ITS TRACKING SIGNAL.
I COULD CONTACT THE MINISTRY AND HAVE MOTHER SEND ALL THE SPECS ON THE OTHER HOMING PENS WE SEIZED. THAT MAY HELP?
IT CERTAINLY WOULD! TIME IS OF THE ESSENCE!
"IF WE'RE GOING TO FIND OUT WHO'S BEHIND THIS AND WHO KIDNAPPED MISS GOUGH, WE HAVE TO MOVE FAST."
IT'S ME.
AH, I WAS WONDERING WHEN I'D HEAR FROM YOU.
GET EVERYTHING READY. I'M COMING HOME.
SO SOON?
THE WHITE STAR WAS A FAKE, A LURE. THE REAL ONE IS STILL IN THE TOWER OF LONDON. THEY SET A TRAP.
I DID WARN YOU ABOUT GOING TO GOTHAM. THE BATMAN IS NOT TO BE UNDERESTIMATED.

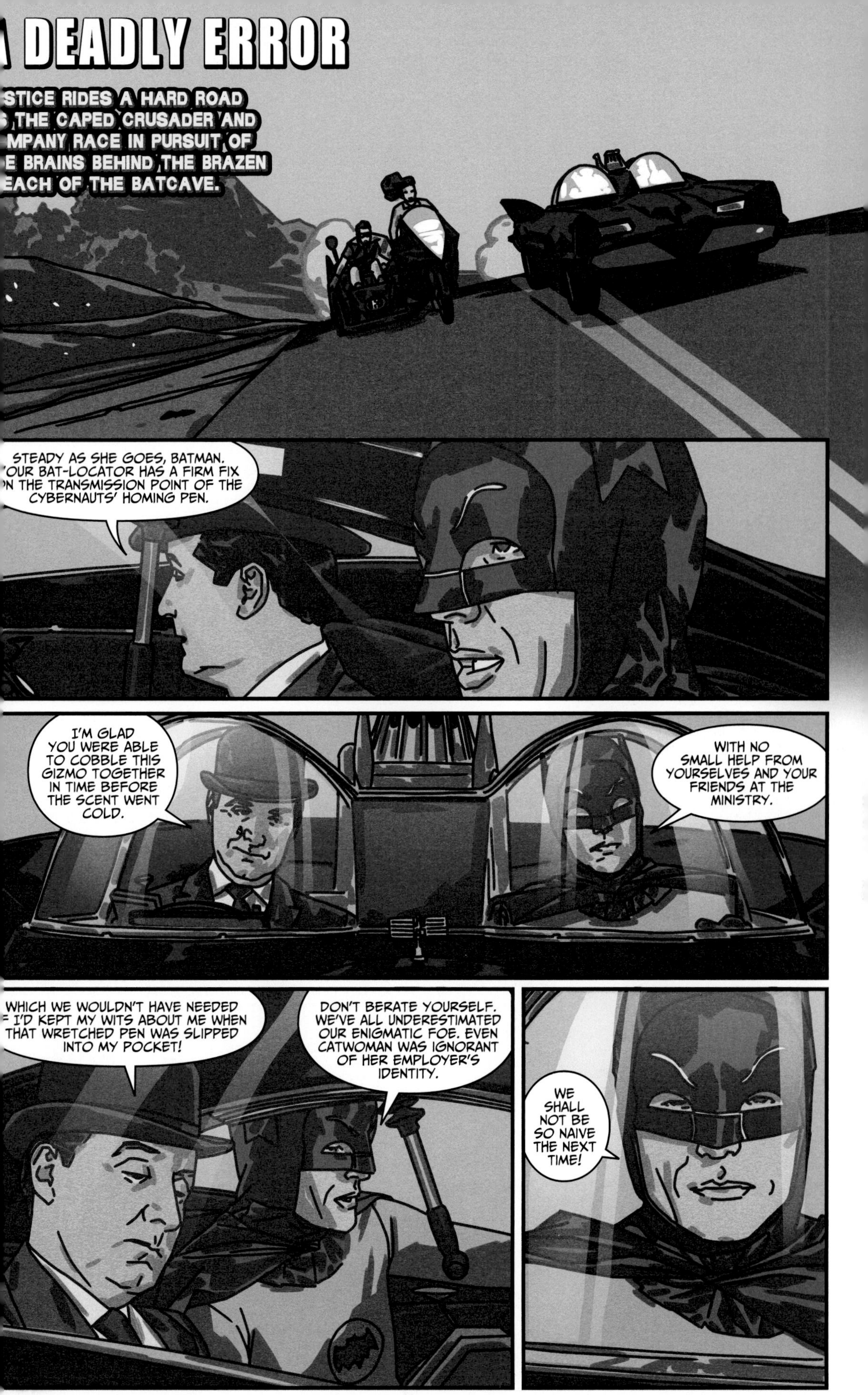
A DEADLY ERROR
STICE RIDES A HARD ROAD
THE CAPED CRUSADER AND
MPANY RACE IN PURSUIT OF
E BRAINS BEHIND THE BRAZEN
EACH OF THE BATCAVE.
STEADY AS SHE GOES, BATMAN. 'OUR BAT-LOCATOR HAS A FIRM FIX 'N THE TRANSMISSION POINT OF THE CYBERNAUTS' HOMING PEN.
I'M GLAD YOU WERE ABLE TO COBBLE THIS GIZMO TOGETHER IN TIME BEFORE THE SCENT WENT COLD.
WITH NO SMALL HELP FROM YOURSELVES AND YOUR FRIENDS AT THE MINISTRY.
WHICH WE WOULDN'T HAVE NEEDED F I'D KEPT MY WITS ABOUT ME WHEN THAT WRETCHED PEN WAS SLIPPED INTO MY POCKET!
DON'T BERATE YOURSELF. WE'VE ALL UNDERESTIMATED OUR ENIGMATIC FOE. EVEN CATWOMAN WAS IGNORANT OF HER EMPLOYER'S IDENTITY.
WE SHALL NOT BE SO NAIVE THE NEXT TIME!

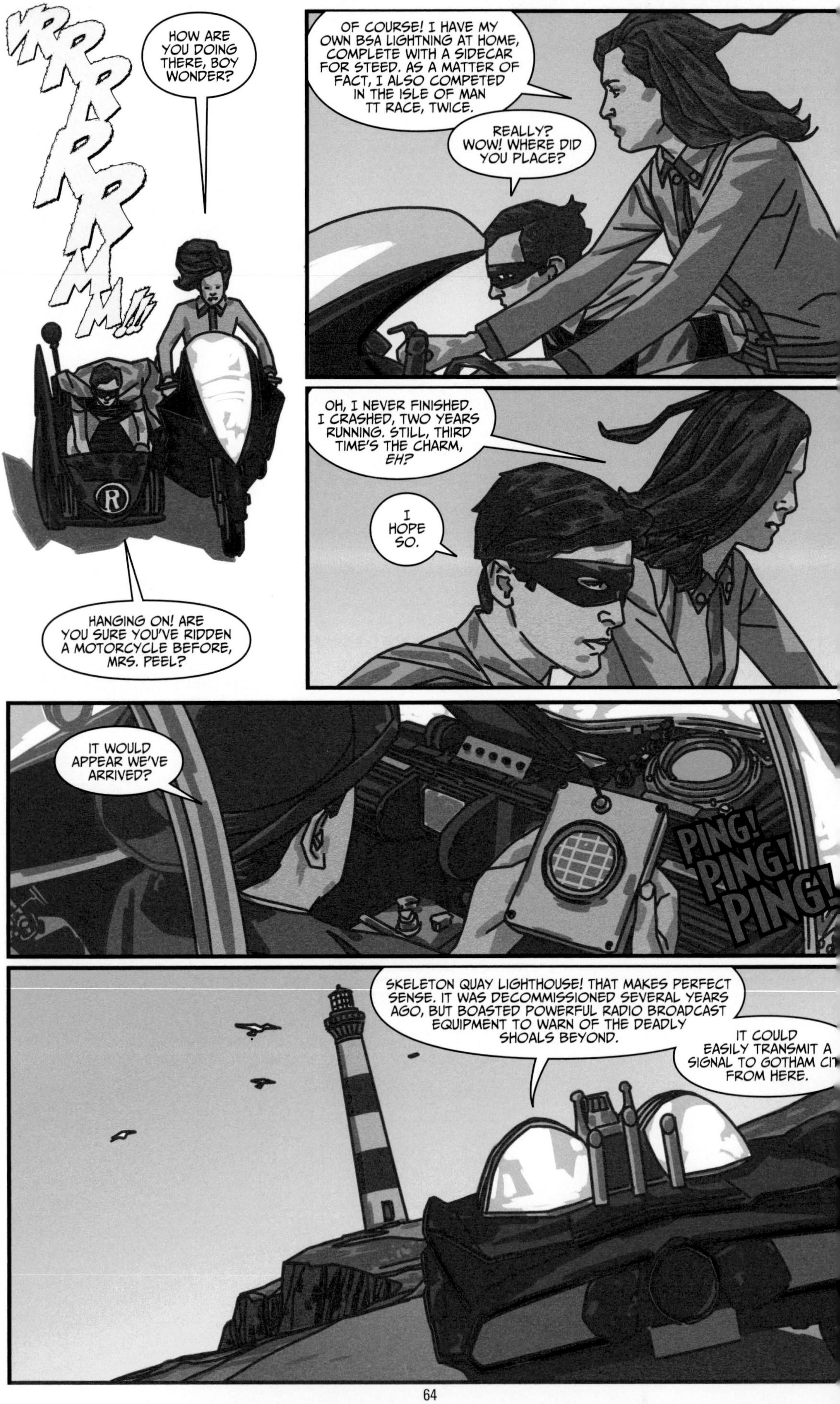
VRRRRRRUMM!!!
HOW ARE YOU DOING THERE, BOY WONDER?
HANGING ON! ARE YOU SURE YOU'VE RIDDEN A MOTORCYCLE BEFORE, MRS. PEEL?
OF COURSE! I HAVE MY OWN BSA LIGHTNING AT HOME, COMPLETE WITH A SIDECAR FOR STEED. AS A MATTER OF FACT, I ALSO COMPETED IN THE ISLE OF MAN TT RACE, TWICE.
REALLY? WOW! WHERE DID YOU PLACE?
OH, I NEVER FINISHED. I CRASHED, TWO YEARS RUNNING. STILL, THIRD TIME'S THE CHARM, EH?
I HOPE SO.
IT WOULD APPEAR WE'VE ARRIVED?
PING! PING! PING!
SKELETON QUAY LIGHTHOUSE! THAT MAKES PERFECT SENSE. IT WAS DECOMMISSIONED SEVERAL YEARS AGO, BUT BOASTED POWERFUL RADIO BROADCAST EQUIPMENT TO WARN OF THE DEADLY SHOALS BEYOND.
IT COULD EASILY TRANSMIT A SIGNAL TO GOTHAM CI FROM HERE.

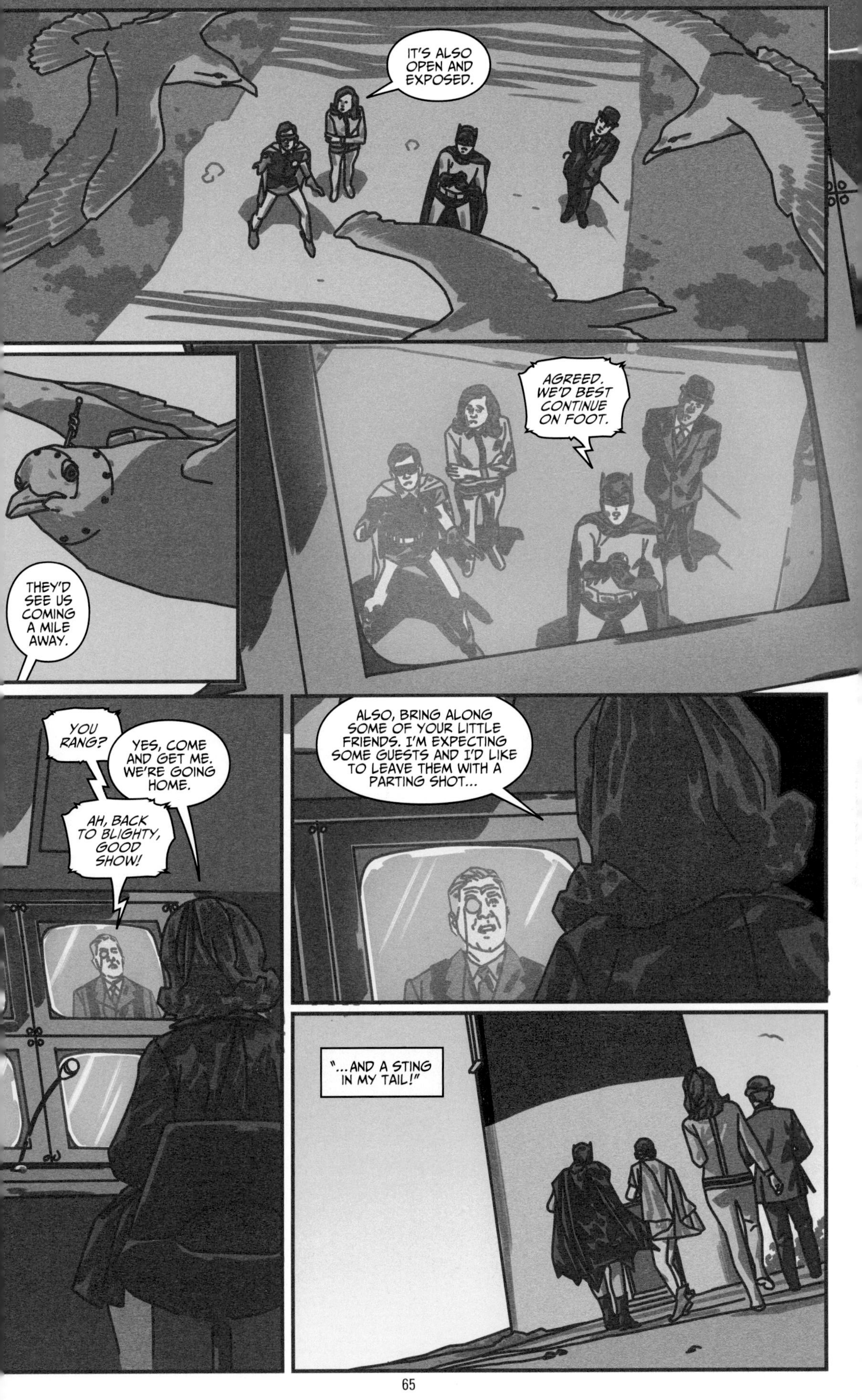
IT'S ALSO OPEN AND EXPOSED.
THEY'D SEE US COMING A MILE AWAY.
AGREED. WE'D BEST CONTINUE ON FOOT.
YOU RANG?
YES, COME AND GET ME. WE'RE GOING HOME.
AH, BACK TO BLIGHTY, GOOD SHOW!
ALSO, BRING ALONG SOME OF YOUR LITTLE FRIENDS. I'M EXPECTING SOME GUESTS AND I'D LIKE TO LEAVE THEM WITH A PARTING SHOT...
"...AND A STING IN MY TAIL!"

SO FAR, SO GOOD.

WE'LL TAKE THEM ON TWO FRONTS--ROBIN AND I FROM ABOVE, YOURSELVES FROM BELOW.

THAT WORKS FOR ME. I HAVE AN AWFUL HEAD FOR HEIGHTS. GOOD LUCK!

LADIES FIRST.

CHARMED, I'M SURE!

BATMAN, THIS IS TOO EASY. IT COULD BE A TRAP?

STEADY, OLD CHUM. KEEP YOUR NERVE. FOCUS ON THE TASK AT HAND.

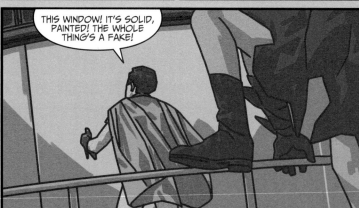

THIS WINDOW! IT'S SOLID, PAINTED! THE WHOLE THING'S A FAKE!

CREEEAK

WELCOME, CAPED CRUSADERS. I'VE BEEN WAITING FOR YOU.

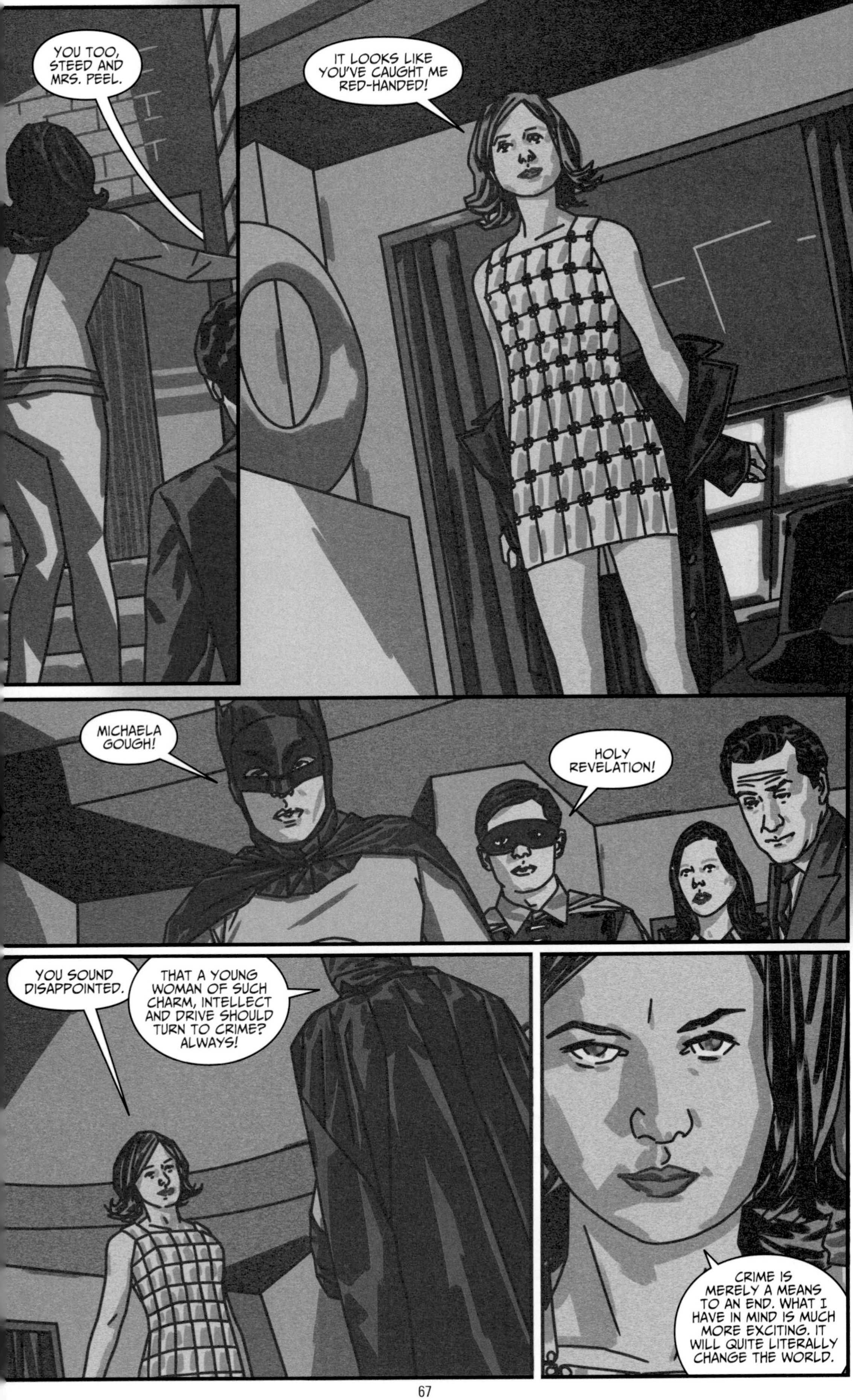
YOU TOO, STEED AND MRS. PEEL.
IT LOOKS LIKE YOU'VE CAUGHT ME RED-HANDED!
MICHAELA GOUGH!
HOLY REVELATION!
YOU SOUND DISAPPOINTED.
THAT A YOUNG WOMAN OF SUCH CHARM, INTELLECT AND DRIVE SHOULD TURN TO CRIME? ALWAYS!
CRIME IS MERELY A MEANS TO AN END. WHAT I HAVE IN MIND IS MUCH MORE EXCITING. IT WILL QUITE LITERALLY CHANGE THE WORLD.

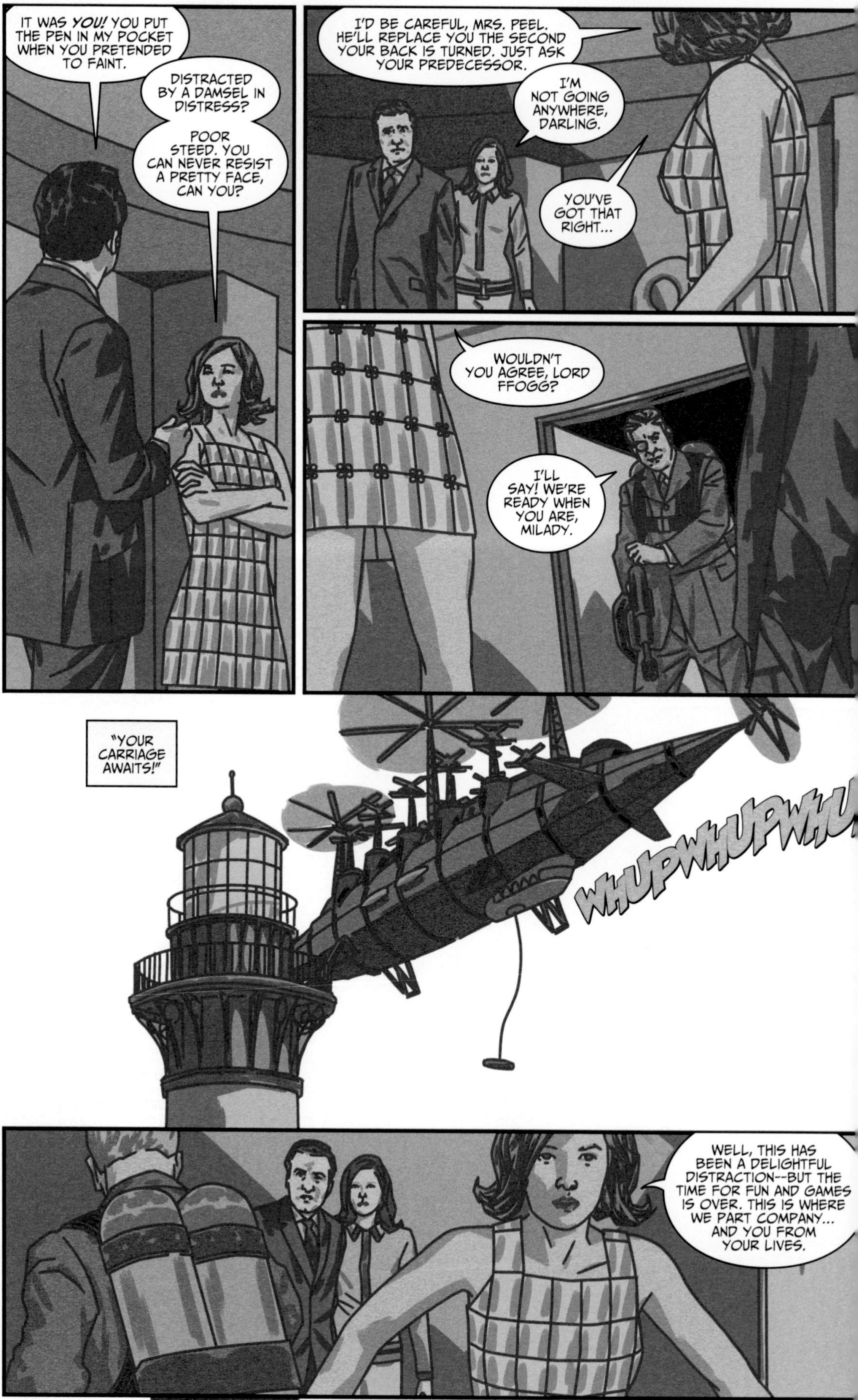

IT WAS *YOU!* YOU PUT THE PEN IN MY POCKET WHEN YOU PRETENDED TO FAINT.
DISTRACTED BY A DAMSEL IN DISTRESS?
POOR STEED. YOU CAN NEVER RESIST A PRETTY FACE, CAN YOU?
I'D BE CAREFUL, MRS. PEEL. HE'LL REPLACE YOU THE SECOND YOUR BACK IS TURNED. JUST ASK YOUR PREDECESSOR.
I'M NOT GOING ANYWHERE, DARLING.
YOU'VE GOT THAT RIGHT...
WOULDN'T YOU AGREE, LORD FFOGG?
I'LL SAY! WE'RE READY WHEN YOU ARE, MILADY.
"YOUR CARRIAGE AWAITS!"
WHUPWHUPWHU
WELL, THIS HAS BEEN A DELIGHTFUL DISTRACTION--BUT THE TIME FOR FUN AND GAMES IS OVER. THIS IS WHERE WE PART COMPANY... AND YOU FROM YOUR LIVES.

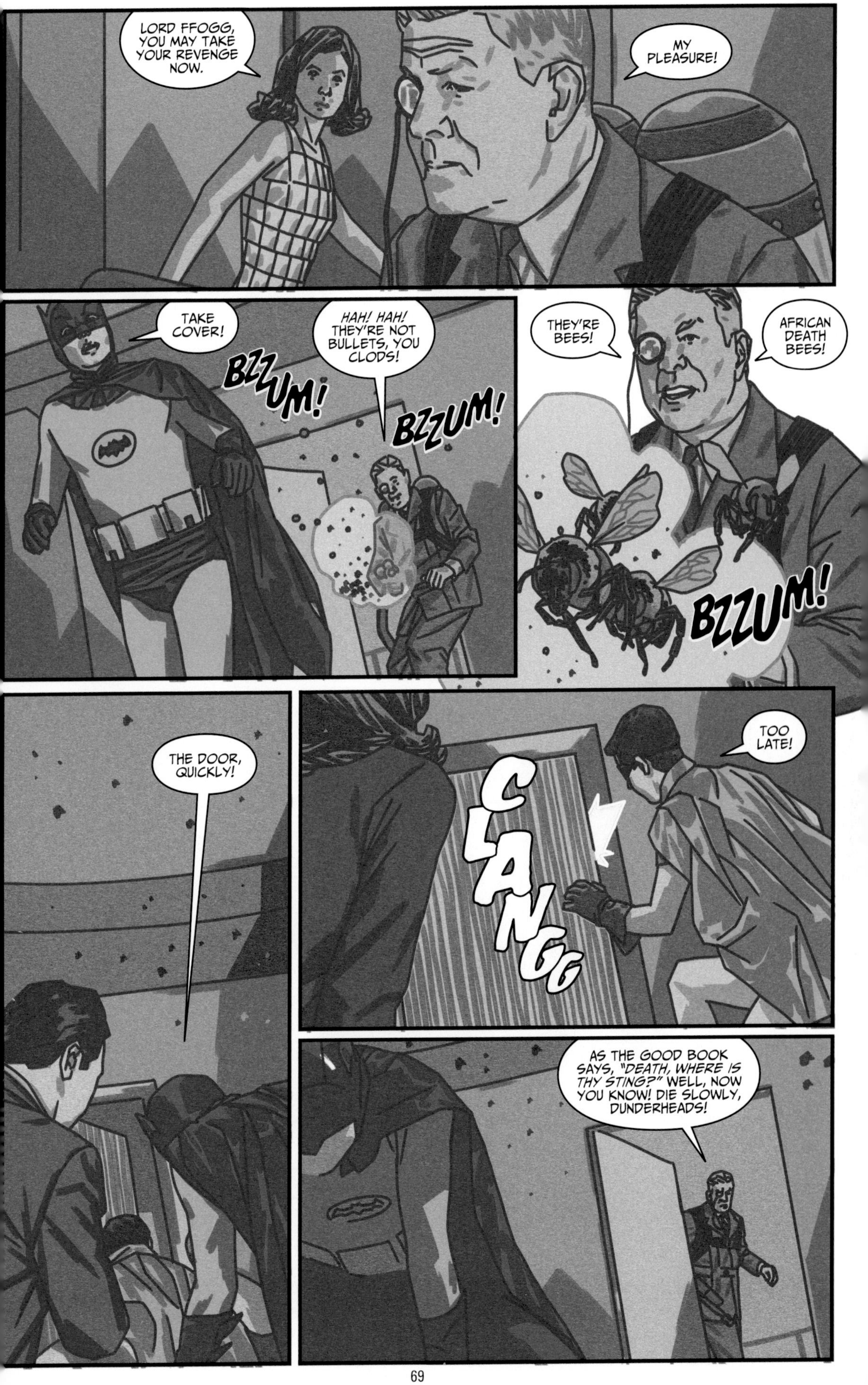
LORD FFOGG, YOU MAY TAKE YOUR REVENGE NOW.
MY PLEASURE!
TAKE COVER!
BZZUM!
HAH! HAH! THEY'RE NOT BULLETS, YOU CLODS!
BZZUM!
THEY'RE BEES!
AFRICAN DEATH BEES!
BZZUM!
THE DOOR, QUICKLY!
CLANGG
TOO LATE!
AS THE GOOD BOOK SAYS, "DEATH, WHERE IS THY STING?" WELL, NOW YOU KNOW! DIE SLOWLY, DUNDERHEADS!

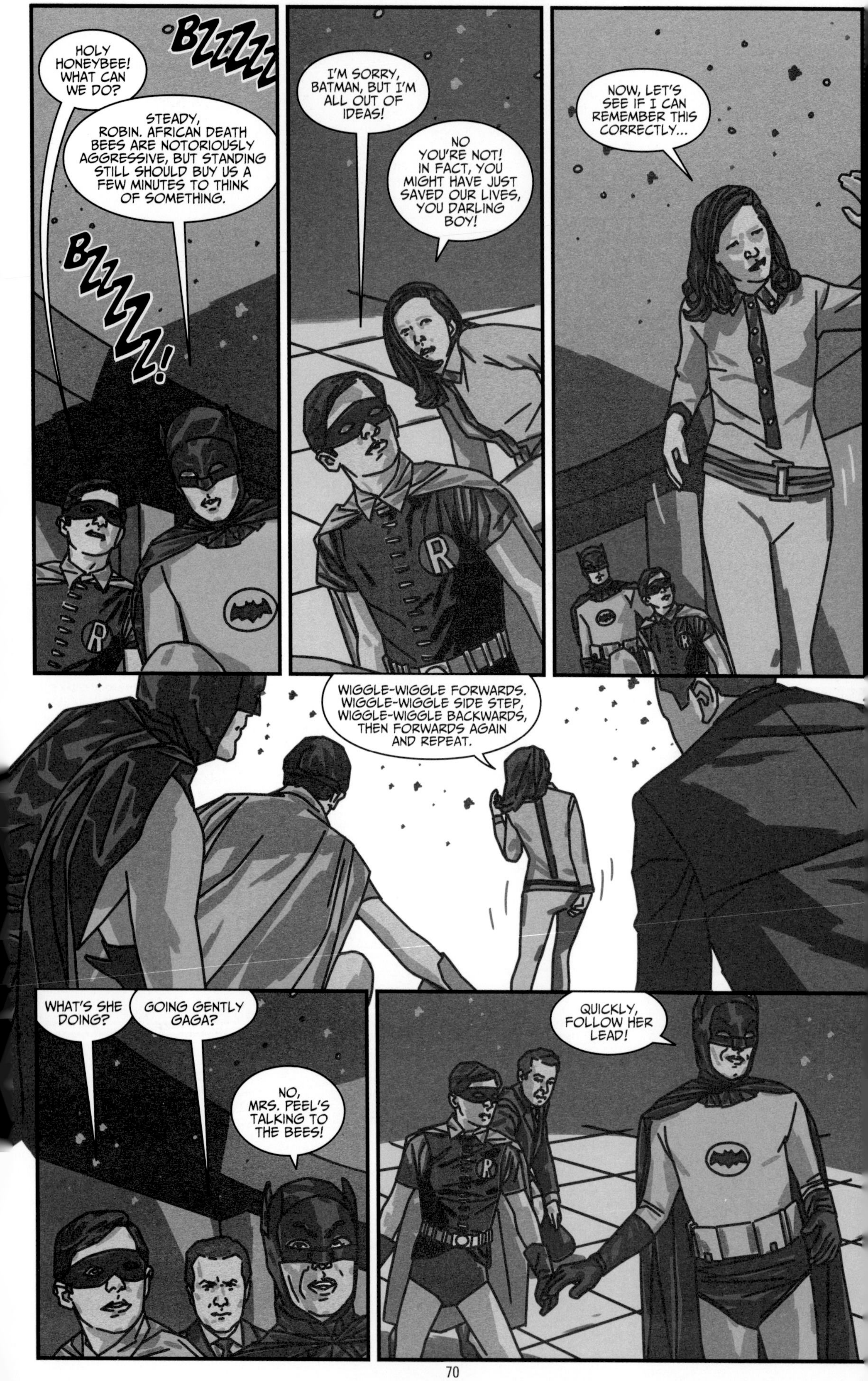
BZZZZZ
HOLY HONEYBEE! WHAT CAN WE DO?
STEADY, ROBIN. AFRICAN DEATH BEES ARE NOTORIOUSLY AGGRESSIVE, BUT STANDING STILL SHOULD BUY US A FEW MINUTES TO THINK OF SOMETHING.
BZZZZZ!
I'M SORRY, BATMAN, BUT I'M ALL OUT OF IDEAS!
NO YOU'RE NOT! IN FACT, YOU MIGHT HAVE JUST SAVED OUR LIVES, YOU DARLING BOY!
NOW, LET'S SEE IF I CAN REMEMBER THIS CORRECTLY...
WIGGLE-WIGGLE FORWARDS. WIGGLE-WIGGLE SIDE STEP, WIGGLE-WIGGLE BACKWARDS, THEN FORWARDS AGAIN AND REPEAT.
WHAT'S SHE DOING?
GOING GENTLY GAGA?
NO, MRS. PEEL'S TALKING TO THE BEES!
QUICKLY, FOLLOW HER LEAD!

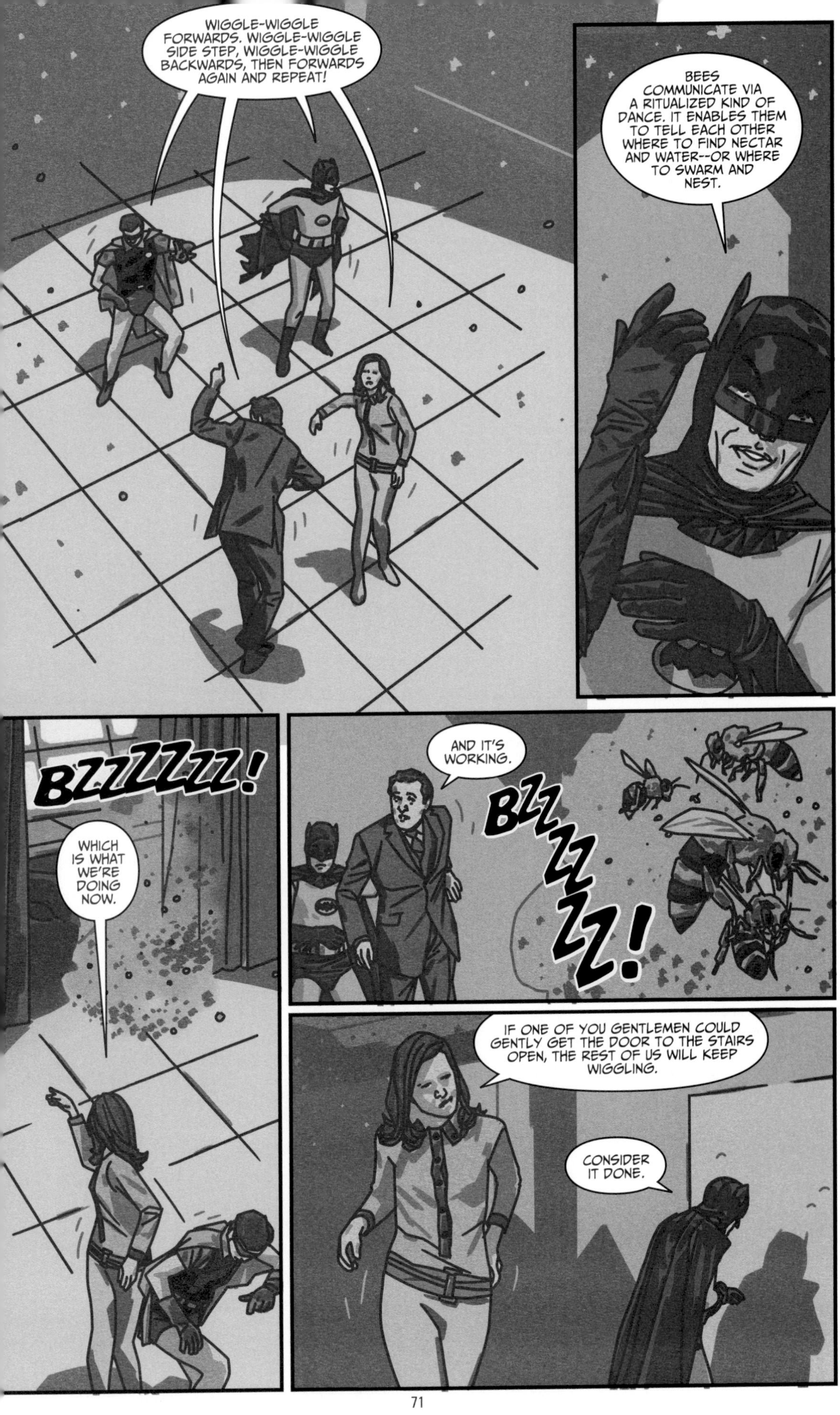
WIGGLE-WIGGLE FORWARDS. WIGGLE-WIGGLE SIDE STEP, WIGGLE-WIGGLE BACKWARDS, THEN FORWARDS AGAIN AND REPEAT!
BEES COMMUNICATE VIA A RITUALIZED KIND OF DANCE. IT ENABLES THEM TO TELL EACH OTHER WHERE TO FIND NECTAR AND WATER--OR WHERE TO SWARM AND NEST.
BZZZZZZZ!
WHICH IS WHAT WE'RE DOING NOW.
AND IT'S WORKING.
BZZZZ!
IF ONE OF YOU GENTLEMEN COULD GENTLY GET THE DOOR TO THE STAIRS OPEN, THE REST OF US WILL KEEP WIGGLING.
CONSIDER IT DONE.

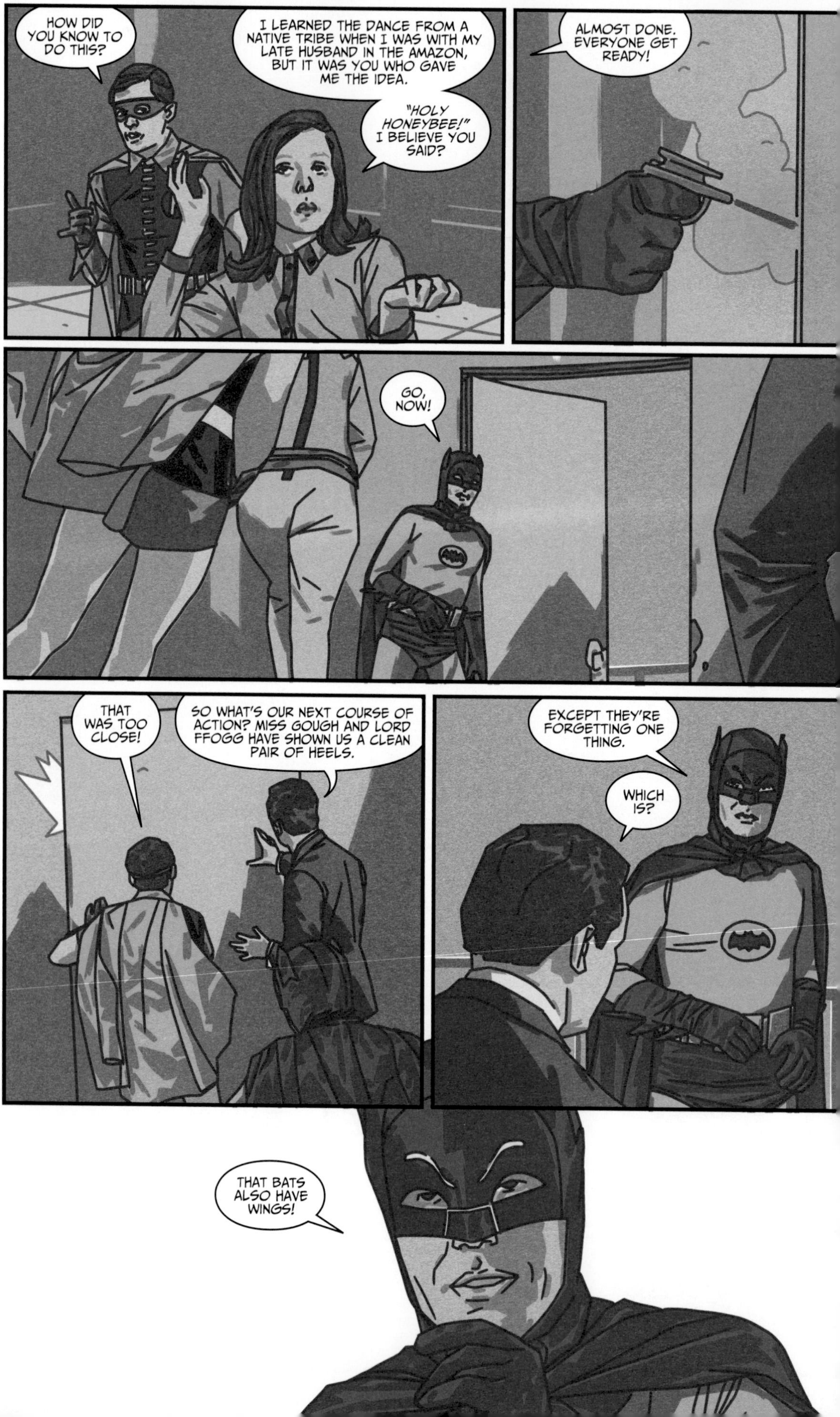
HOW DID YOU KNOW TO DO THIS?
I LEARNED THE DANCE FROM A NATIVE TRIBE WHEN I WAS WITH MY LATE HUSBAND IN THE AMAZON, BUT IT WAS YOU WHO GAVE ME THE IDEA.
"HOLY HONEYBEE!" I BELIEVE YOU SAID?
ALMOST DONE. EVERYONE GET READY!
GO, NOW!
THAT WAS TOO CLOSE!
SO WHAT'S OUR NEXT COURSE OF ACTION? MISS GOUGH AND LORD FFOGG HAVE SHOWN US A CLEAN PAIR OF HEELS.
EXCEPT THEY'RE FORGETTING ONE THING.
WHICH IS?
THAT BATS ALSO HAVE WINGS!

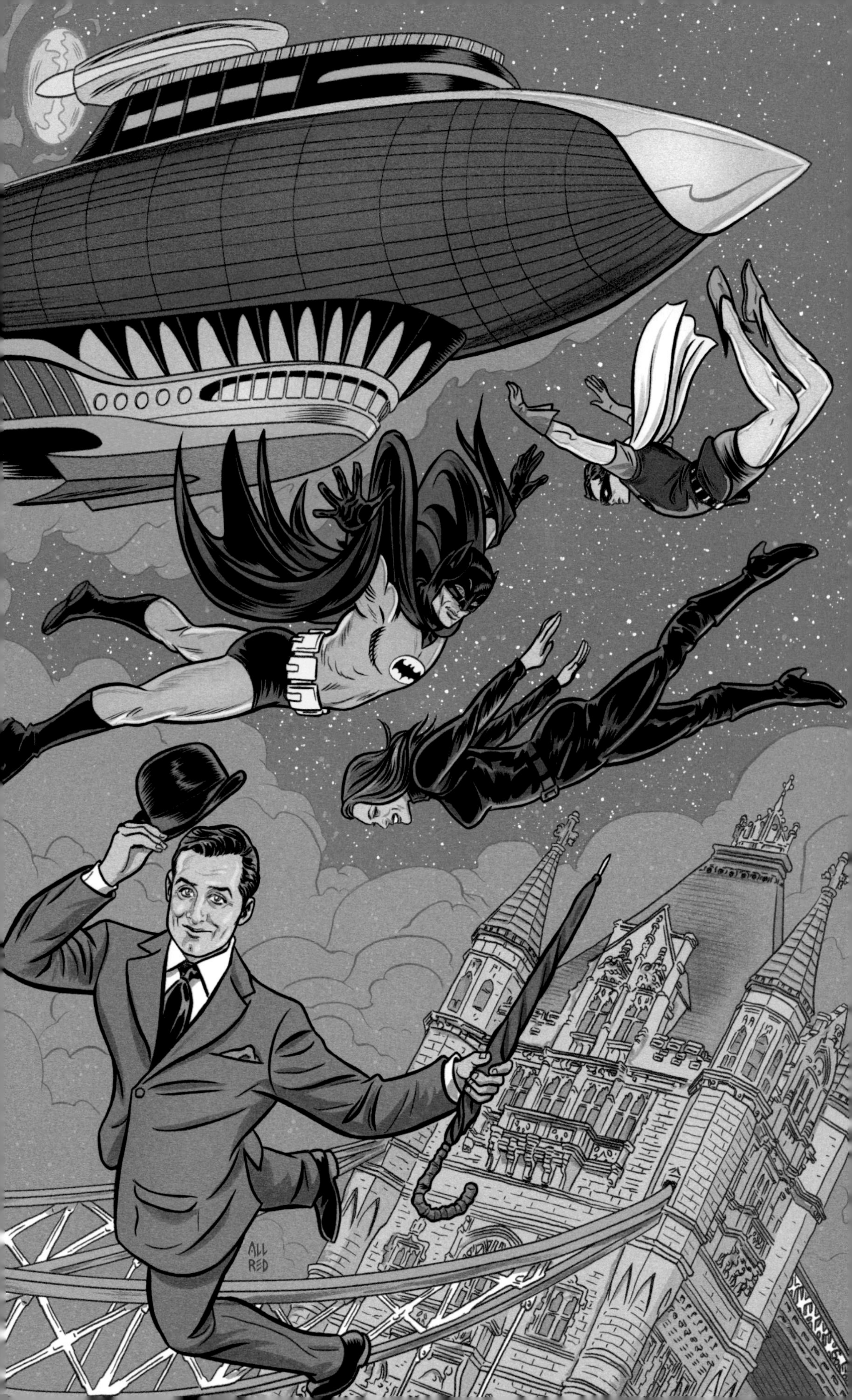
ALL
RED

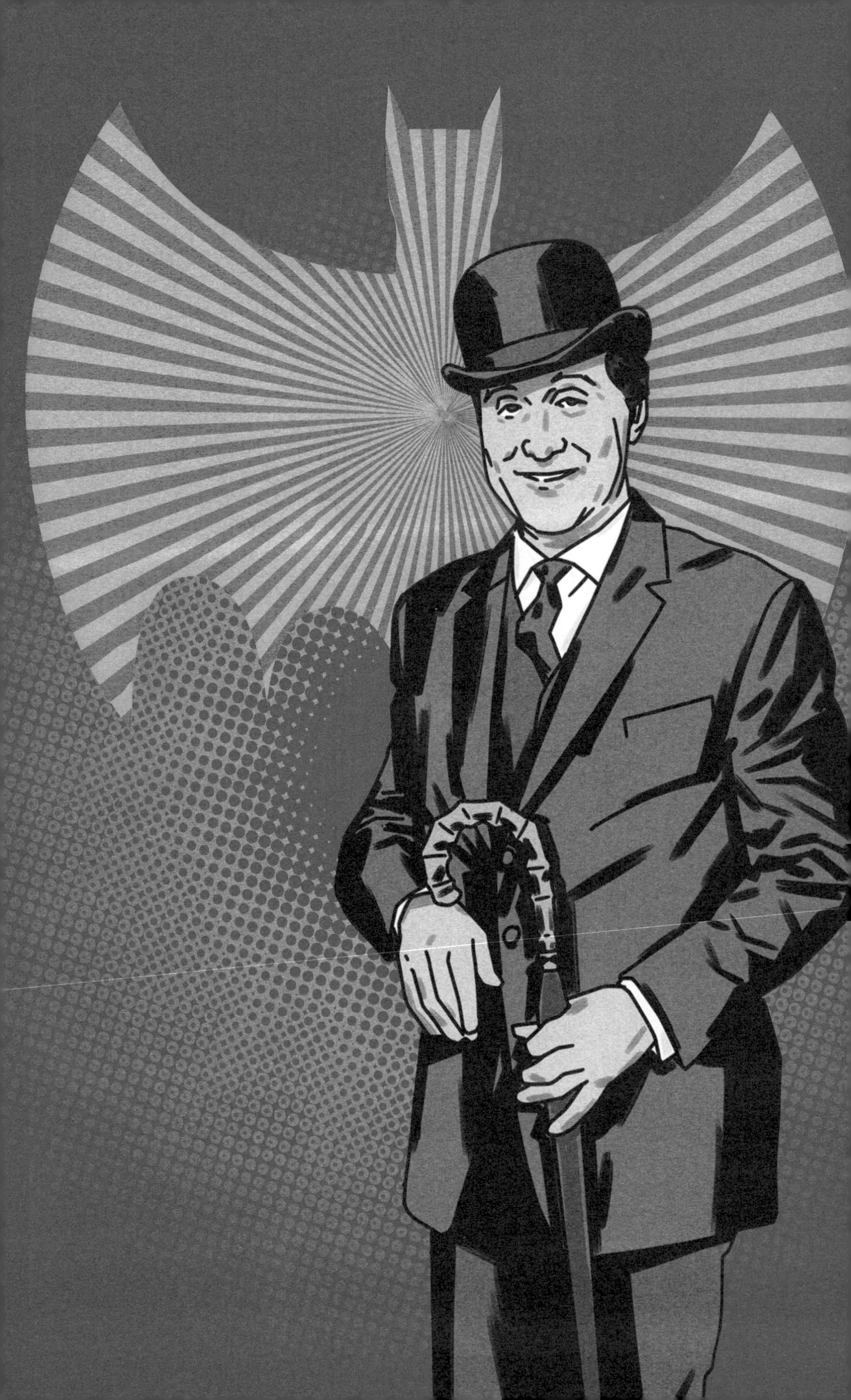

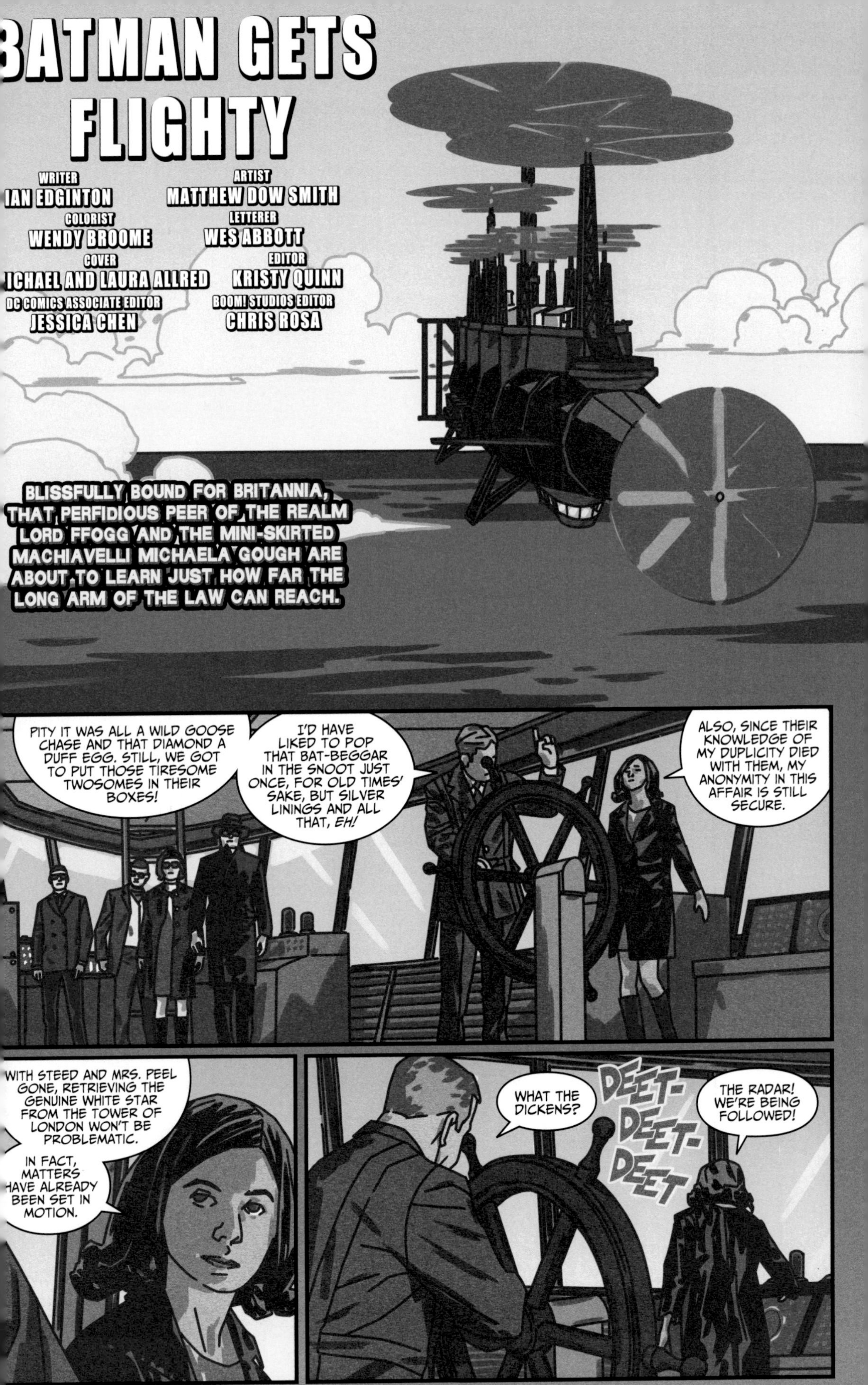

BATMAN GETS FLIGHTY
WRITER IAN EDGINTON
ARTIST MATTHEW DOW SMITH
COLORIST WENDY BROOME
LETTERER WES ABBOTT
COVER ICHAEL AND LAURA ALLRED
EDITOR KRISTY QUINN
DC COMICS ASSOCIATE EDITOR JESSICA CHEN
BOOM! STUDIOS EDITOR CHRIS ROSA
BLISSFULLY BOUND FOR BRITANNIA, THAT PERFIDIOUS PEER OF THE REALM LORD FFOGG AND THE MINI-SKIRTED MACHIAVELLI MICHAELA GOUGH ARE ABOUT TO LEARN JUST HOW FAR THE LONG ARM OF THE LAW CAN REACH.
PITY IT WAS ALL A WILD GOOSE CHASE AND THAT DIAMOND A DUFF EGG. STILL, WE GOT TO PUT THOSE TIRESOME TWOSOMES IN THEIR BOXES!
I'D HAVE LIKED TO POP THAT BAT-BEGGAR IN THE SNOOT JUST ONCE, FOR OLD TIMES' SAKE, BUT SILVER LININGS AND ALL THAT, *EH!*
ALSO, SINCE THEIR KNOWLEDGE OF MY DUPLICITY DIED WITH THEM, MY ANONYMITY IN THIS AFFAIR IS STILL SECURE.
WITH STEED AND MRS. PEEL GONE, RETRIEVING THE GENUINE WHITE STAR FROM THE TOWER OF LONDON WON'T BE PROBLEMATIC.
IN FACT, MATTERS HAVE ALREADY BEEN SET IN MOTION.
WHAT THE DICKENS?
DEET-DEET-DEET
THE RADAR! WE'RE BEING FOLLOWED!

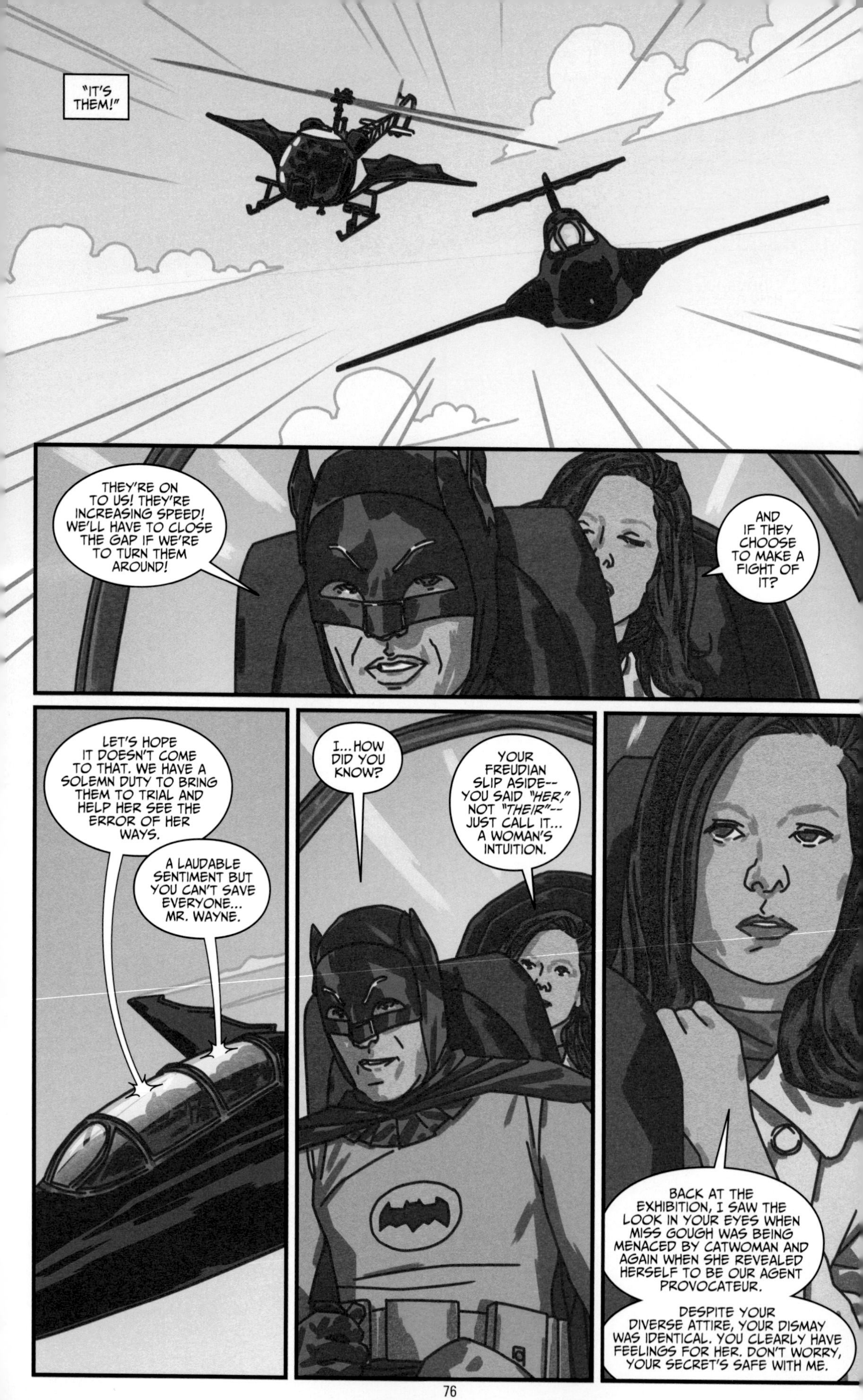
"IT'S THEM!"
THEY'RE ON TO US! THEY'RE INCREASING SPEED! WE'LL HAVE TO CLOSE THE GAP IF WE'RE TO TURN THEM AROUND!
AND IF THEY CHOOSE TO MAKE A FIGHT OF IT?
LET'S HOPE IT DOESN'T COME TO THAT. WE HAVE A SOLEMN DUTY TO BRING THEM TO TRIAL AND HELP HER SEE THE ERROR OF HER WAYS.
A LAUDABLE SENTIMENT BUT YOU CAN'T SAVE EVERYONE... MR. WAYNE.
I...HOW DID YOU KNOW?
YOUR FREUDIAN SLIP ASIDE-- YOU SAID *"HER,"* NOT *"THEIR"*-- JUST CALL IT... A WOMAN'S INTUITION.
BACK AT THE EXHIBITION, I SAW THE LOOK IN YOUR EYES WHEN MISS GOUGH WAS BEING MENACED BY CATWOMAN AND AGAIN WHEN SHE REVEALED HERSELF TO BE OUR AGENT PROVOCATEUR.
DESPITE YOUR DIVERSE ATTIRE, YOUR DISMAY WAS IDENTICAL. YOU CLEARLY HAVE FEELINGS FOR HER. DON'T WORRY, YOUR SECRET'S SAFE WITH ME.

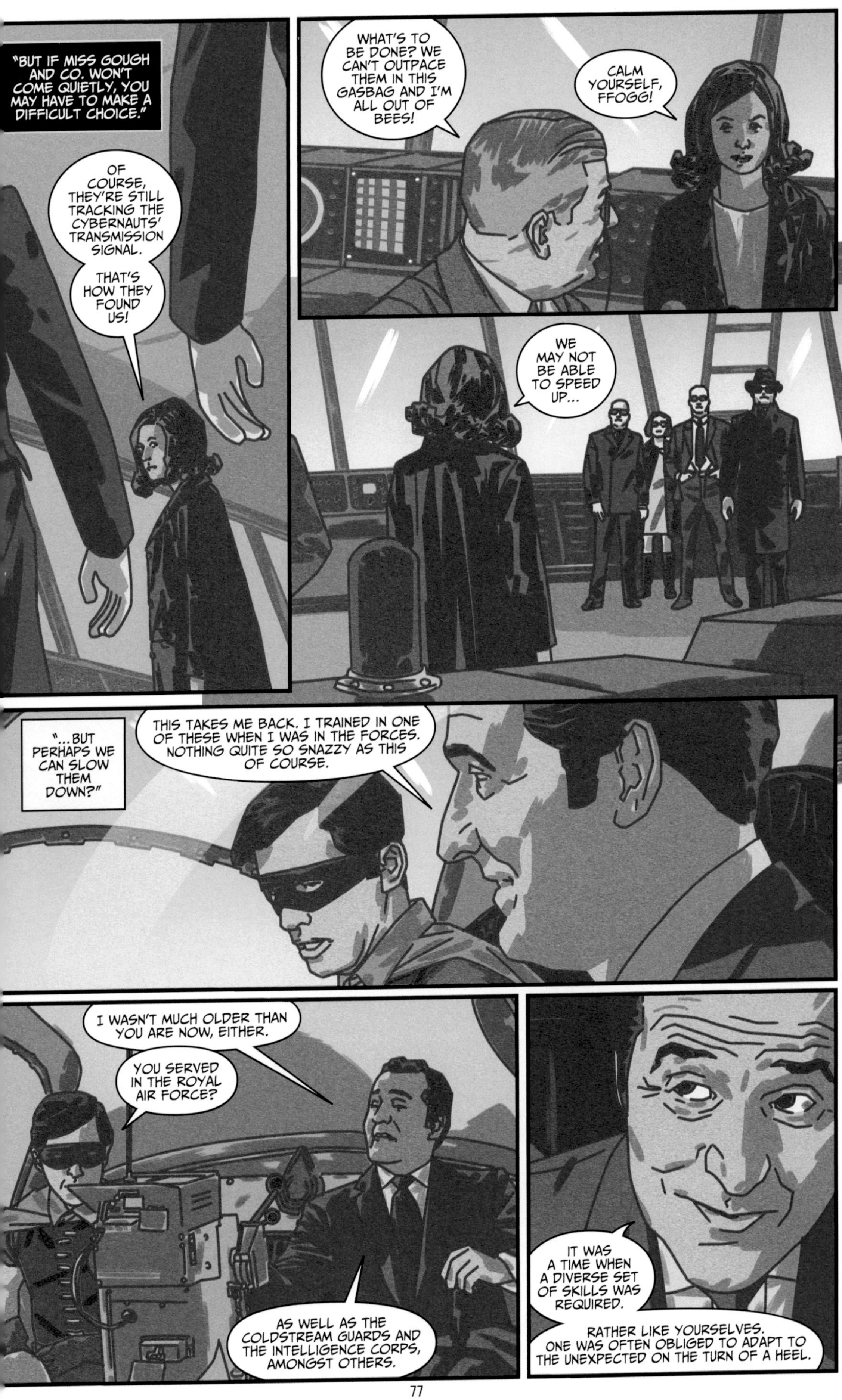
"BUT IF MISS GOUGH AND CO. WON'T COME QUIETLY, YOU MAY HAVE TO MAKE A DIFFICULT CHOICE."
OF COURSE, THEY'RE STILL TRACKING THE CYBERNAUTS' TRANSMISSION SIGNAL.
THAT'S HOW THEY FOUND US!
WHAT'S TO BE DONE? WE CAN'T OUTPACE THEM IN THIS GASBAG AND I'M ALL OUT OF BEES!
CALM YOURSELF, FFOGG!
WE MAY NOT BE ABLE TO SPEED UP...
"...BUT PERHAPS WE CAN SLOW THEM DOWN?"
THIS TAKES ME BACK. I TRAINED IN ONE OF THESE WHEN I WAS IN THE FORCES. NOTHING QUITE SO SNAZZY AS THIS OF COURSE.
I WASN'T MUCH OLDER THAN YOU ARE NOW, EITHER.
YOU SERVED IN THE ROYAL AIR FORCE?
AS WELL AS THE COLDSTREAM GUARDS AND THE INTELLIGENCE CORPS, AMONGST OTHERS.
IT WAS A TIME WHEN A DIVERSE SET OF SKILLS WAS REQUIRED.
RATHER LIKE YOURSELVES. ONE WAS OFTEN OBLIGED TO ADAPT TO THE UNEXPECTED ON THE TURN OF A HEEL.

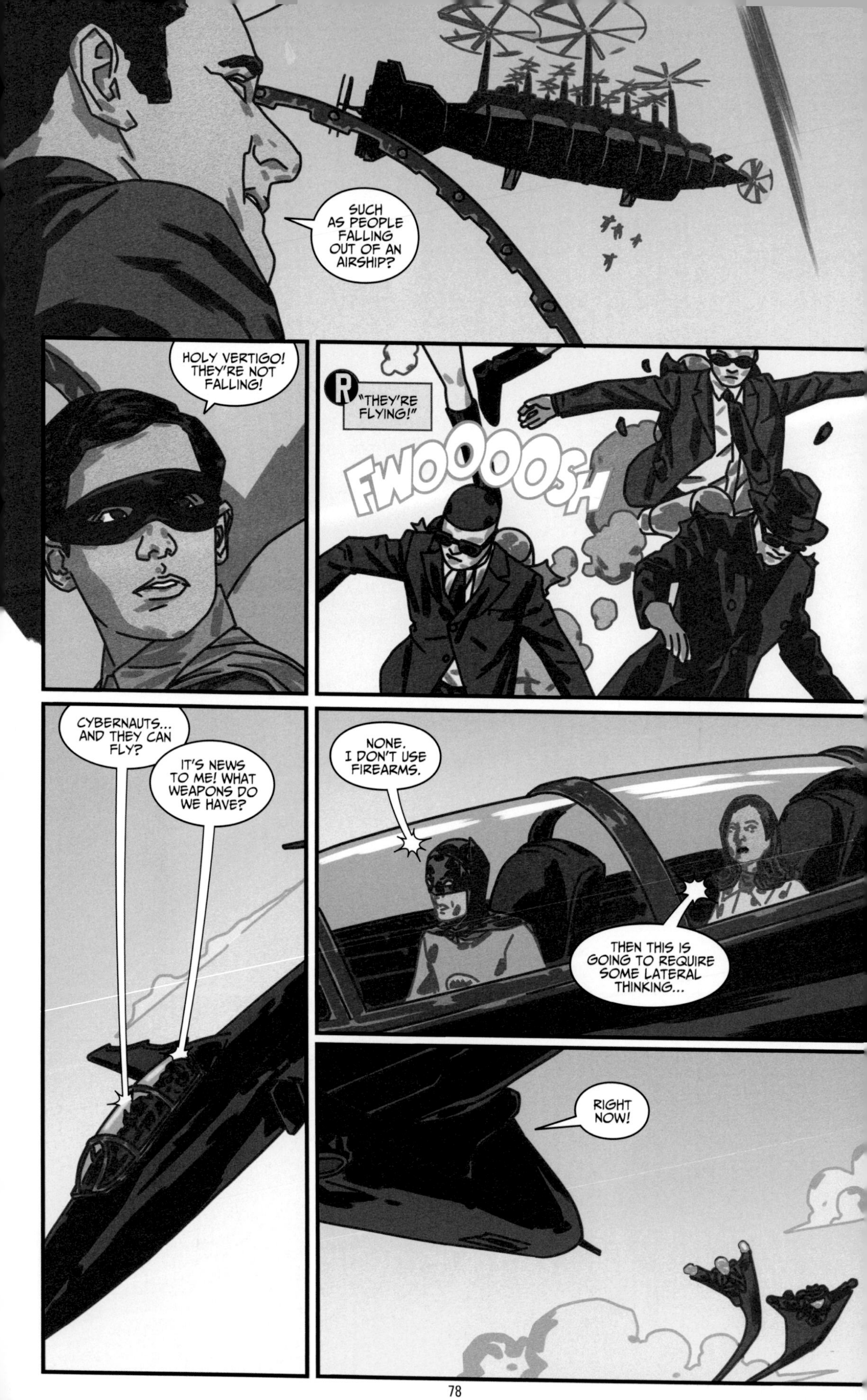
SUCH AS PEOPLE FALLING OUT OF AN AIRSHIP?
HOLY VERTIGO! THEY'RE NOT FALLING!
"THEY'RE FLYING!"
FWOOOOOSH
CYBERNAUTS... AND THEY CAN FLY?
IT'S NEWS TO ME! WHAT WEAPONS DO WE HAVE?
NONE. I DON'T USE FIREARMS.
THEN THIS IS GOING TO REQUIRE SOME LATERAL THINKING...
RIGHT NOW!

WHSSH FSSHHHH

IMPRESSIVE! WE'LL NEED A FEW MORE BRIGHT IDEAS LIKE THAT.

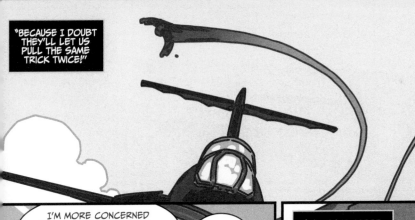

"BECAUSE I DOUBT THEY'LL LET US PULL THE SAME TRICK TWICE!"

I'M MORE CONCERNED ABOUT STEED AND ROBIN-- THEY DON'T HAVE OUR SPEED OR MANEUVERABILITY! THEY'RE SITTING DUCKS!

OH, I WOULDN'T WORRY UNDULY.

"I'M SURE STEED HAS THE SITUATION WELL IN HAND."

ANY SUGGESTIONS?

I...

79

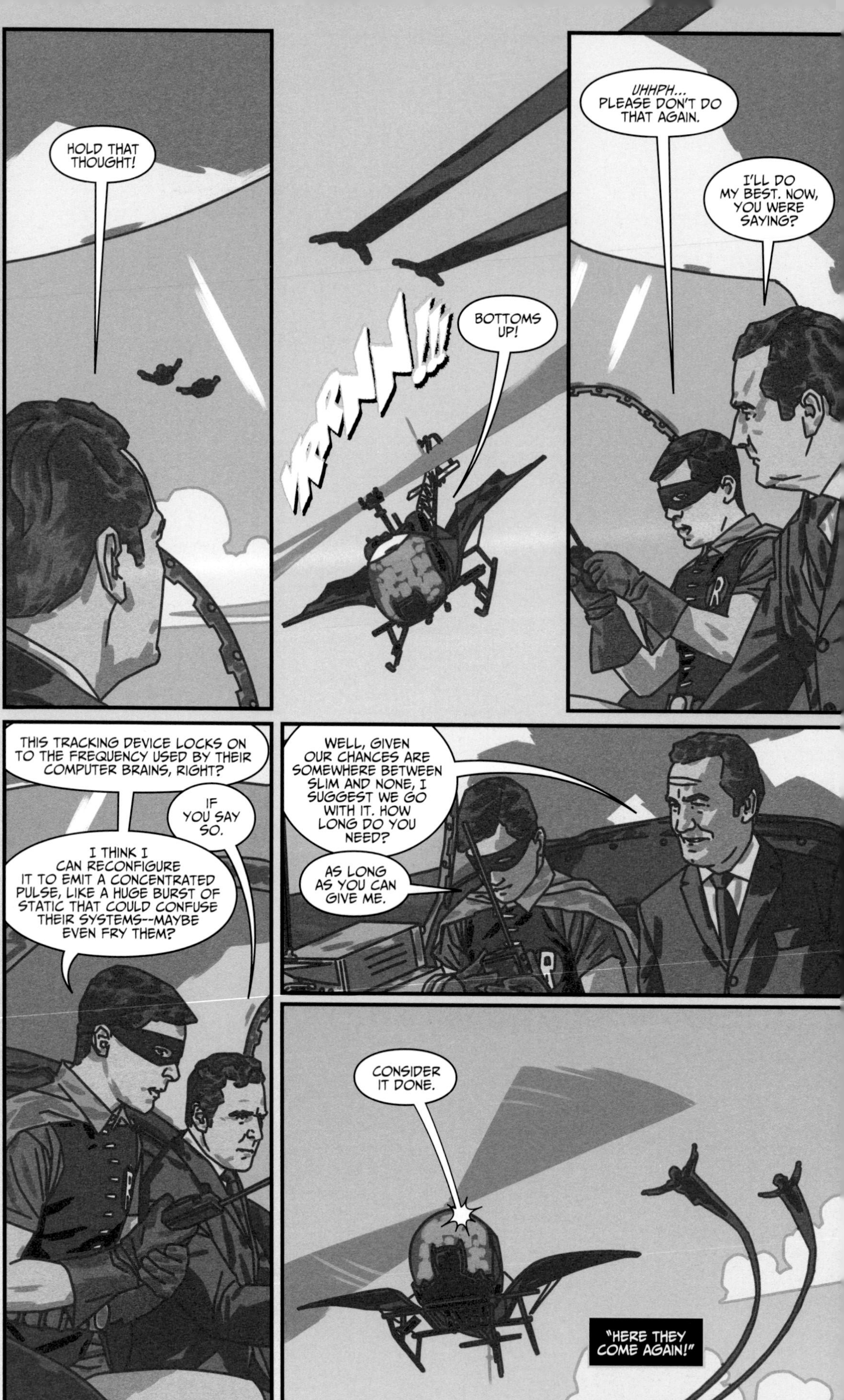
HOLD THAT THOUGHT!
WRRRMM!!!
BOTTOMS UP!
UHHPH... PLEASE DON'T DO THAT AGAIN.
I'LL DO MY BEST. NOW, YOU WERE SAYING?
THIS TRACKING DEVICE LOCKS ON TO THE FREQUENCY USED BY THEIR COMPUTER BRAINS, RIGHT?
IF YOU SAY SO.
I THINK I CAN RECONFIGURE IT TO EMIT A CONCENTRATED PULSE, LIKE A HUGE BURST OF STATIC THAT COULD CONFUSE THEIR SYSTEMS--MAYBE EVEN FRY THEM?
WELL, GIVEN OUR CHANCES ARE SOMEWHERE BETWEEN SLIM AND NONE, I SUGGEST WE GO WITH IT. HOW LONG DO YOU NEED?
AS LONG AS YOU CAN GIVE ME.
CONSIDER IT DONE.
"HERE THEY COME AGAIN!"

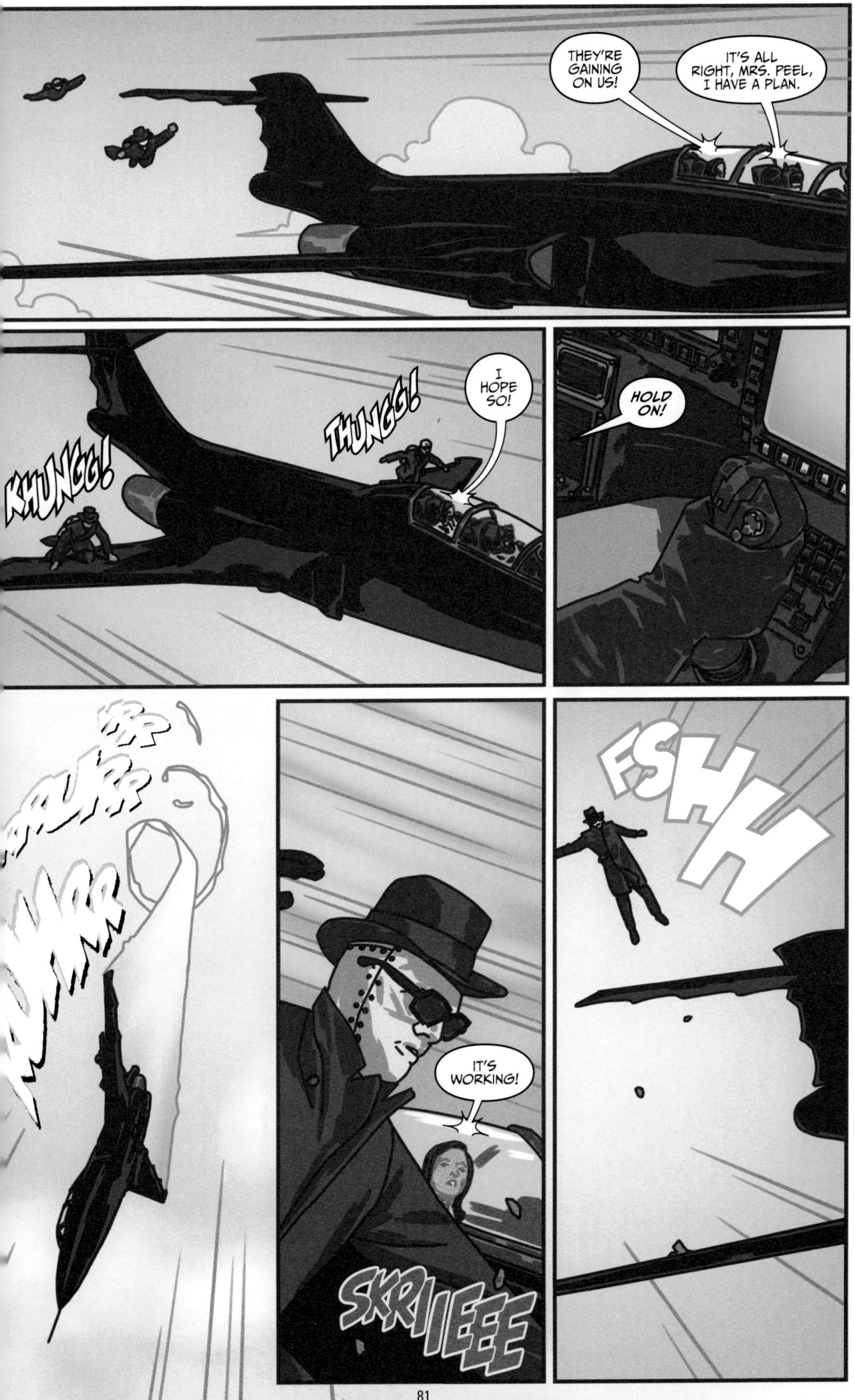
THEY'RE GAINING ON US!
IT'S ALL RIGHT, MRS. PEEL, I HAVE A PLAN.
KHUNGG!
THUNGG!
I HOPE SO!
HOLD ON!
IT'S WORKING!
SKRIIEEE
FSHH

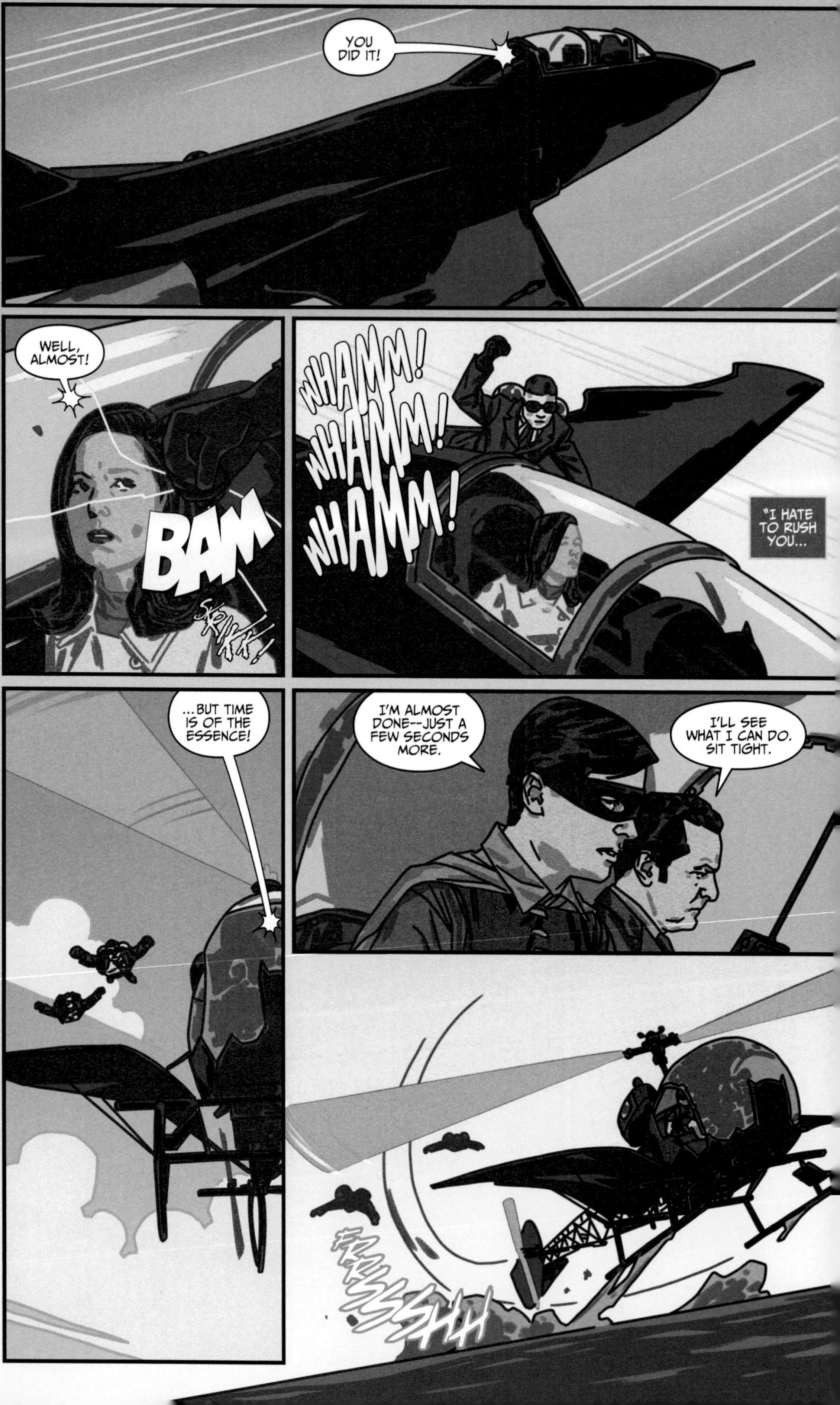
YOU DID IT!
WELL, ALMOST!
BAM
SKRIKK!
WHAMM! WHAMM! WHAMM!
"I HATE TO RUSH YOU...
...BUT TIME IS OF THE ESSENCE!
I'M ALMOST DONE--JUST A FEW SECONDS MORE.
I'LL SEE WHAT I CAN DO. SIT TIGHT.
FRSSSHH

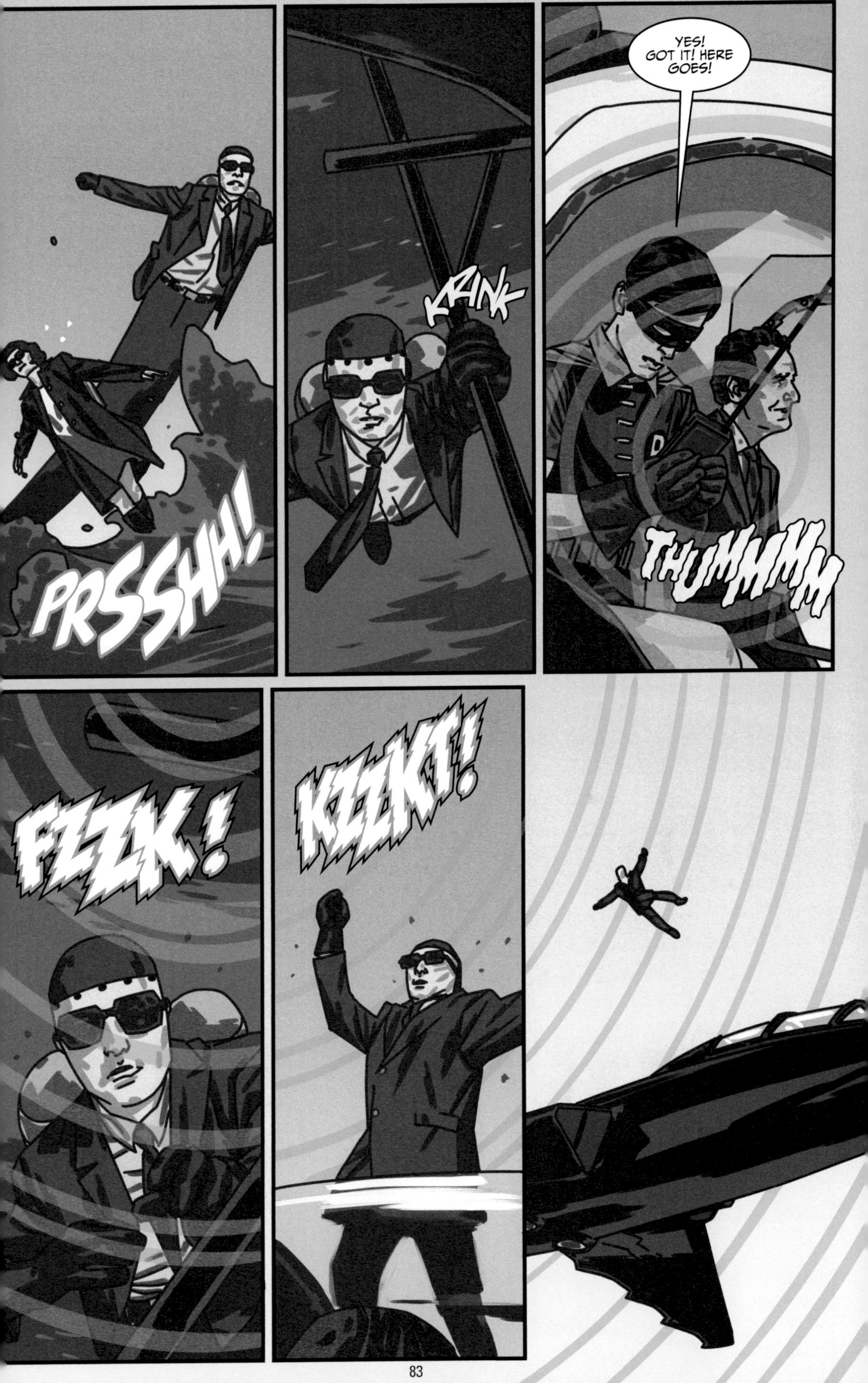
PRSSHH!
KRINK
YES! GOT IT! HERE GOES!
THUMMMM
FZZK!
KZZKT!

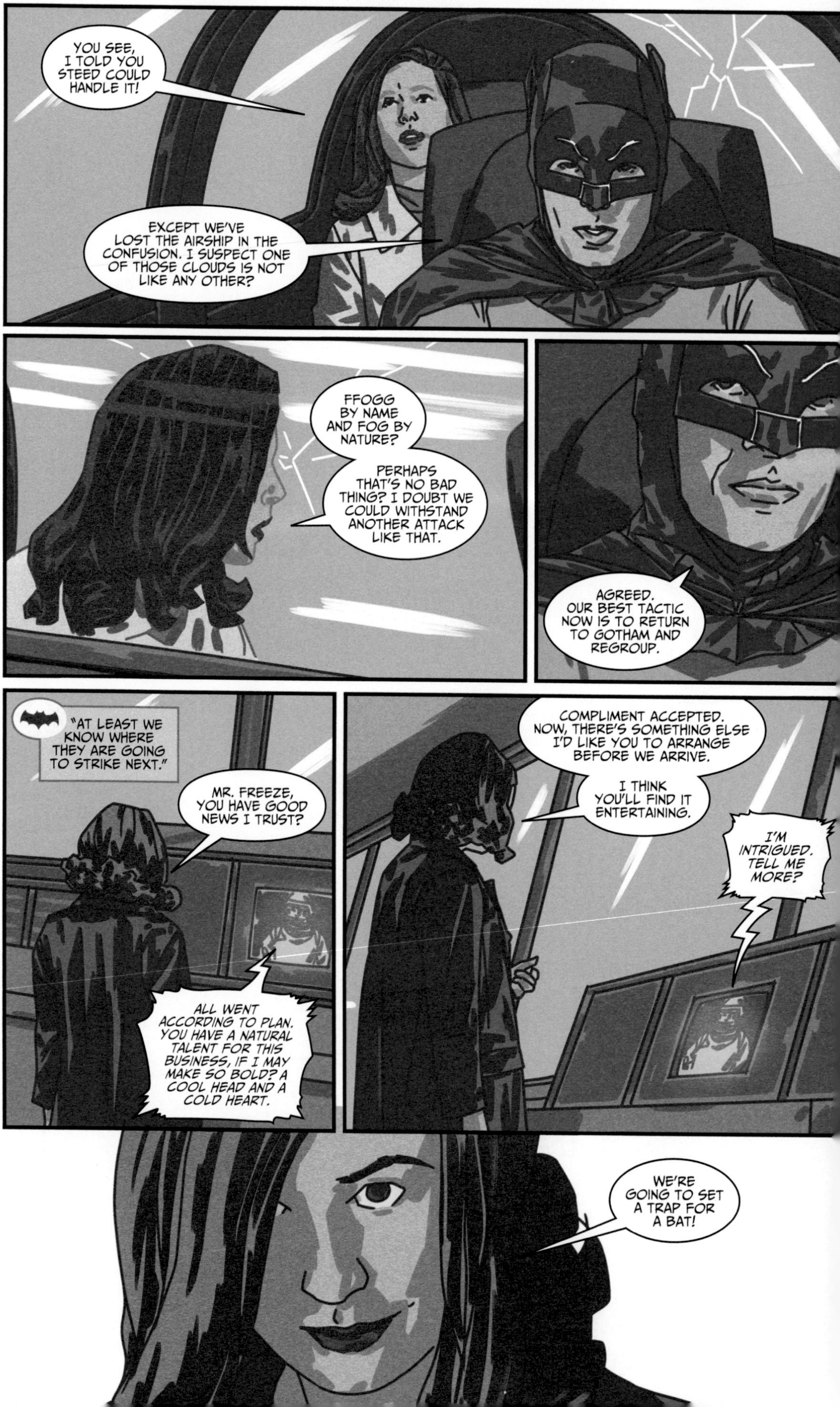
YOU SEE, I TOLD YOU STEED COULD HANDLE IT!
EXCEPT WE'VE LOST THE AIRSHIP IN THE CONFUSION. I SUSPECT ONE OF THOSE CLOUDS IS NOT LIKE ANY OTHER?
FFOGG BY NAME AND FOG BY NATURE?
PERHAPS THAT'S NO BAD THING? I DOUBT WE COULD WITHSTAND ANOTHER ATTACK LIKE THAT.
AGREED. OUR BEST TACTIC NOW IS TO RETURN TO GOTHAM AND REGROUP.
"AT LEAST WE KNOW WHERE THEY ARE GOING TO STRIKE NEXT."
MR. FREEZE, YOU HAVE GOOD NEWS I TRUST?
ALL WENT ACCORDING TO PLAN. YOU HAVE A NATURAL TALENT FOR THIS BUSINESS, IF I MAY MAKE SO BOLD? A COOL HEAD AND A COLD HEART.
COMPLIMENT ACCEPTED. NOW, THERE'S SOMETHING ELSE I'D LIKE YOU TO ARRANGE BEFORE WE ARRIVE.
I THINK YOU'LL FIND IT ENTERTAINING.
I'M INTRIGUED. TELL ME MORE?
WE'RE GOING TO SET A TRAP FOR A BAT!

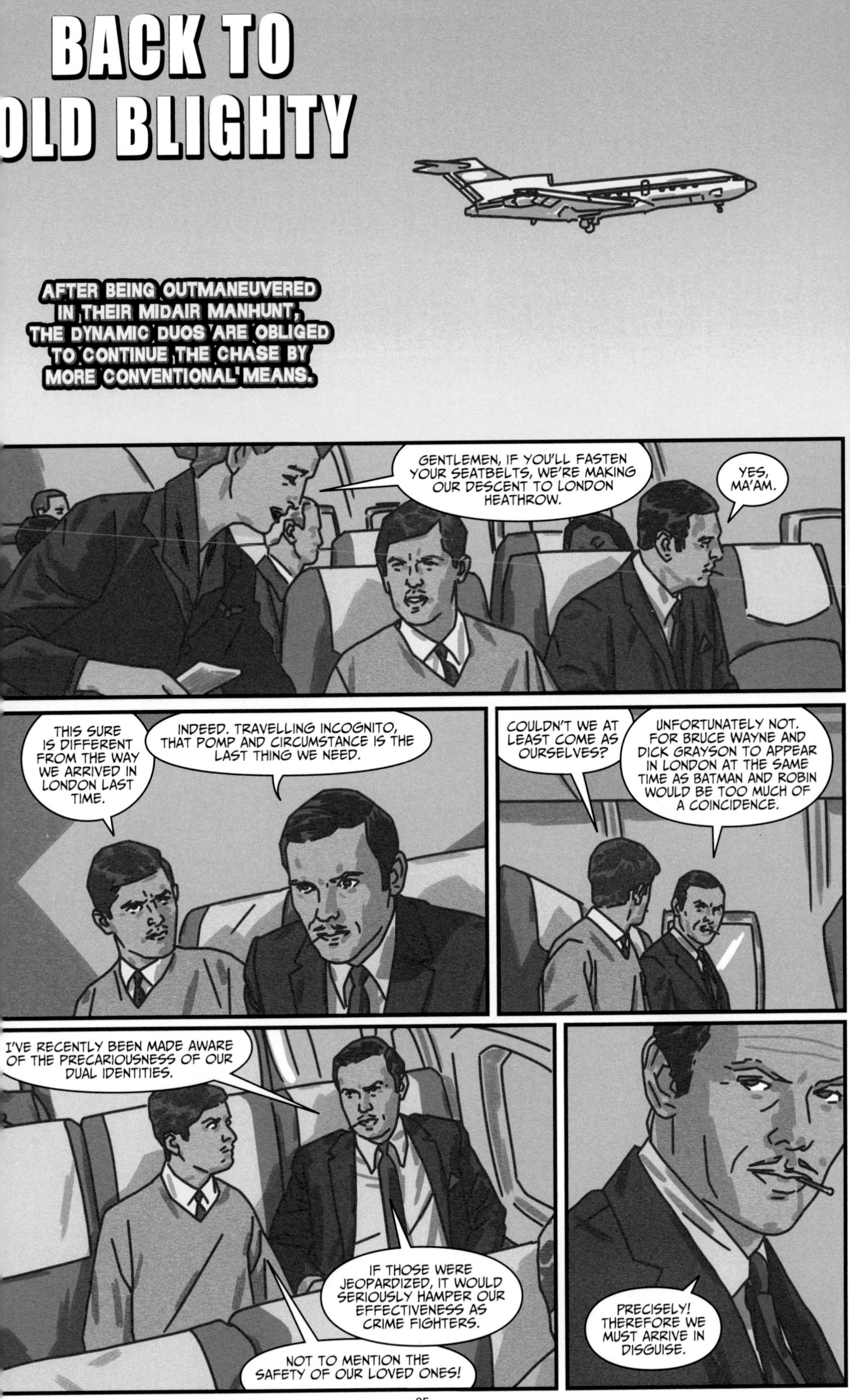
BACK TO OLD BLIGHTY
AFTER BEING OUTMANEUVERED IN THEIR MIDAIR MANHUNT, THE DYNAMIC DUOS ARE OBLIGED TO CONTINUE THE CHASE BY MORE CONVENTIONAL MEANS.
GENTLEMEN, IF YOU'LL FASTEN YOUR SEATBELTS, WE'RE MAKING OUR DESCENT TO LONDON HEATHROW.
YES, MA'AM.
THIS SURE IS DIFFERENT FROM THE WAY WE ARRIVED IN LONDON LAST TIME.
INDEED. TRAVELLING INCOGNITO, THAT POMP AND CIRCUMSTANCE IS THE LAST THING WE NEED.
COULDN'T WE AT LEAST COME AS OURSELVES?
UNFORTUNATELY NOT. FOR BRUCE WAYNE AND DICK GRAYSON TO APPEAR IN LONDON AT THE SAME TIME AS BATMAN AND ROBIN WOULD BE TOO MUCH OF A COINCIDENCE.
I'VE RECENTLY BEEN MADE AWARE OF THE PRECARIOUSNESS OF OUR DUAL IDENTITIES.
IF THOSE WERE JEOPARDIZED, IT WOULD SERIOUSLY HAMPER OUR EFFECTIVENESS AS CRIME FIGHTERS.
NOT TO MENTION THE SAFETY OF OUR LOVED ONES!
PRECISELY! THEREFORE WE MUST ARRIVE IN DISGUISE.

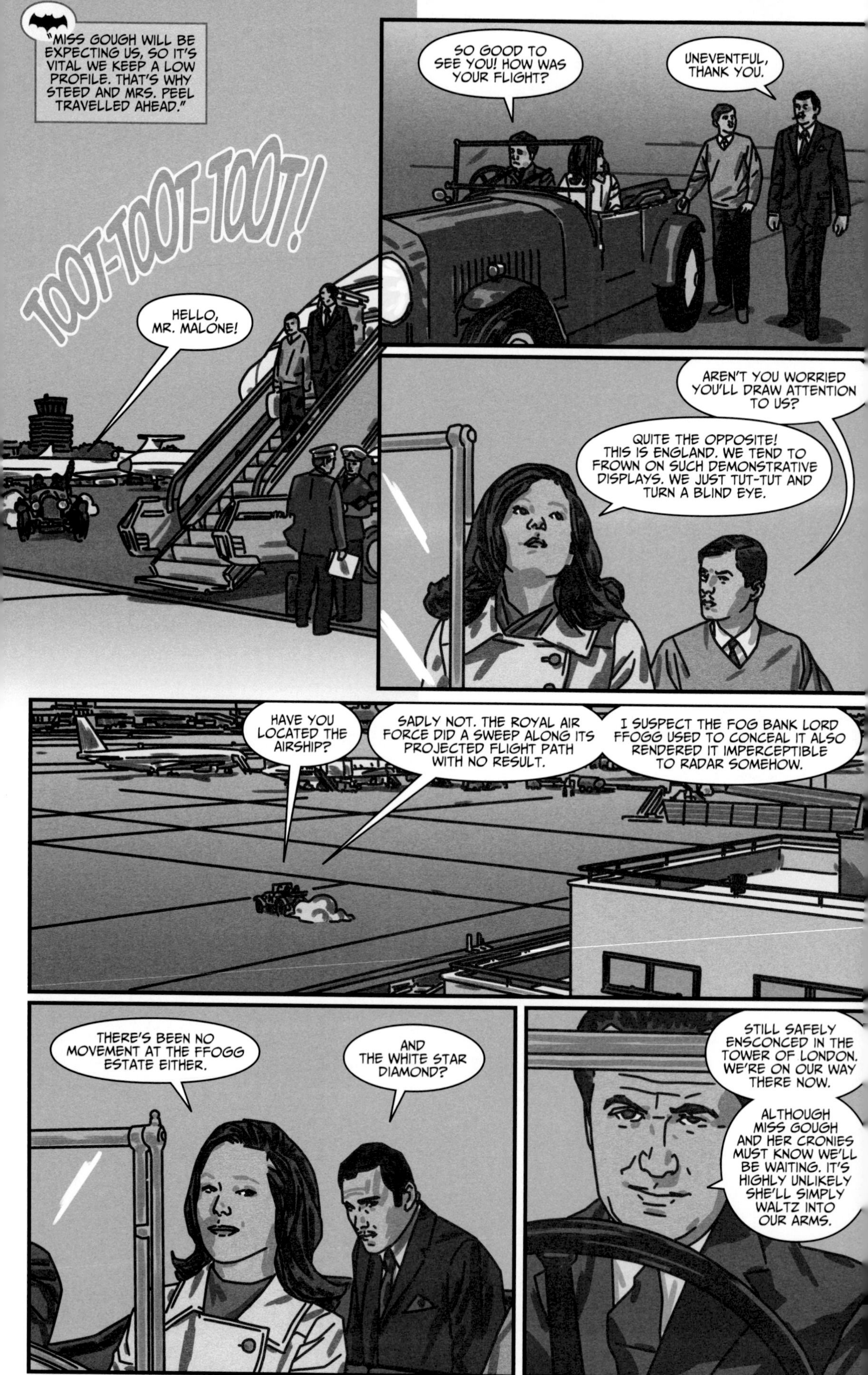
"MISS GOUGH WILL BE EXPECTING US, SO IT'S VITAL WE KEEP A LOW PROFILE. THAT'S WHY STEED AND MRS. PEEL TRAVELLED AHEAD."
TOOT-TOOT-TOOT!
HELLO, MR. MALONE!
SO GOOD TO SEE YOU! HOW WAS YOUR FLIGHT?
UNEVENTFUL, THANK YOU.
AREN'T YOU WORRIED YOU'LL DRAW ATTENTION TO US?
QUITE THE OPPOSITE! THIS IS ENGLAND. WE TEND TO FROWN ON SUCH DEMONSTRATIVE DISPLAYS. WE JUST TUT-TUT AND TURN A BLIND EYE.
HAVE YOU LOCATED THE AIRSHIP?
SADLY NOT. THE ROYAL AIR FORCE DID A SWEEP ALONG ITS PROJECTED FLIGHT PATH WITH NO RESULT.
I SUSPECT THE FOG BANK LORD FFOGG USED TO CONCEAL IT ALSO RENDERED IT IMPERCEPTIBLE TO RADAR SOMEHOW.
THERE'S BEEN NO MOVEMENT AT THE FFOGG ESTATE EITHER.
AND THE WHITE STAR DIAMOND?
STILL SAFELY ENSCONCED IN THE TOWER OF LONDON. WE'RE ON OUR WAY THERE NOW.
ALTHOUGH MISS GOUGH AND HER CRONIES MUST KNOW WE'LL BE WAITING. IT'S HIGHLY UNLIKELY SHE'LL SIMPLY WALTZ INTO OUR ARMS.

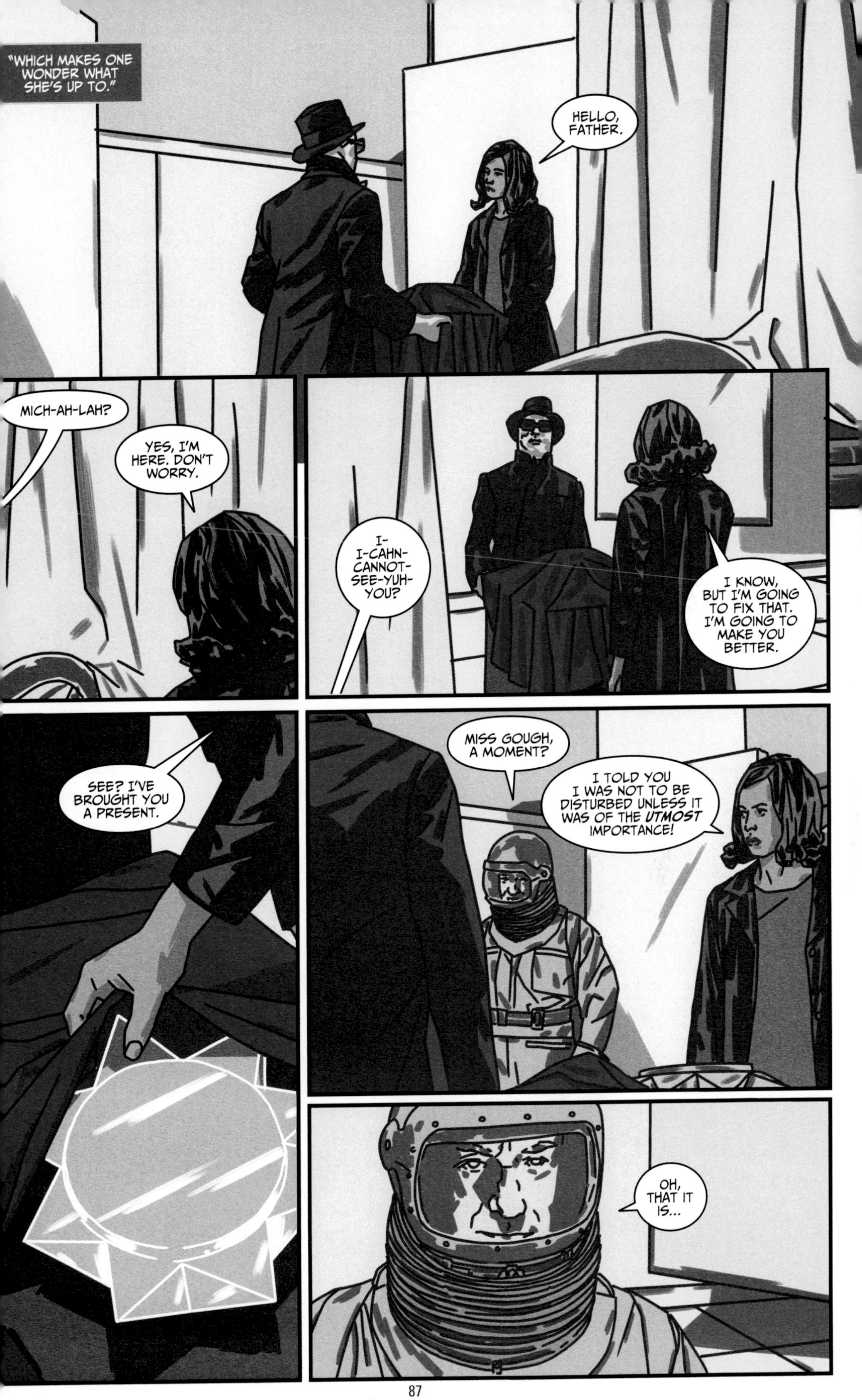
"WHICH MAKES ONE WONDER WHAT SHE'S UP TO."
HELLO, FATHER.
MICH-AH-LAH?
YES, I'M HERE. DON'T WORRY.
I-I-CAHN-CANNOT-SEE-YUH-YOU?
I KNOW, BUT I'M GOING TO FIX THAT. I'M GOING TO MAKE YOU BETTER.
SEE? I'VE BROUGHT YOU A PRESENT.
MISS GOUGH, A MOMENT?
I TOLD YOU I WAS NOT TO BE DISTURBED UNLESS IT WAS OF THE *UTMOST* IMPORTANCE!
OH, THAT IT IS...

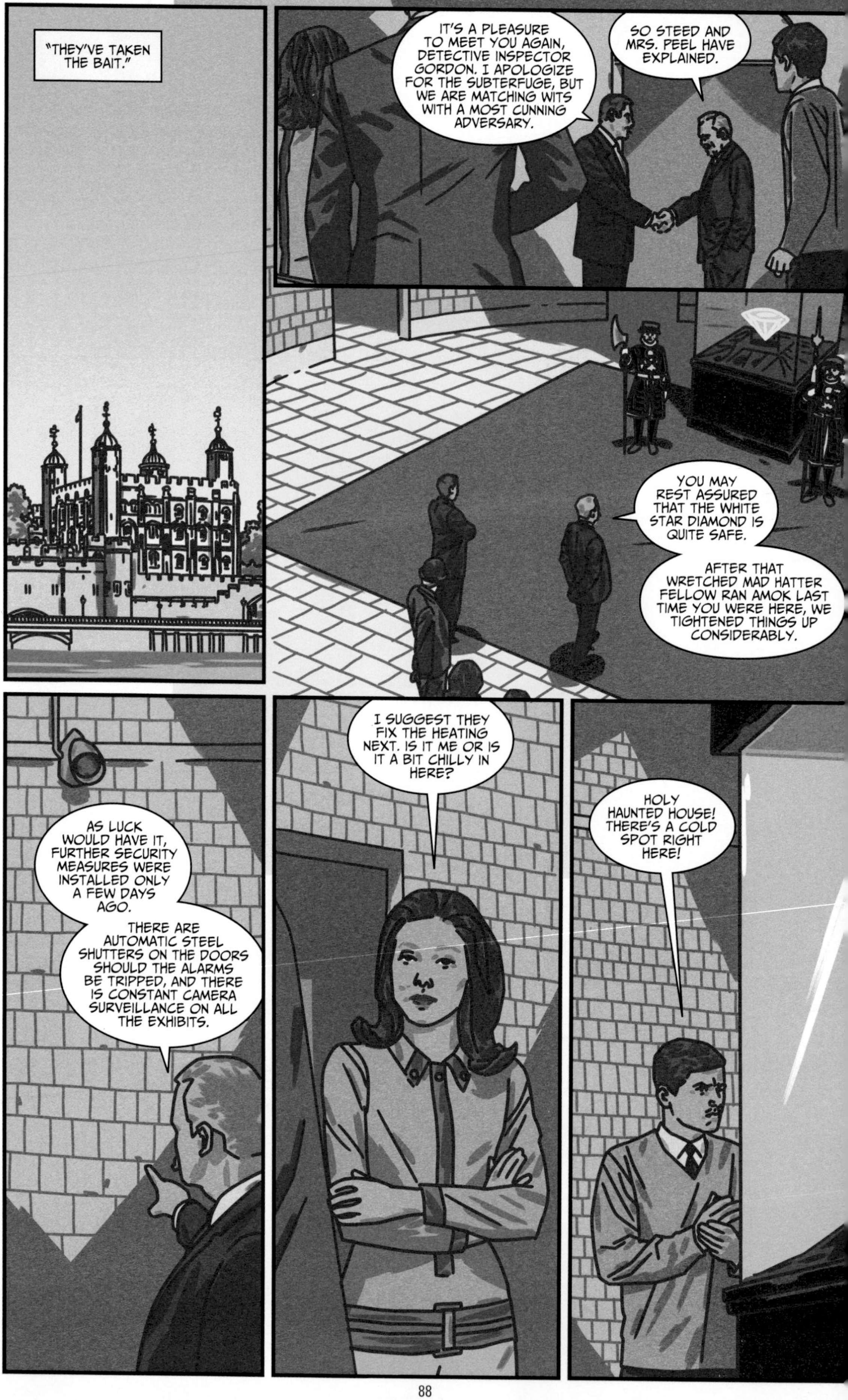
"THEY'VE TAKEN THE BAIT."
IT'S A PLEASURE TO MEET YOU AGAIN, DETECTIVE INSPECTOR GORDON. I APOLOGIZE FOR THE SUBTERFUGE, BUT WE ARE MATCHING WITS WITH A MOST CUNNING ADVERSARY.
SO STEED AND MRS. PEEL HAVE EXPLAINED.
YOU MAY REST ASSURED THAT THE WHITE STAR DIAMOND IS QUITE SAFE.
AFTER THAT WRETCHED MAD HATTER FELLOW RAN AMOK LAST TIME YOU WERE HERE, WE TIGHTENED THINGS UP CONSIDERABLY.
AS LUCK WOULD HAVE IT, FURTHER SECURITY MEASURES WERE INSTALLED ONLY A FEW DAYS AGO.
THERE ARE AUTOMATIC STEEL SHUTTERS ON THE DOORS SHOULD THE ALARMS BE TRIPPED, AND THERE IS CONSTANT CAMERA SURVEILLANCE ON ALL THE EXHIBITS.
I SUGGEST THEY FIX THE HEATING NEXT. IS IT ME OR IS IT A BIT CHILLY IN HERE?
HOLY HAUNTED HOUSE! THERE'S A COLD SPOT RIGHT HERE!

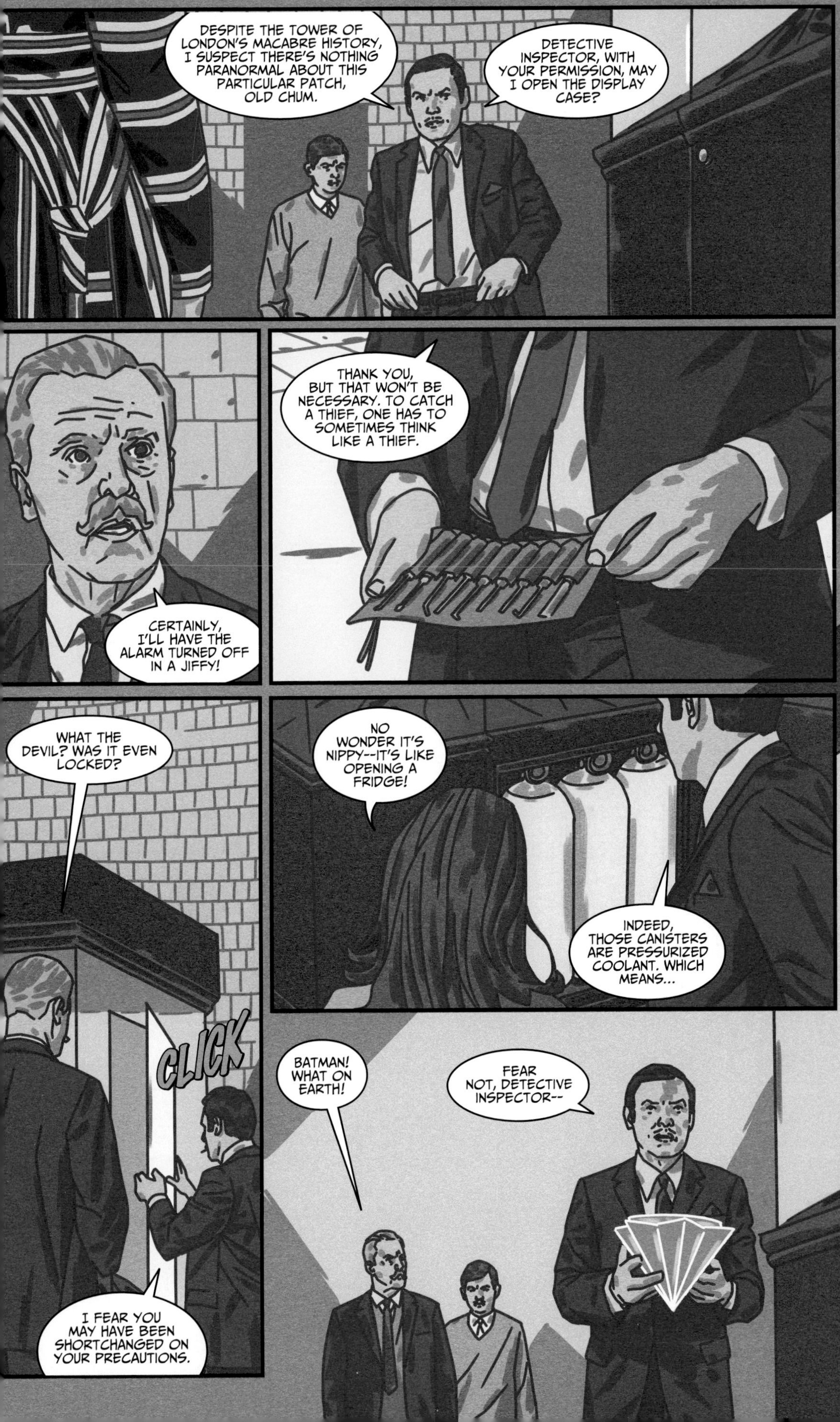
DESPITE THE TOWER OF LONDON'S MACABRE HISTORY, I SUSPECT THERE'S NOTHING PARANORMAL ABOUT THIS PARTICULAR PATCH, OLD CHUM.
DETECTIVE INSPECTOR, WITH YOUR PERMISSION, MAY I OPEN THE DISPLAY CASE?
CERTAINLY, I'LL HAVE THE ALARM TURNED OFF IN A JIFFY!
THANK YOU, BUT THAT WON'T BE NECESSARY. TO CATCH A THIEF, ONE HAS TO SOMETIMES THINK LIKE A THIEF.
WHAT THE DEVIL? WAS IT EVEN LOCKED?
CLICK
I FEAR YOU MAY HAVE BEEN SHORTCHANGED ON YOUR PRECAUTIONS.
NO WONDER IT'S NIPPY--IT'S LIKE OPENING A FRIDGE!
INDEED, THOSE CANISTERS ARE PRESSURIZED COOLANT. WHICH MEANS...
BATMAN! WHAT ON EARTH!
FEAR NOT, DETECTIVE INSPECTOR--

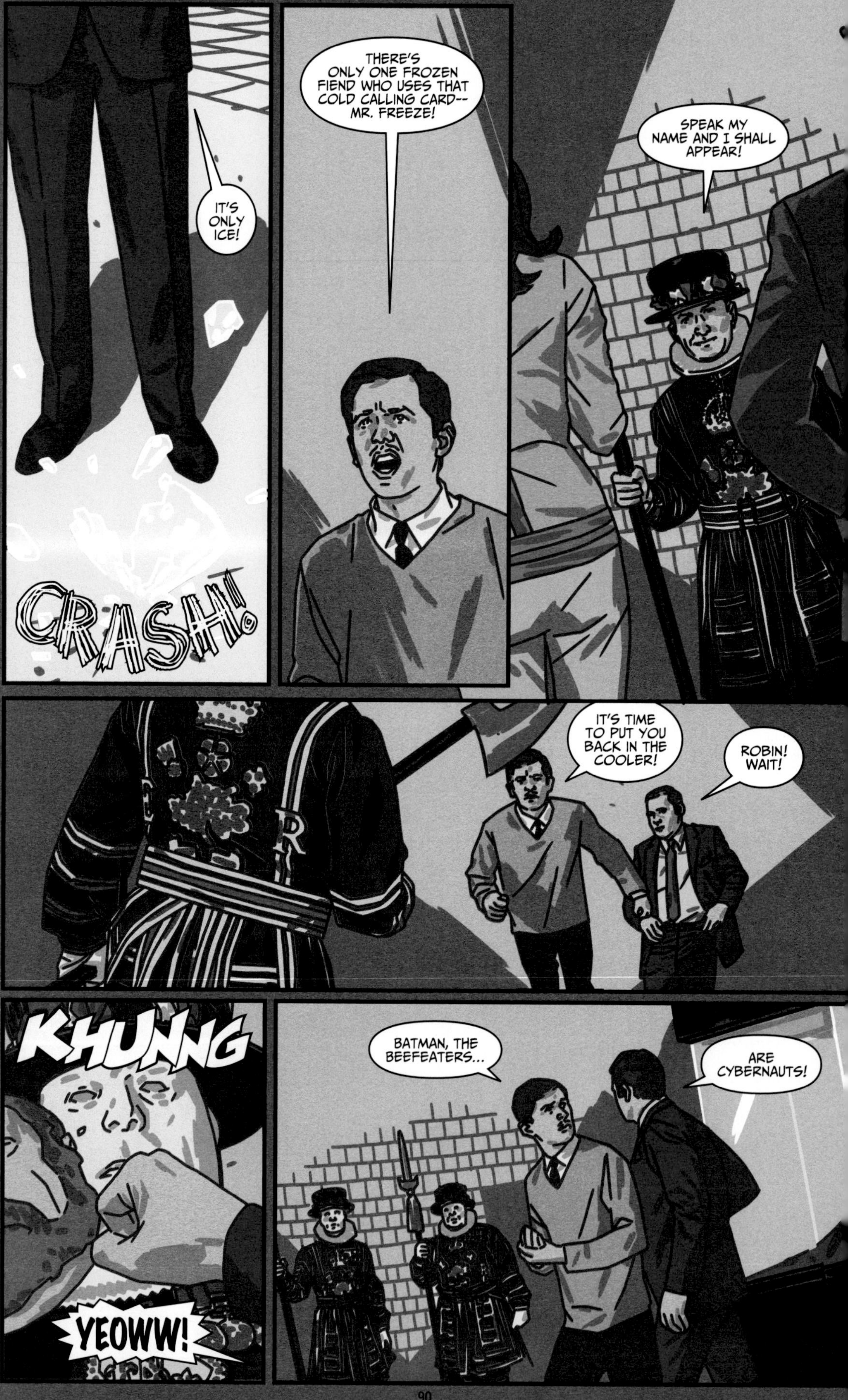

IT'S ONLY ICE!
CRASH!
THERE'S ONLY ONE FROZEN FIEND WHO USES THAT COLD CALLING CARD-- MR. FREEZE!
SPEAK MY NAME AND I SHALL APPEAR!
IT'S TIME TO PUT YOU BACK IN THE COOLER!
ROBIN! WAIT!
KHUNNG
YEOWW!
BATMAN, THE BEEFEATERS...
ARE CYBERNAUTS!

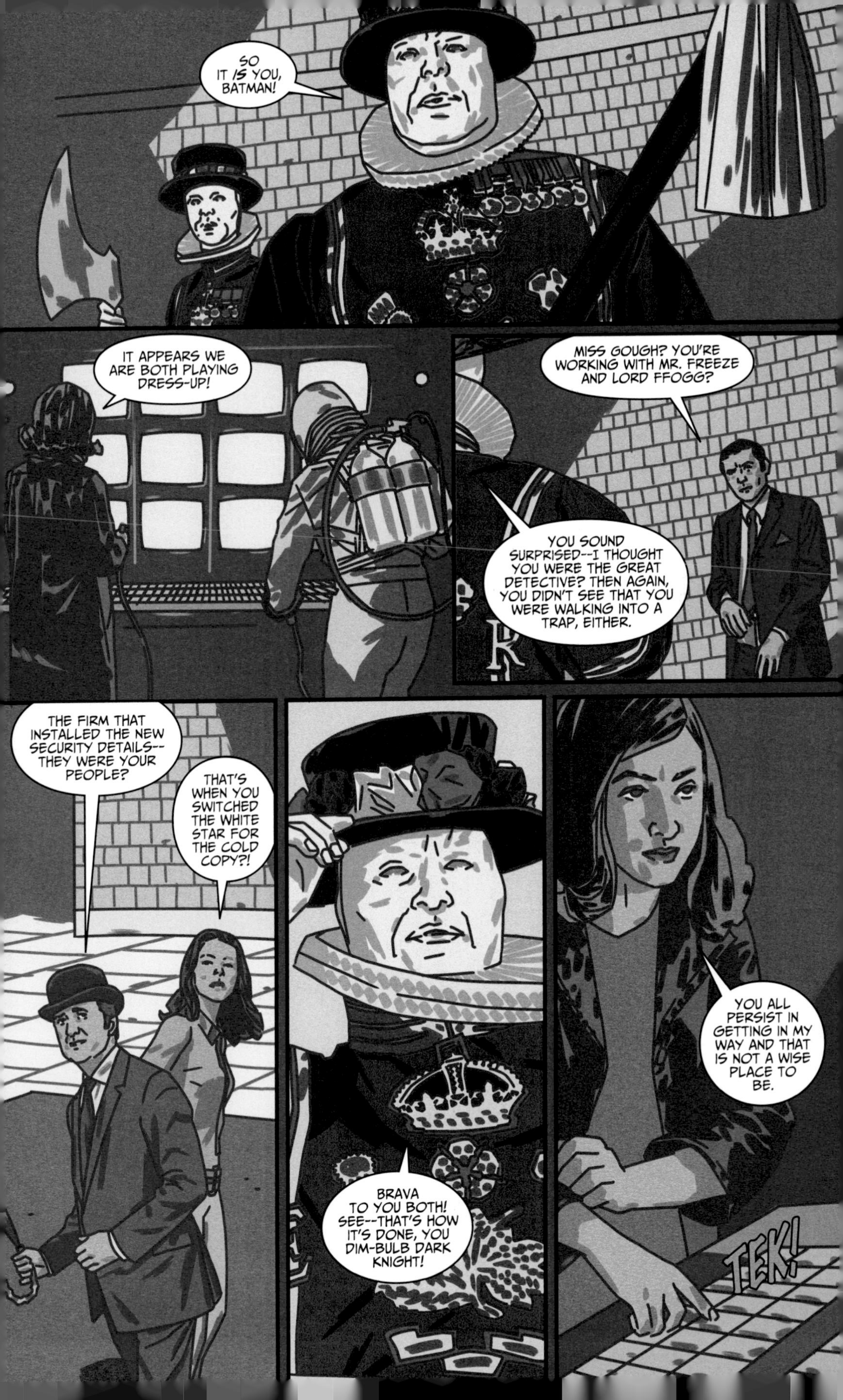
SO IT IS YOU, BATMAN!
IT APPEARS WE ARE BOTH PLAYING DRESS-UP!
MISS GOUGH? YOU'RE WORKING WITH MR. FREEZE AND LORD FFOGG?
YOU SOUND SURPRISED--I THOUGHT YOU WERE THE GREAT DETECTIVE? THEN AGAIN, YOU DIDN'T SEE THAT YOU WERE WALKING INTO A TRAP, EITHER.
THE FIRM THAT INSTALLED THE NEW SECURITY DETAILS-- THEY WERE YOUR PEOPLE?
THAT'S WHEN YOU SWITCHED THE WHITE STAR FOR THE COLD COPY?!
BRAVA TO YOU BOTH! SEE--THAT'S HOW IT'S DONE, YOU DIM-BULB DARK KNIGHT!
YOU ALL PERSIST IN GETTING IN MY WAY AND THAT IS NOT A WISE PLACE TO BE.
TEK!

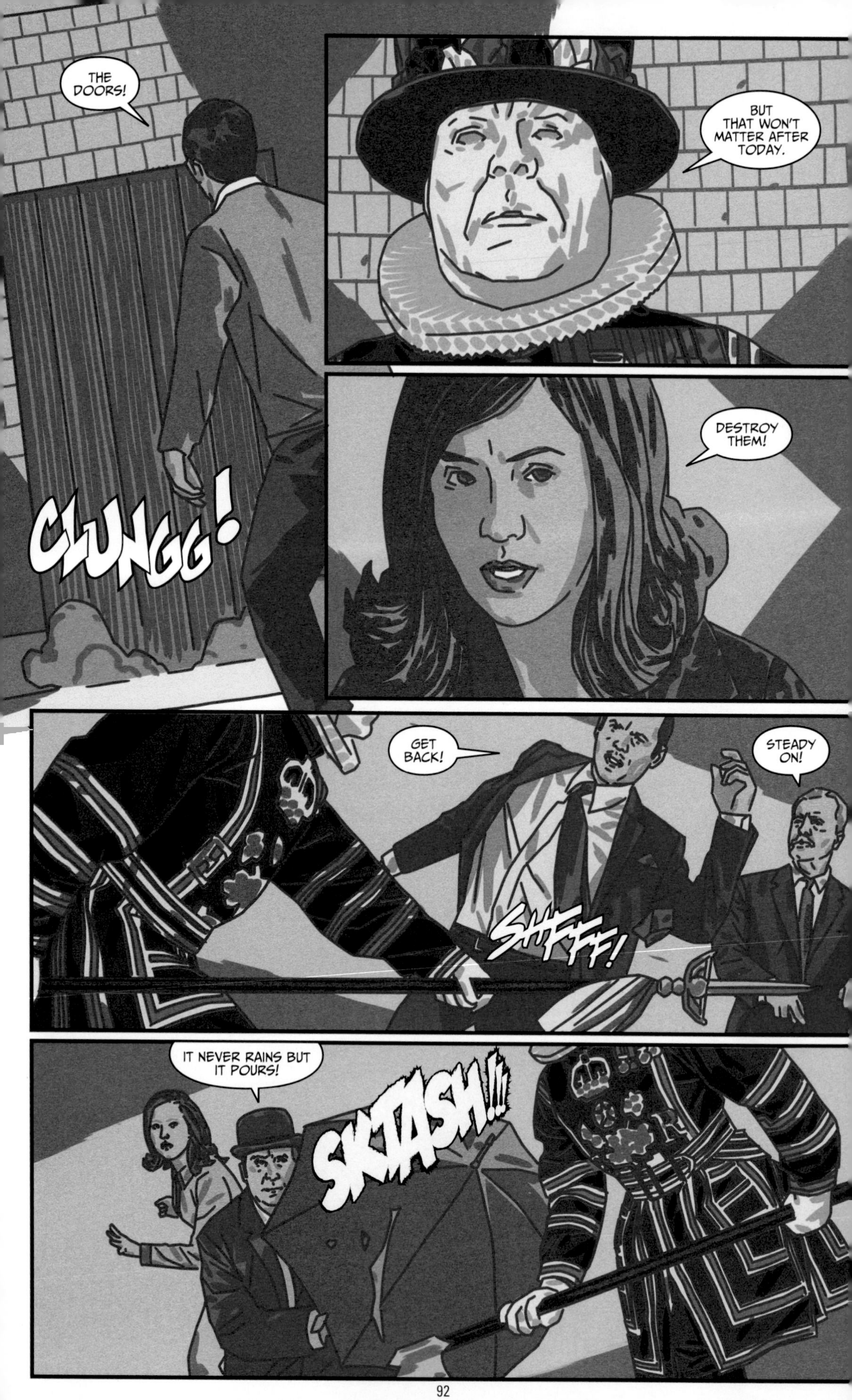
THE DOORS!
BUT THAT WON'T MATTER AFTER TODAY.
CLUNGG!
DESTROY THEM!
GET BACK!
STEADY ON!
SHFFF!
IT NEVER RAINS BUT IT POURS!
SKTASH!!!

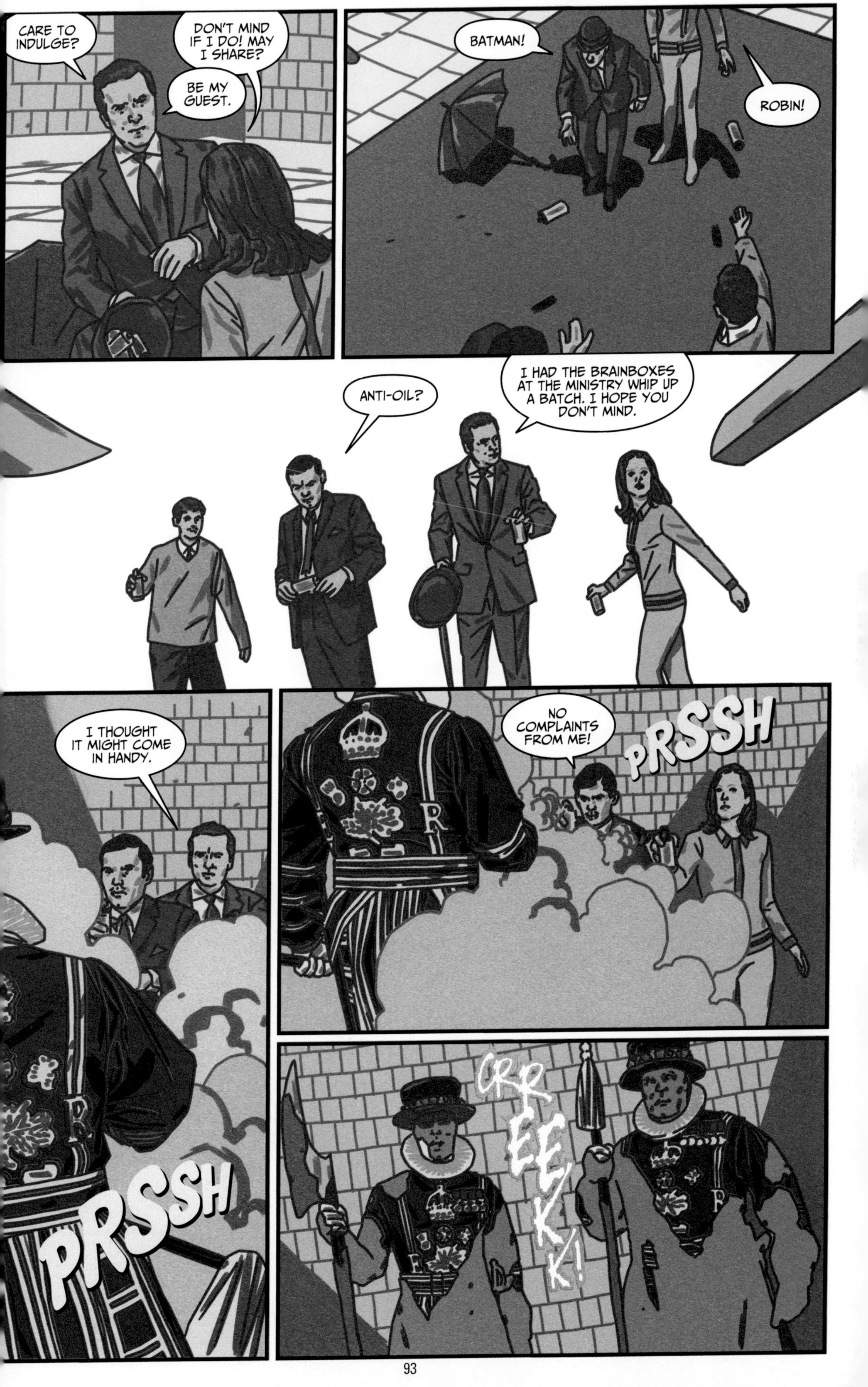
CARE TO INDULGE?
DON'T MIND IF I DO! MAY I SHARE?
BE MY GUEST.
BATMAN!
ROBIN!
ANTI-OIL?
I HAD THE BRAINBOXES AT THE MINISTRY WHIP UP A BATCH. I HOPE YOU DON'T MIND.
I THOUGHT IT MIGHT COME IN HANDY.
PRSSH
NO COMPLAINTS FROM ME!
PRSSH
CRRREEEK!

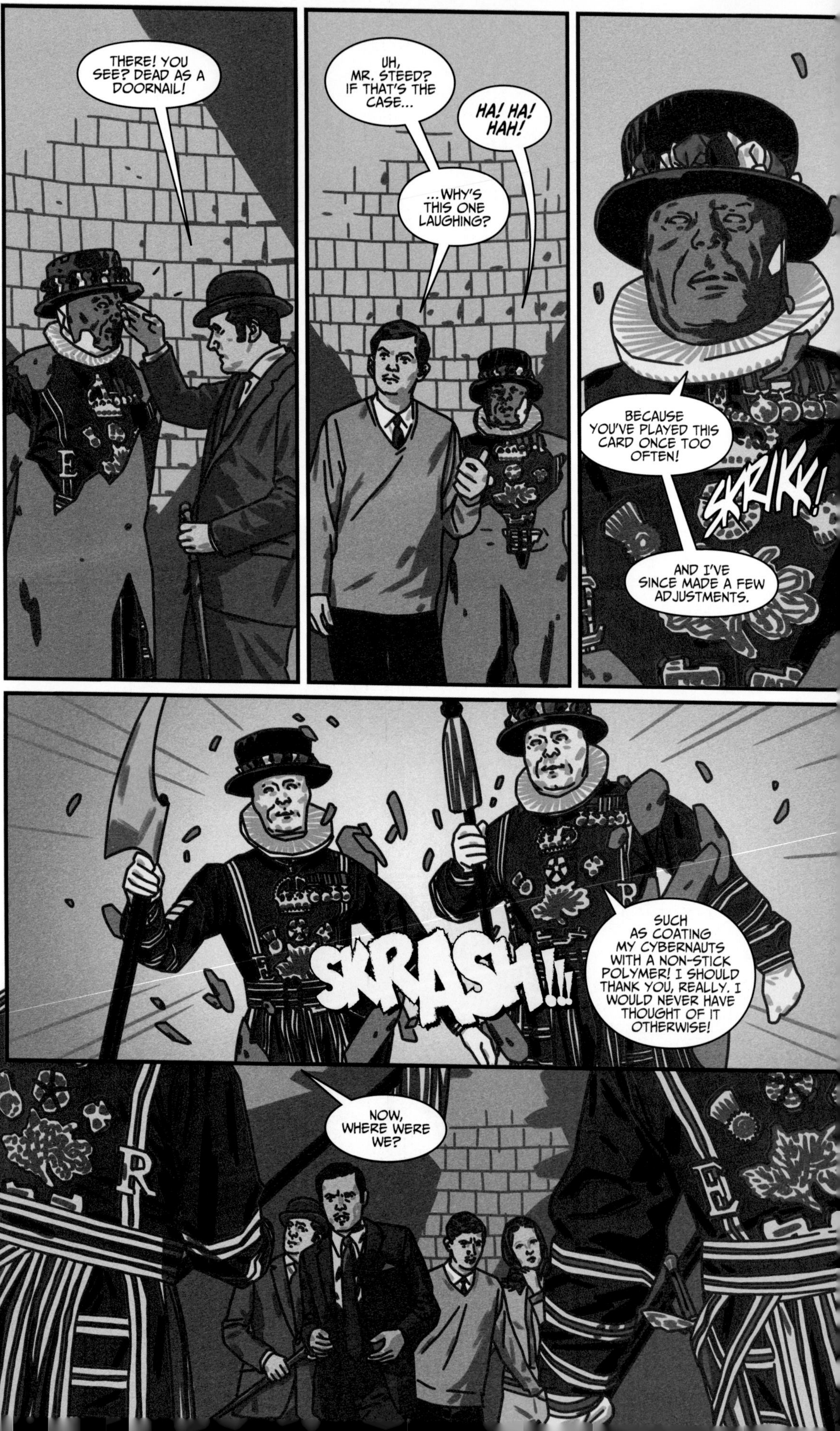
THERE! YOU SEE? DEAD AS A DOORNAIL!
UH, MR. STEED? IF THAT'S THE CASE...
...WHY'S THIS ONE LAUGHING?
HA! HA! HAH!
BECAUSE YOU'VE PLAYED THIS CARD ONCE TOO OFTEN!
SKRIKK!
AND I'VE SINCE MADE A FEW ADJUSTMENTS.
SKRASH!!!
SUCH AS COATING MY CYBERNAUTS WITH A NON-STICK POLYMER! I SHOULD THANK YOU, REALLY. I WOULD NEVER HAVE THOUGHT OF IT OTHERWISE!
NOW, WHERE WERE WE?

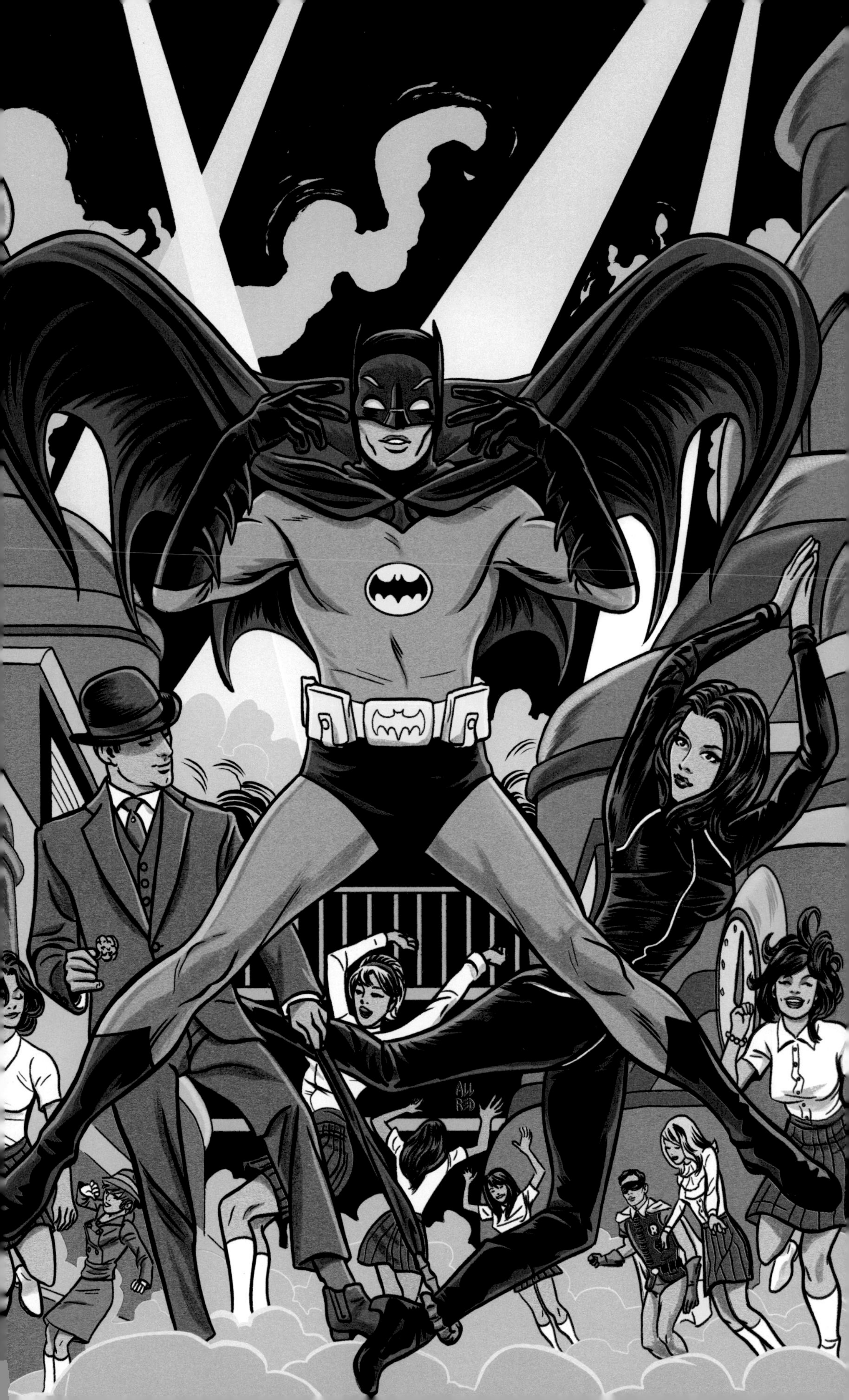
ALL
RED

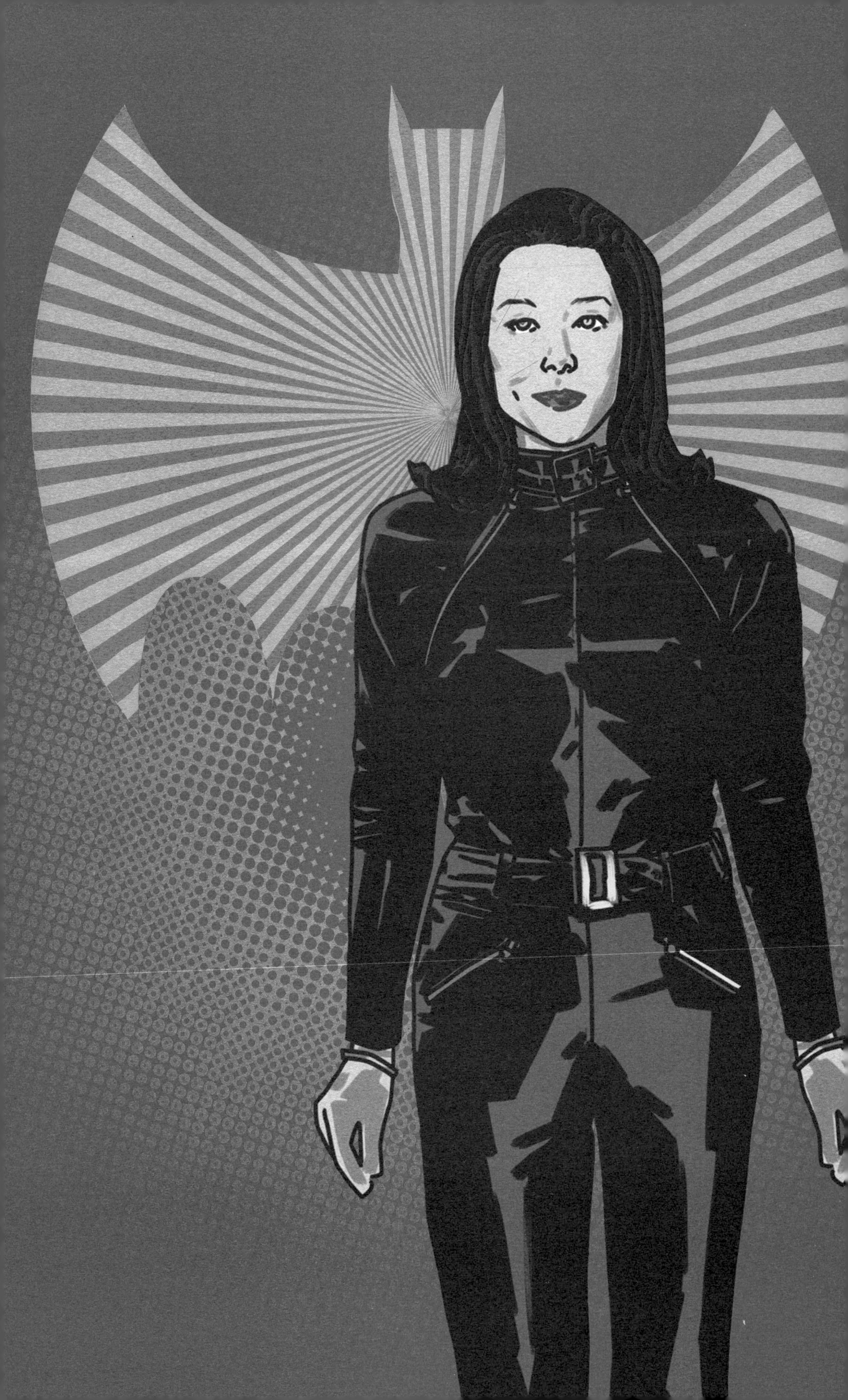

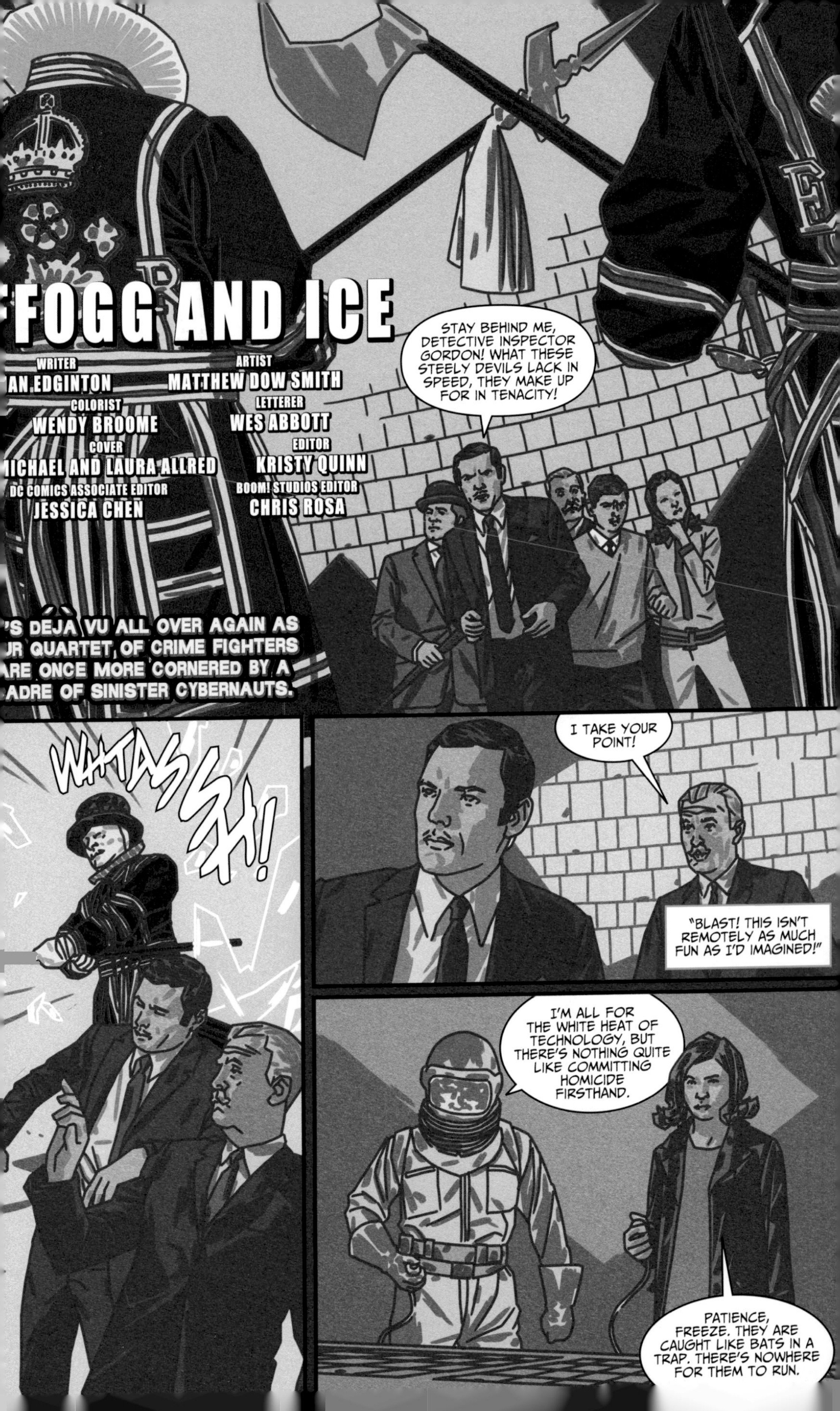

FOGG AND ICE
WRITER
AN EDGINTON
ARTIST
MATTHEW DOW SMITH
COLORIST
WENDY BROOME
LETTERER
WES ABBOTT
COVER
ICHAEL AND LAURA ALLRED
EDITOR
KRISTY QUINN
DC COMICS ASSOCIATE EDITOR
JESSICA CHEN
BOOM! STUDIOS EDITOR
CHRIS ROSA
'S DÉJÀ VU ALL OVER AGAIN AS R QUARTET OF CRIME FIGHTERS ARE ONCE MORE CORNERED BY A ADRE OF SINISTER CYBERNAUTS.
STAY BEHIND ME, DETECTIVE INSPECTOR GORDON! WHAT THESE STEELY DEVILS LACK IN SPEED, THEY MAKE UP FOR IN TENACITY!
WHTASSH!
I TAKE YOUR POINT!
"BLAST! THIS ISN'T REMOTELY AS MUCH FUN AS I'D IMAGINED!"
I'M ALL FOR THE WHITE HEAT OF TECHNOLOGY, BUT THERE'S NOTHING QUITE LIKE COMMITTING HOMICIDE FIRSTHAND.
PATIENCE, FREEZE. THEY ARE CAUGHT LIKE BATS IN A TRAP. THERE'S NOWHERE FOR THEM TO RUN.

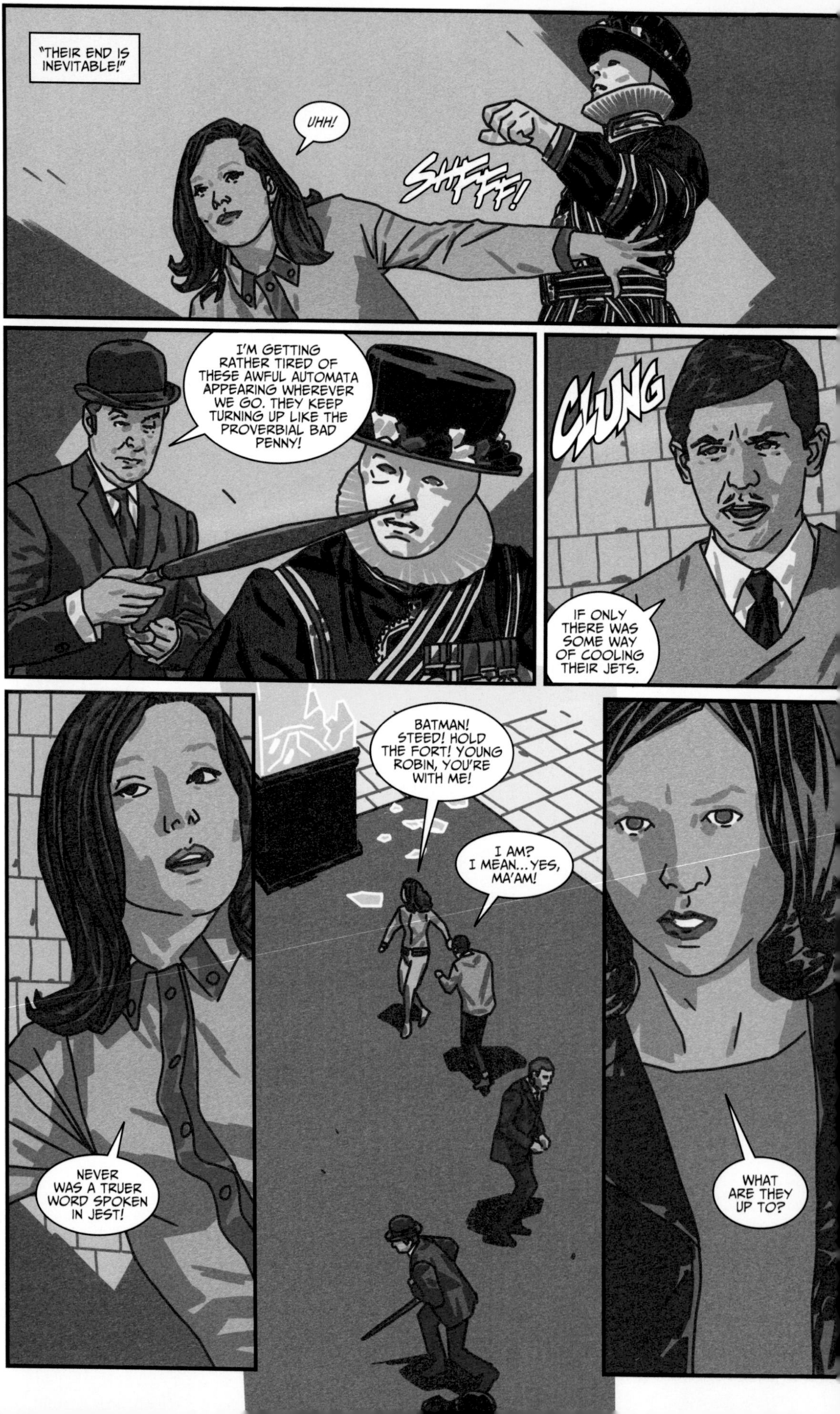
"THEIR END IS INEVITABLE!"
UHH!
SHFFFF!
I'M GETTING RATHER TIRED OF THESE AWFUL AUTOMATA APPEARING WHEREVER WE GO. THEY KEEP TURNING UP LIKE THE PROVERBIAL BAD PENNY!
CLUNG
IF ONLY THERE WAS SOME WAY OF COOLING THEIR JETS.
NEVER WAS A TRUER WORD SPOKEN IN JEST!
BATMAN! STEED! HOLD THE FORT! YOUNG ROBIN, YOU'RE WITH ME!
I AM? I MEAN...YES, MA'AM!
WHAT ARE THEY UP TO?

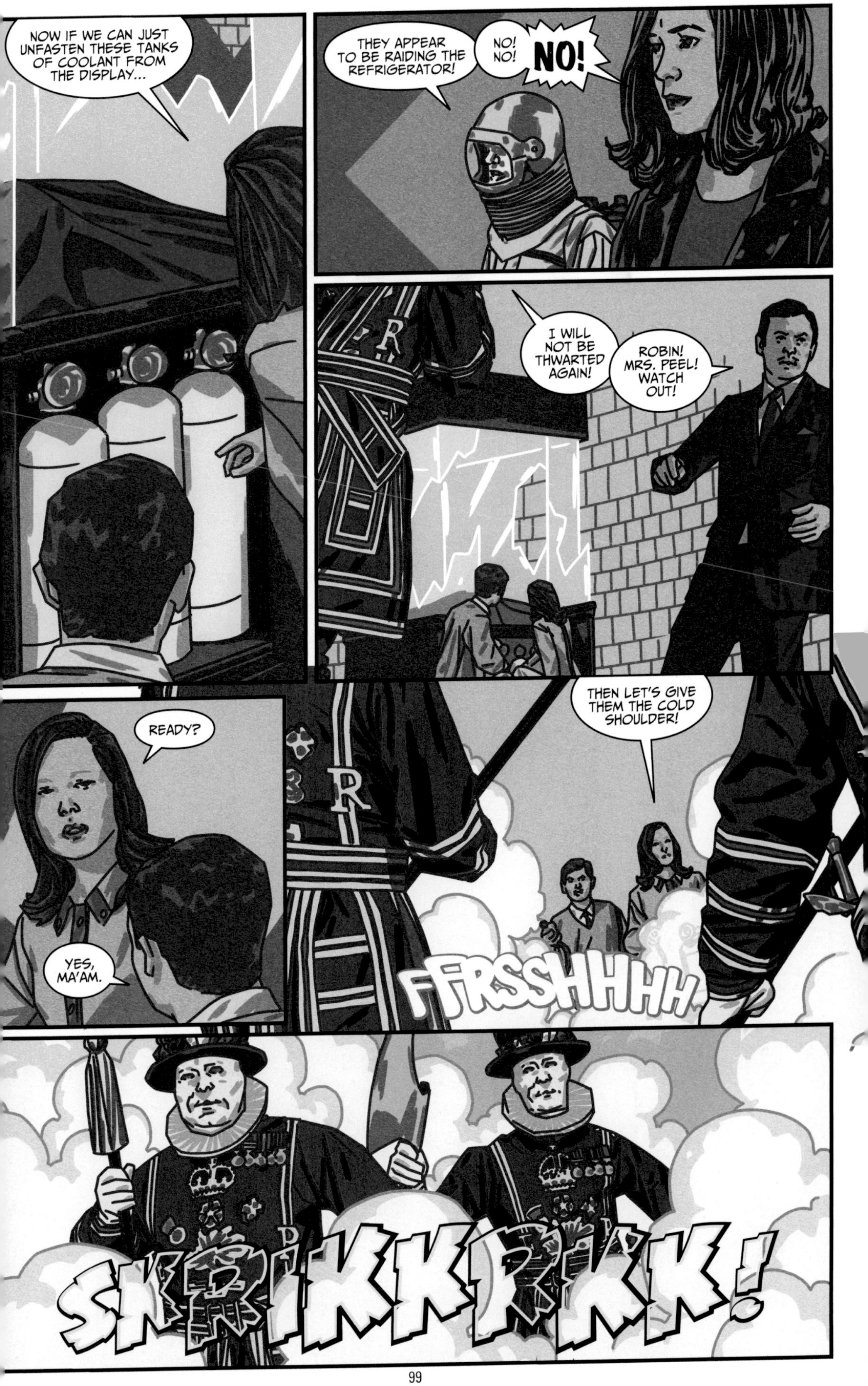

NOW IF WE CAN JUST UNFASTEN THESE TANKS OF COOLANT FROM THE DISPLAY...
THEY APPEAR TO BE RAIDING THE REFRIGERATOR!
NO! NO!
NO!
I WILL NOT BE THWARTED AGAIN!
ROBIN! MRS. PEEL! WATCH OUT!
READY?
YES, MA'AM.
THEN LET'S GIVE THEM THE COLD SHOULDER!
FFRSSHHHH
SKRIKKRKK!

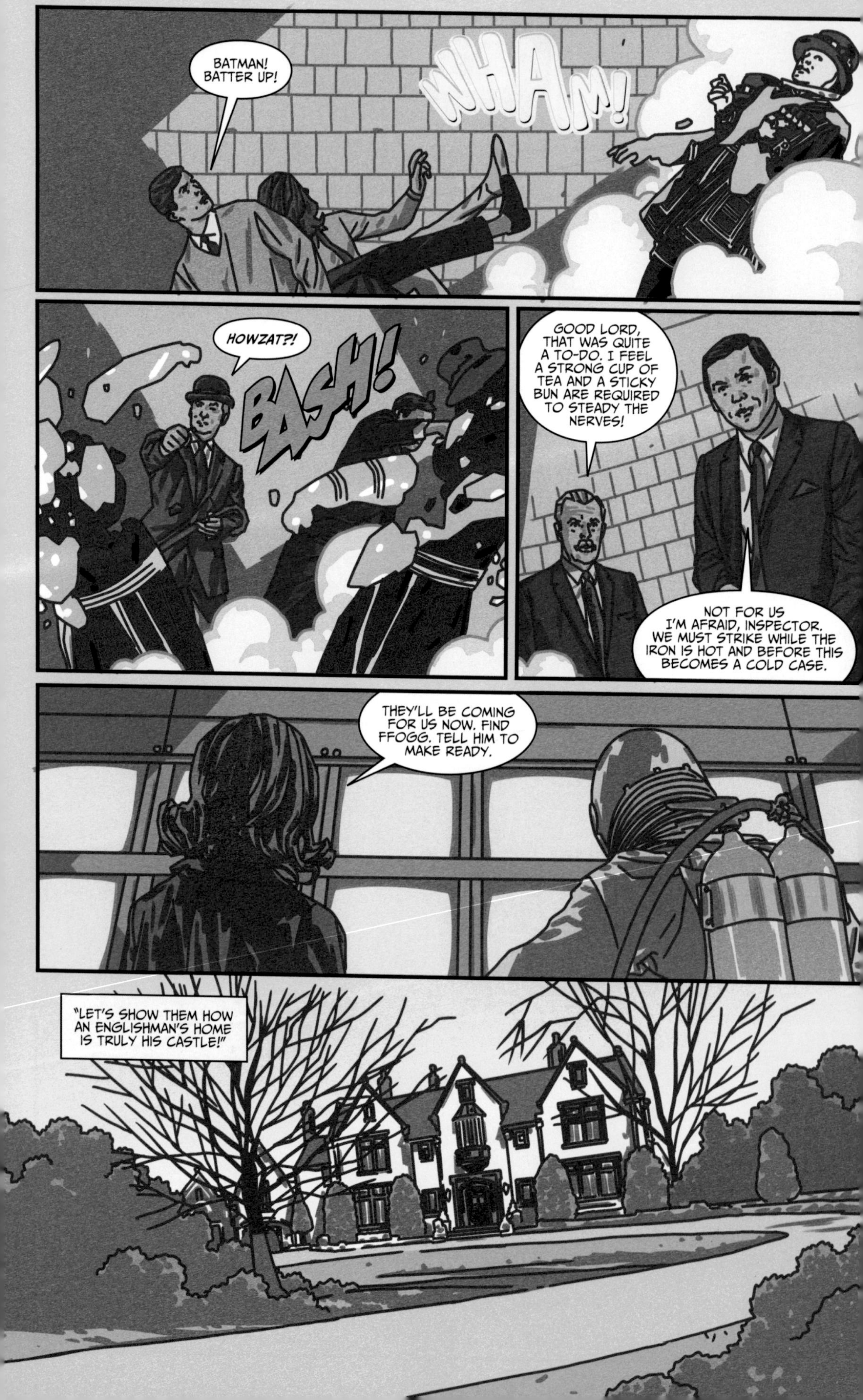
BATMAN! BATTER UP!
WHAM!
HOWZAT?!
BASH!
GOOD LORD, THAT WAS QUITE A TO-DO. I FEEL A STRONG CUP OF TEA AND A STICKY BUN ARE REQUIRED TO STEADY THE NERVES!
NOT FOR US I'M AFRAID, INSPECTOR. WE MUST STRIKE WHILE THE IRON IS HOT AND BEFORE THIS BECOMES A COLD CASE.
THEY'LL BE COMING FOR US NOW. FIND FFOGG. TELL HIM TO MAKE READY.
"LET'S SHOW THEM HOW AN ENGLISHMAN'S HOME IS TRULY HIS CASTLE!"

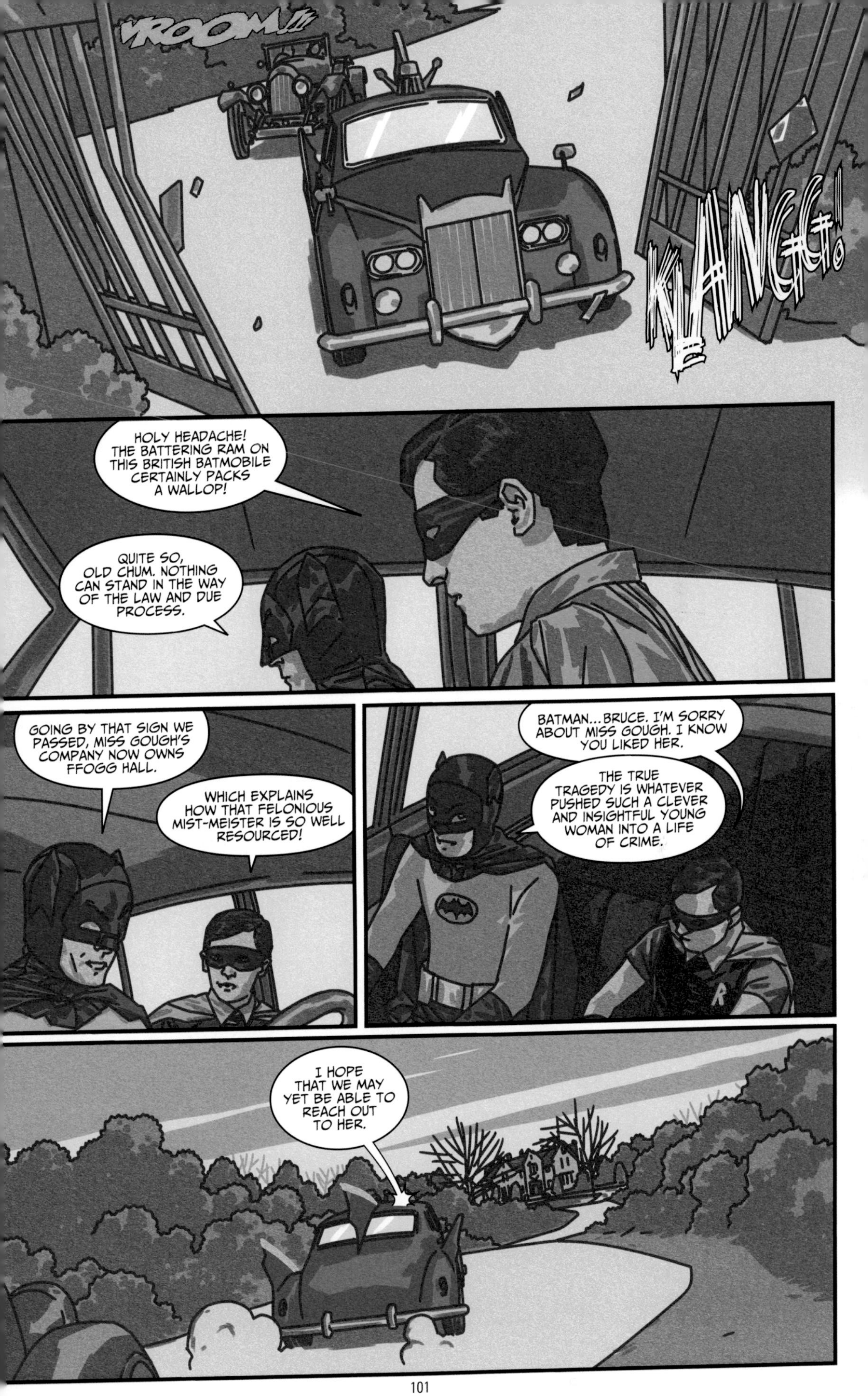
VROOM!!!
KLANGG!
HOLY HEADACHE! THE BATTERING RAM ON THIS BRITISH BATMOBILE CERTAINLY PACKS A WALLOP!
QUITE SO, OLD CHUM. NOTHING CAN STAND IN THE WAY OF THE LAW AND DUE PROCESS.
GOING BY THAT SIGN WE PASSED, MISS GOUGH'S COMPANY NOW OWNS FFOGG HALL.
WHICH EXPLAINS HOW THAT FELONIOUS MIST-MEISTER IS SO WELL RESOURCED!
BATMAN...BRUCE. I'M SORRY ABOUT MISS GOUGH. I KNOW YOU LIKED HER.
THE TRUE TRAGEDY IS WHATEVER PUSHED SUCH A CLEVER AND INSIGHTFUL YOUNG WOMAN INTO A LIFE OF CRIME.
I HOPE THAT WE MAY YET BE ABLE TO REACH OUT TO HER.

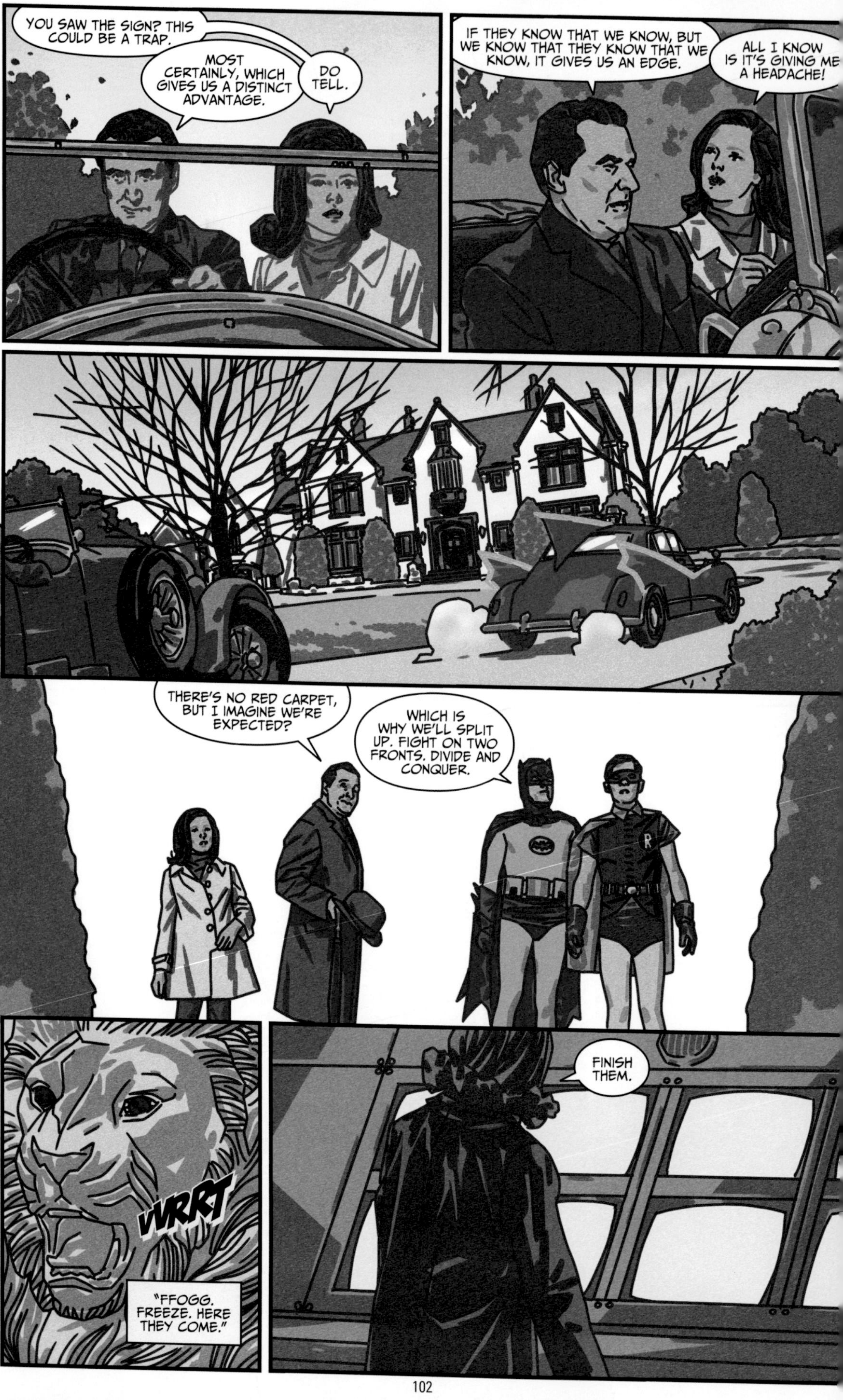
YOU SAW THE SIGN? THIS COULD BE A TRAP.
MOST CERTAINLY, WHICH GIVES US A DISTINCT ADVANTAGE.
DO TELL.
IF THEY KNOW THAT WE KNOW, BUT WE KNOW THAT THEY KNOW THAT WE KNOW, IT GIVES US AN EDGE.
ALL I KNOW IS IT'S GIVING ME A HEADACHE!
THERE'S NO RED CARPET, BUT I IMAGINE WE'RE EXPECTED?
WHICH IS WHY WE'LL SPLIT UP. FIGHT ON TWO FRONTS. DIVIDE AND CONQUER.
VVRRT
"FFOGG. FREEZE. HERE THEY COME."
FINISH THEM.

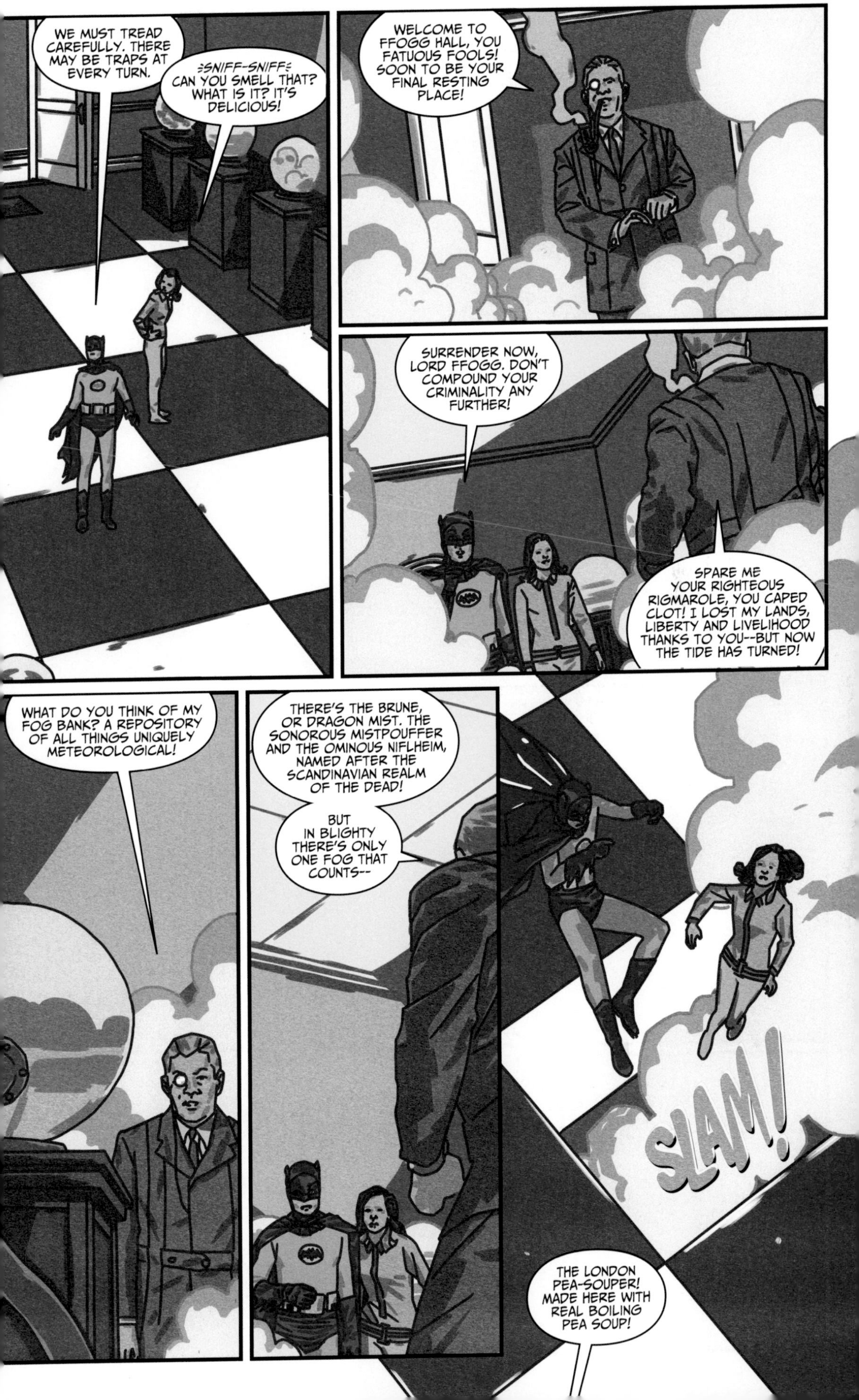
WE MUST TREAD CAREFULLY. THERE MAY BE TRAPS AT EVERY TURN.
=SNIFF-SNIFF= CAN YOU SMELL THAT? WHAT IS IT? IT'S DELICIOUS!
WELCOME TO FFOGG HALL, YOU FATUOUS FOOLS! SOON TO BE YOUR FINAL RESTING PLACE!
SURRENDER NOW, LORD FFOGG. DON'T COMPOUND YOUR CRIMINALITY ANY FURTHER!
SPARE ME YOUR RIGHTEOUS RIGMAROLE, YOU CAPED CLOT! I LOST MY LANDS, LIBERTY AND LIVELIHOOD THANKS TO YOU--BUT NOW THE TIDE HAS TURNED!
WHAT DO YOU THINK OF MY FOG BANK? A REPOSITORY OF ALL THINGS UNIQUELY METEOROLOGICAL!
THERE'S THE BRUNE, OR DRAGON MIST. THE SONOROUS MISTPOUFFER AND THE OMINOUS NIFLHEIM, NAMED AFTER THE SCANDINAVIAN REALM OF THE DEAD!
BUT IN BLIGHTY THERE'S ONLY ONE FOG THAT COUNTS--
SLAM!
THE LONDON PEA-SOUPER! MADE HERE WITH REAL BOILING PEA SOUP!

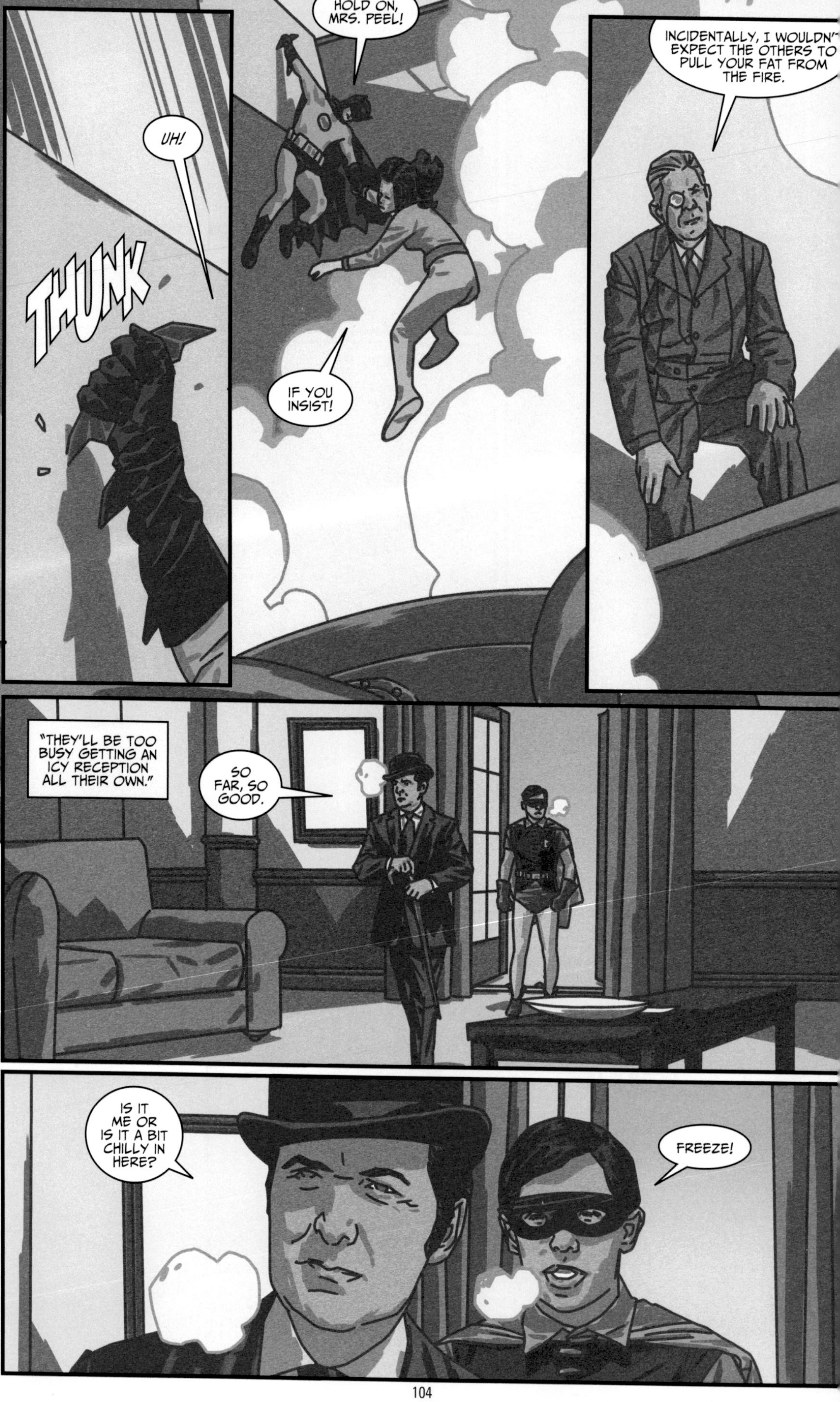

UH!
THUNK
HOLD ON, MRS. PEEL!
IF YOU INSIST!
INCIDENTALLY, I WOULDN'T EXPECT THE OTHERS TO PULL YOUR FAT FROM THE FIRE.
"THEY'LL BE TOO BUSY GETTING AN ICY RECEPTION ALL THEIR OWN."
SO FAR, SO GOOD.
IS IT ME OR IS IT A BIT CHILLY IN HERE?
FREEZE!

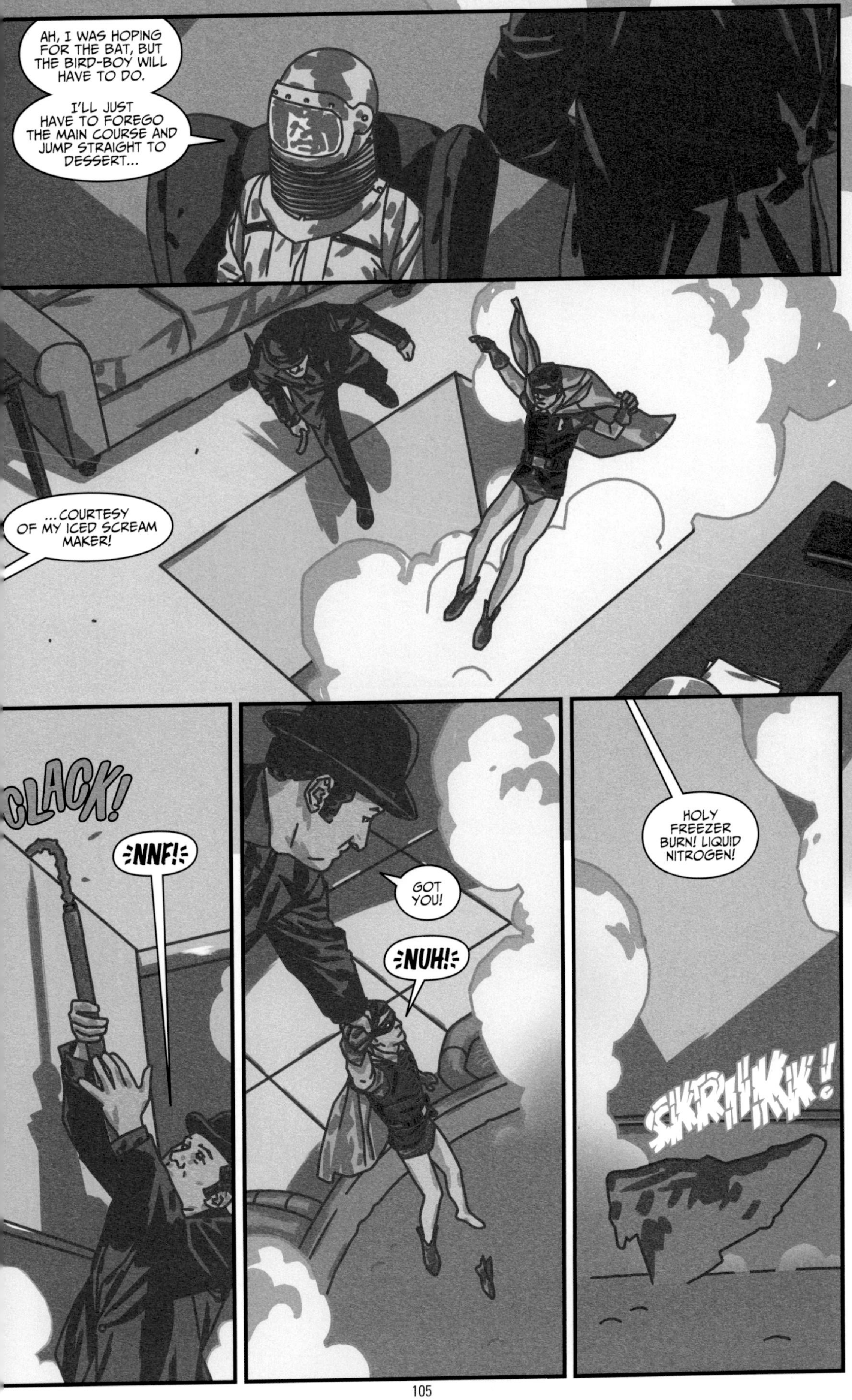
AH, I WAS HOPING FOR THE BAT, BUT THE BIRD-BOY WILL HAVE TO DO.
I'LL JUST HAVE TO FOREGO THE MAIN COURSE AND JUMP STRAIGHT TO DESSERT...
...COURTESY OF MY ICED SCREAM MAKER!
CLACK!
NNF!
GOT YOU!
NUH!
HOLY FREEZER BURN! LIQUID NITROGEN!
SKRIIKK!!

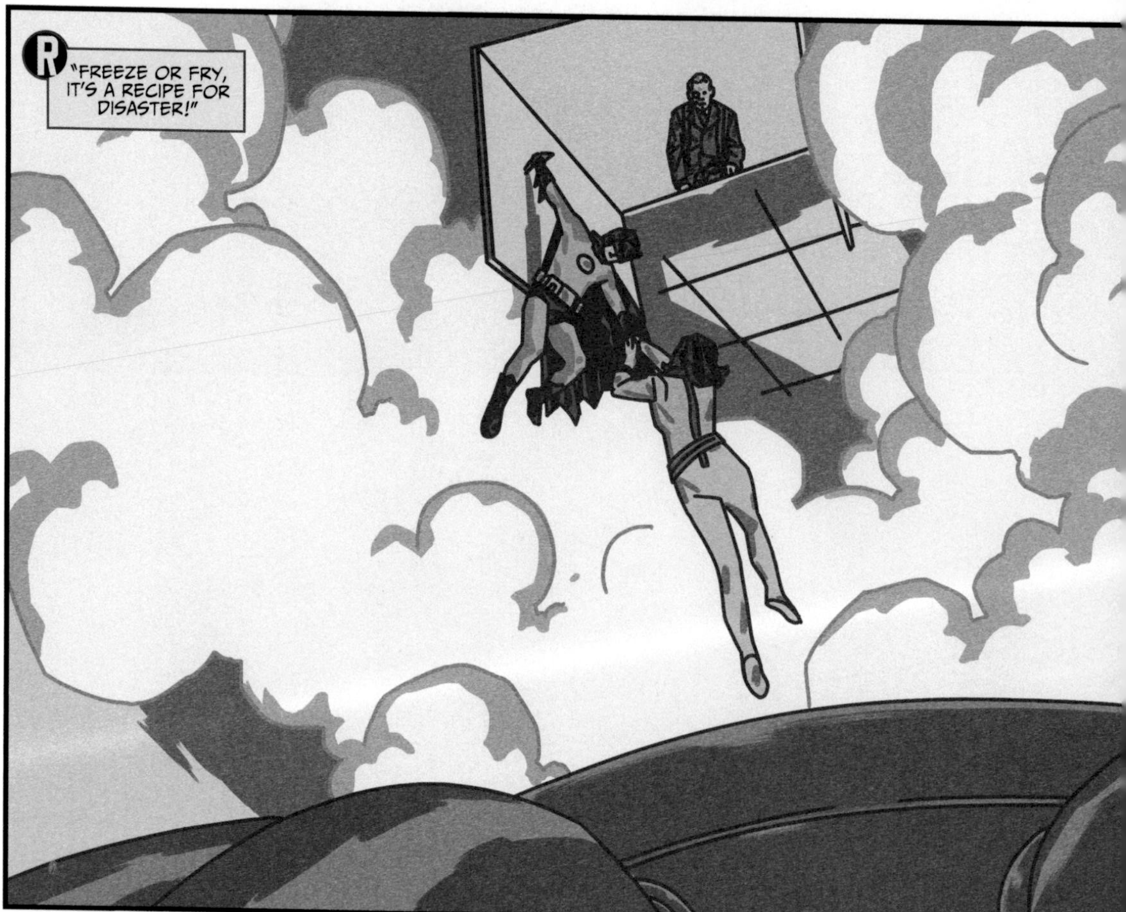
"FREEZE OR FRY, IT'S A RECIPE FOR DISASTER!"

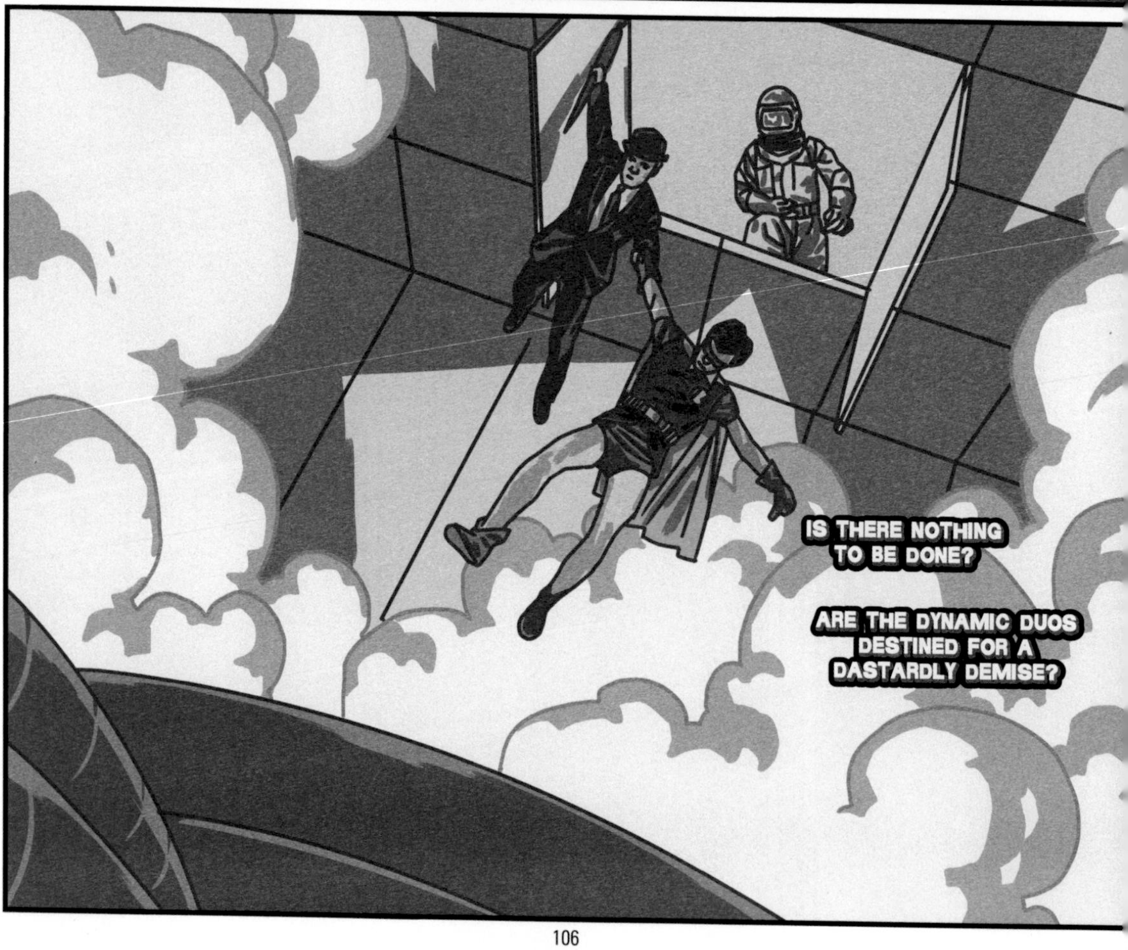
IS THERE NOTHING TO BE DONE?
ARE THE DYNAMIC DUOS DESTINED FOR A DASTARDLY DEMISE?

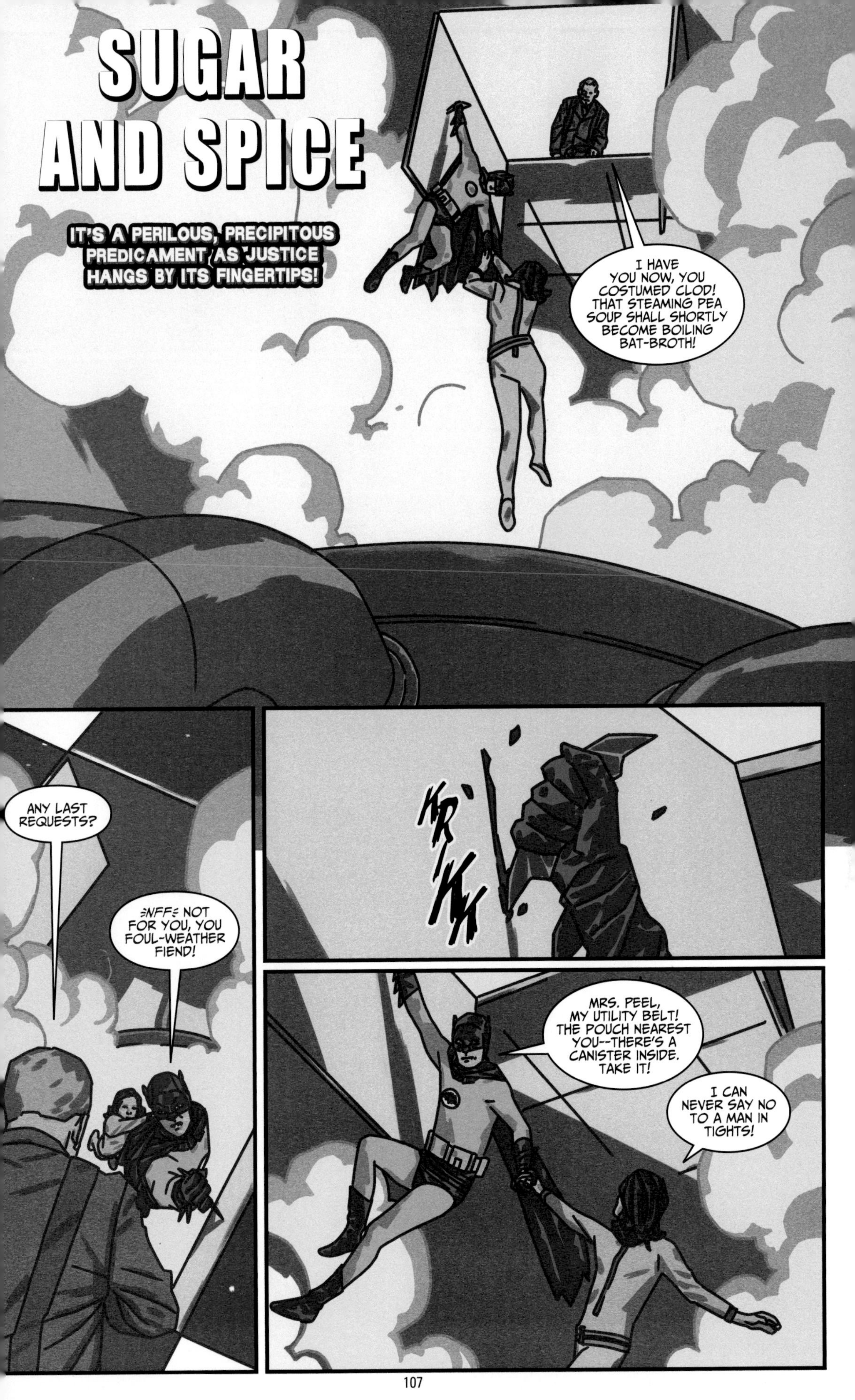
SUGAR AND SPICE
IT'S A PERILOUS, PRECIPITOUS PREDICAMENT AS JUSTICE HANGS BY ITS FINGERTIPS!
I HAVE YOU NOW, YOU COSTUMED CLOD! THAT STEAMING PEA SOUP SHALL SHORTLY BECOME BOILING BAT-BROTH!
ANY LAST REQUESTS?
SNFF NOT FOR YOU, YOU FOUL-WEATHER FIEND!
MRS. PEEL, MY UTILITY BELT! THE POUCH NEAREST YOU--THERE'S A CANISTER INSIDE. TAKE IT!
I CAN NEVER SAY NO TO A MAN IN TIGHTS!

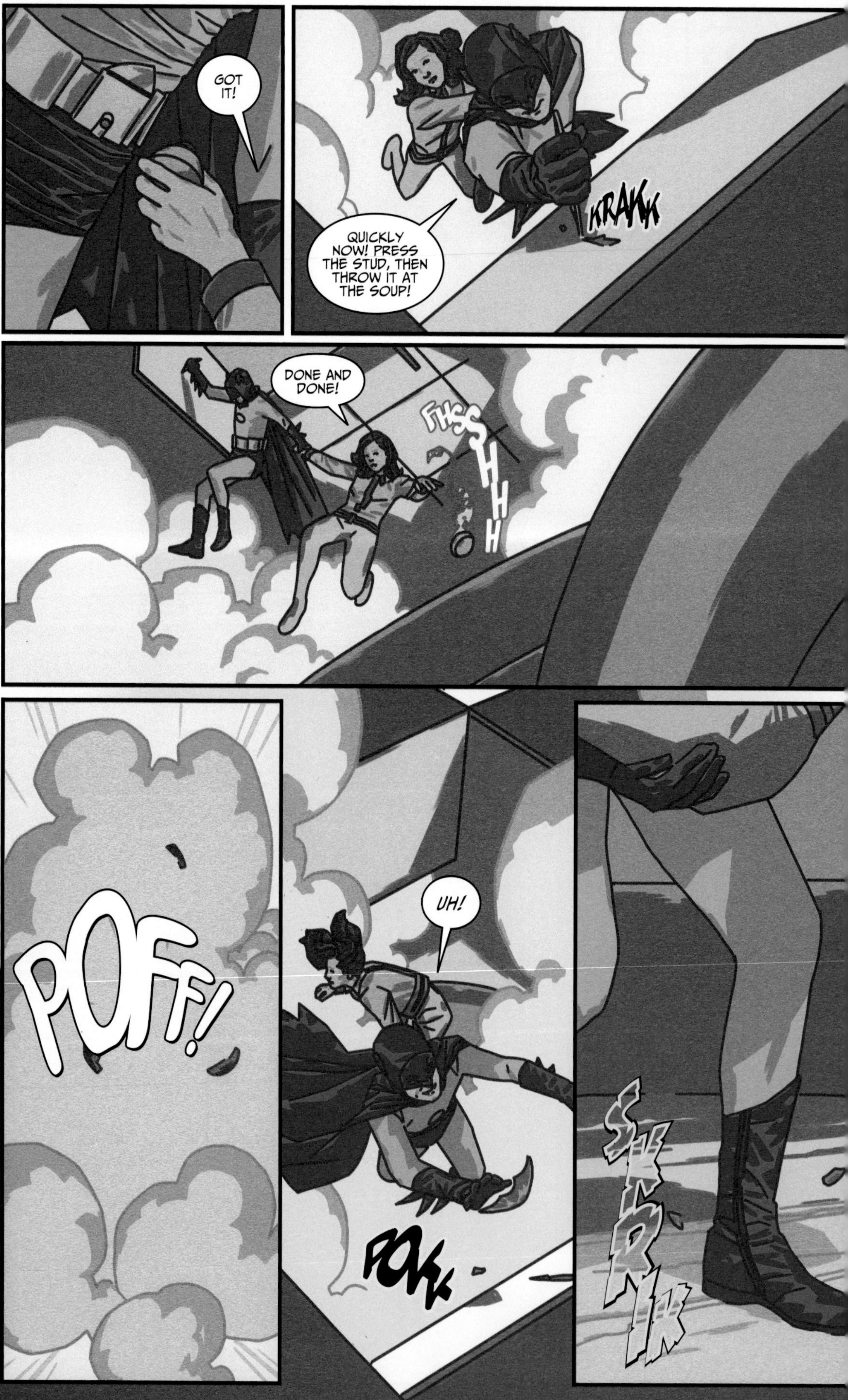
GOT IT!
QUICKLY NOW! PRESS THE STUD, THEN THROW IT AT THE SOUP!
KRAKK
DONE AND DONE!
FHSSHHHH
POFF!
UH!
POKK

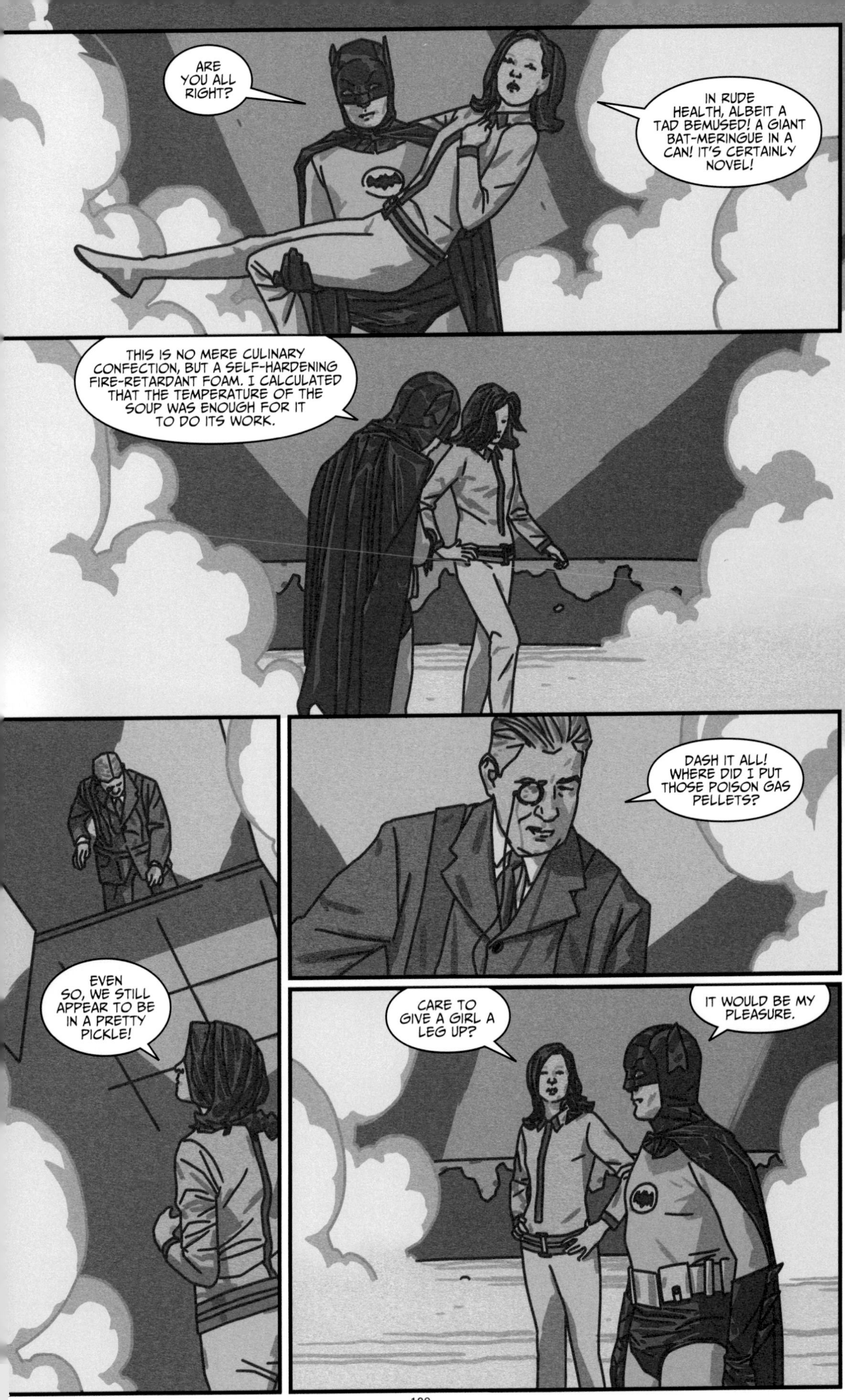
ARE YOU ALL RIGHT?
IN RUDE HEALTH, ALBEIT A TAD BEMUSED! A GIANT BAT-MERINGUE IN A CAN! IT'S CERTAINLY NOVEL!
THIS IS NO MERE CULINARY CONFECTION, BUT A SELF-HARDENING FIRE-RETARDANT FOAM. I CALCULATED THAT THE TEMPERATURE OF THE SOUP WAS ENOUGH FOR IT TO DO ITS WORK.
EVEN SO, WE STILL APPEAR TO BE IN A PRETTY PICKLE!
DASH IT ALL! WHERE DID I PUT THOSE POISON GAS PELLETS?
CARE TO GIVE A GIRL A LEG UP?
IT WOULD BE MY PLEASURE.

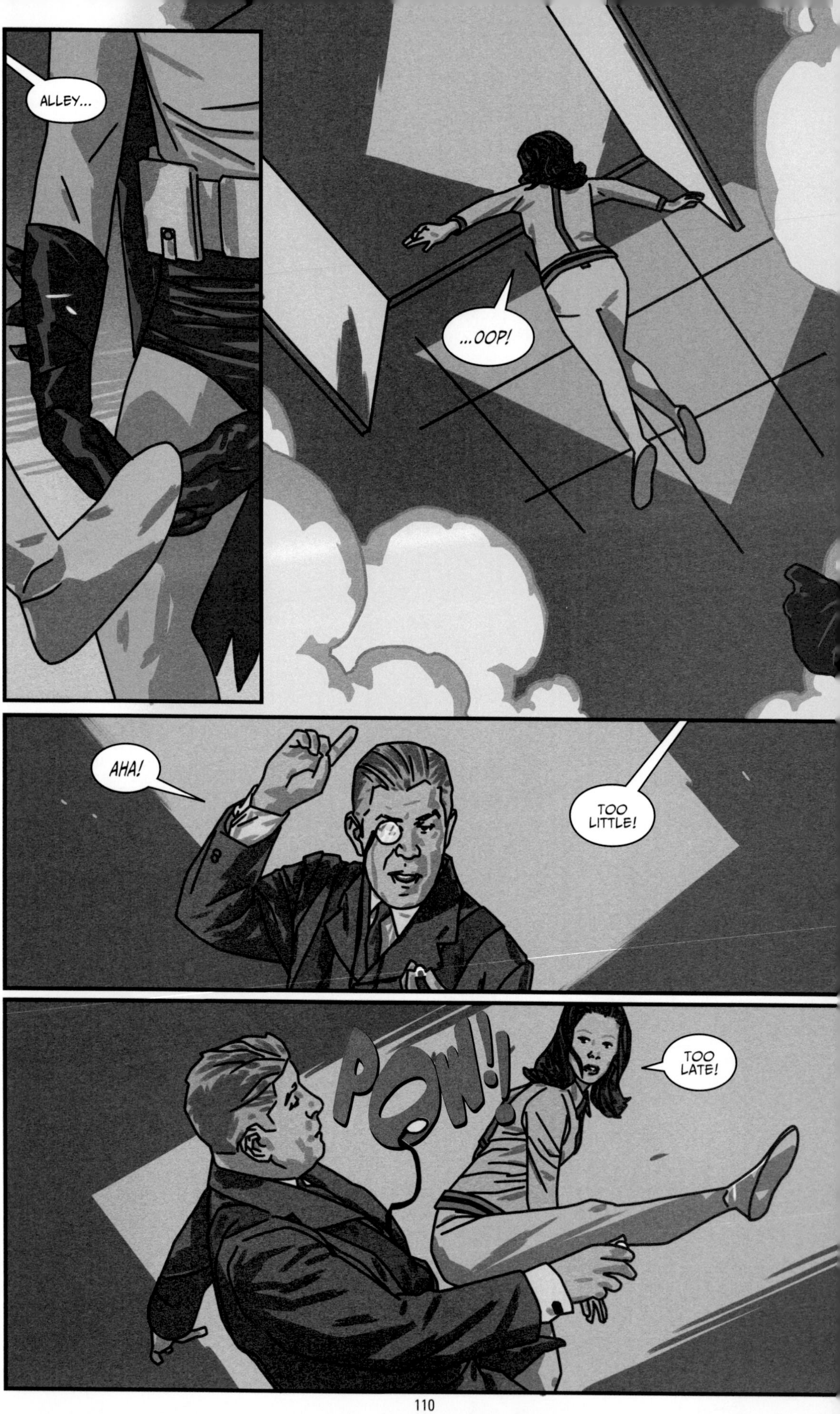
ALLEY...
...OOP!
AHA!
TOO LITTLE!
POW!!
TOO LATE!

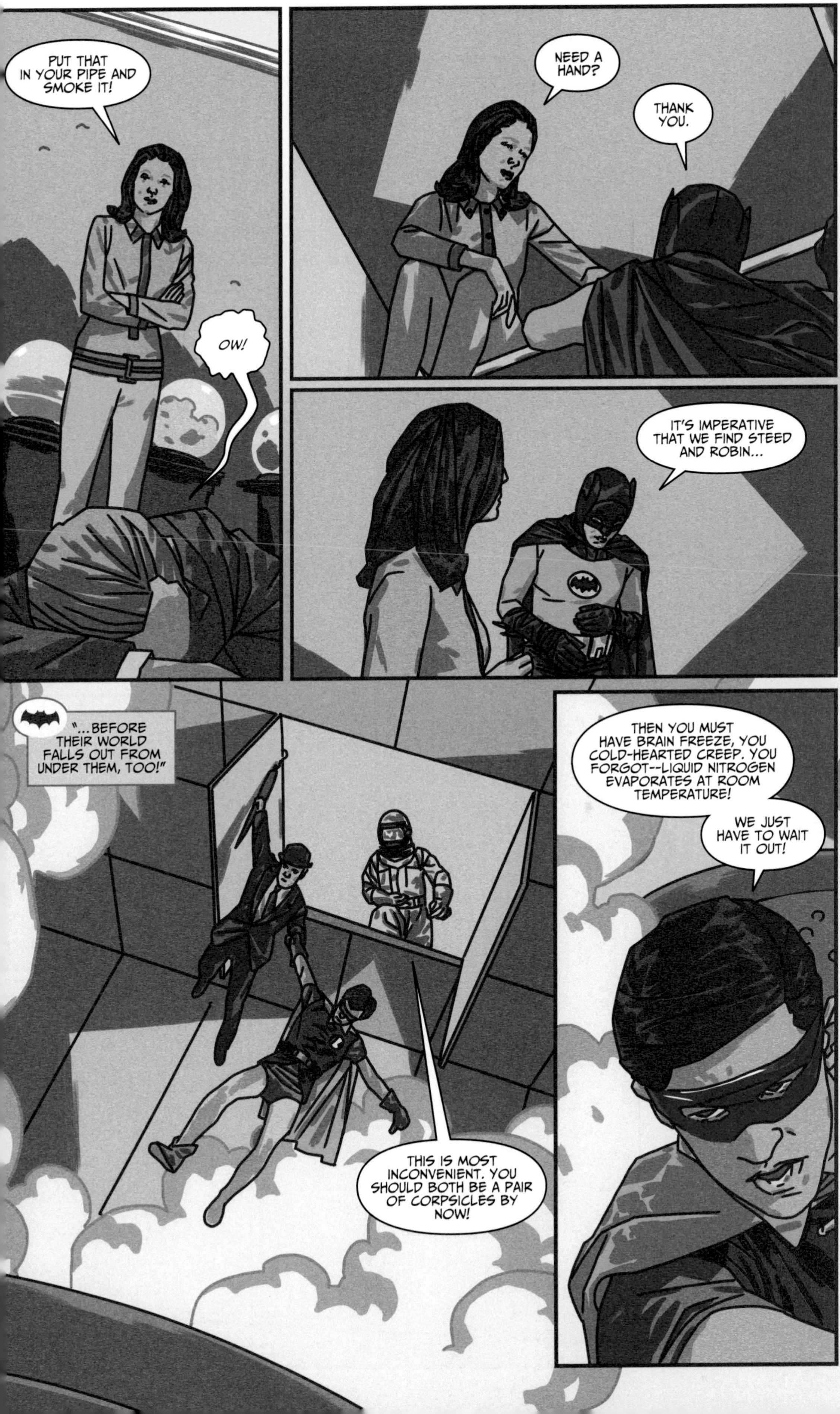
PUT THAT IN YOUR PIPE AND SMOKE IT!
OW!
NEED A HAND?
THANK YOU.
IT'S IMPERATIVE THAT WE FIND STEED AND ROBIN...
"...BEFORE THEIR WORLD FALLS OUT FROM UNDER THEM, TOO!"
THIS IS MOST INCONVENIENT. YOU SHOULD BOTH BE A PAIR OF CORPSICLES BY NOW!
THEN YOU MUST HAVE BRAIN FREEZE, YOU COLD-HEARTED CREEP. YOU FORGOT--LIQUID NITROGEN EVAPORATES AT ROOM TEMPERATURE!
WE JUST HAVE TO WAIT IT OUT!

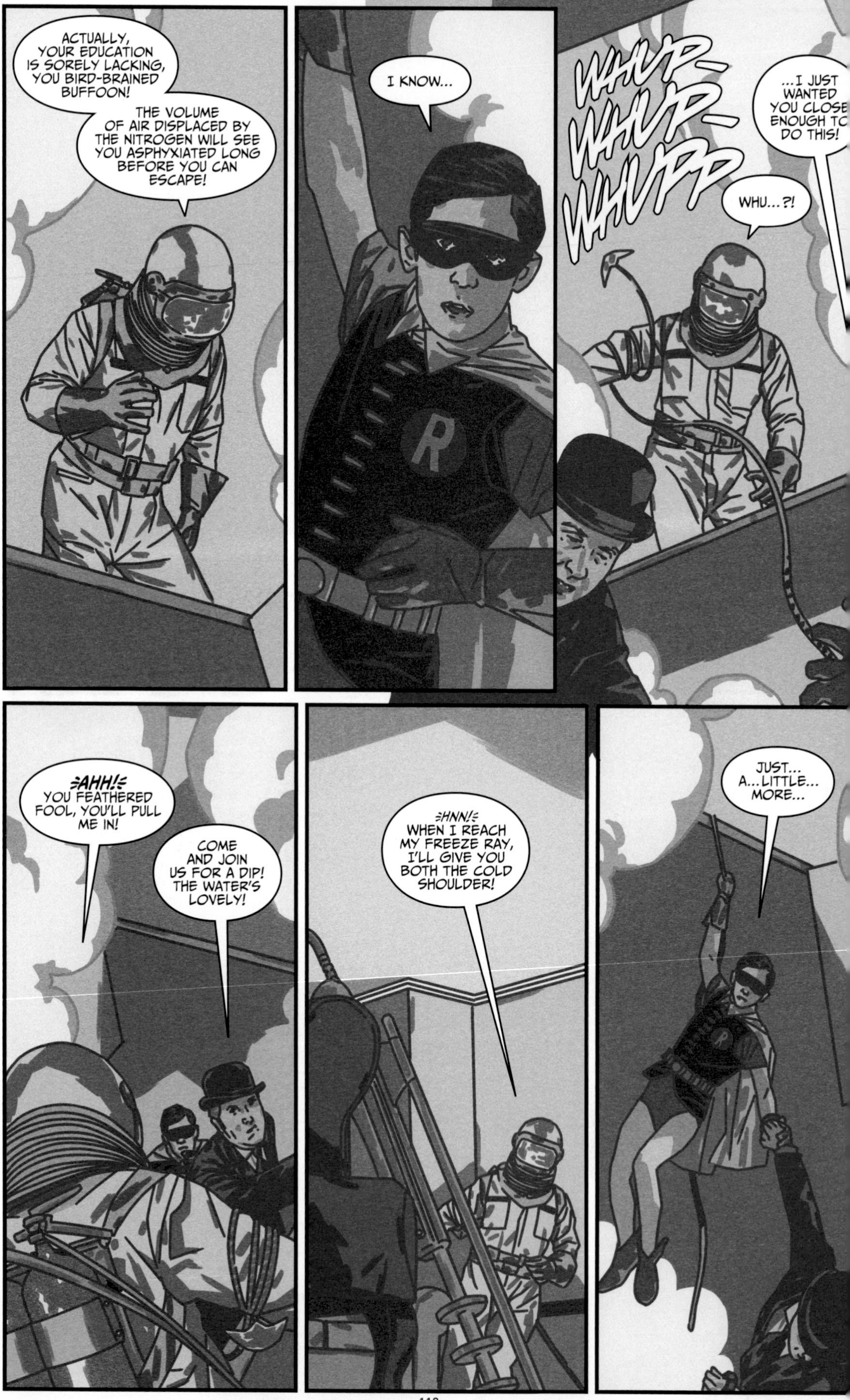
ACTUALLY, YOUR EDUCATION IS SORELY LACKING, YOU BIRD-BRAINED BUFFOON!
THE VOLUME OF AIR DISPLACED BY THE NITROGEN WILL SEE YOU ASPHYXIATED LONG BEFORE YOU CAN ESCAPE!
I KNOW...
...I JUST WANTED YOU CLOSE ENOUGH TO DO THIS!
WHUP-WHUP-WHUPP
WHU...?!
AHH! YOU FEATHERED FOOL, YOU'LL PULL ME IN!
COME AND JOIN US FOR A DIP! THE WATER'S LOVELY!
HNN! WHEN I REACH MY FREEZE RAY, I'LL GIVE YOU BOTH THE COLD SHOULDER!
JUST... A...LITTLE... MORE...

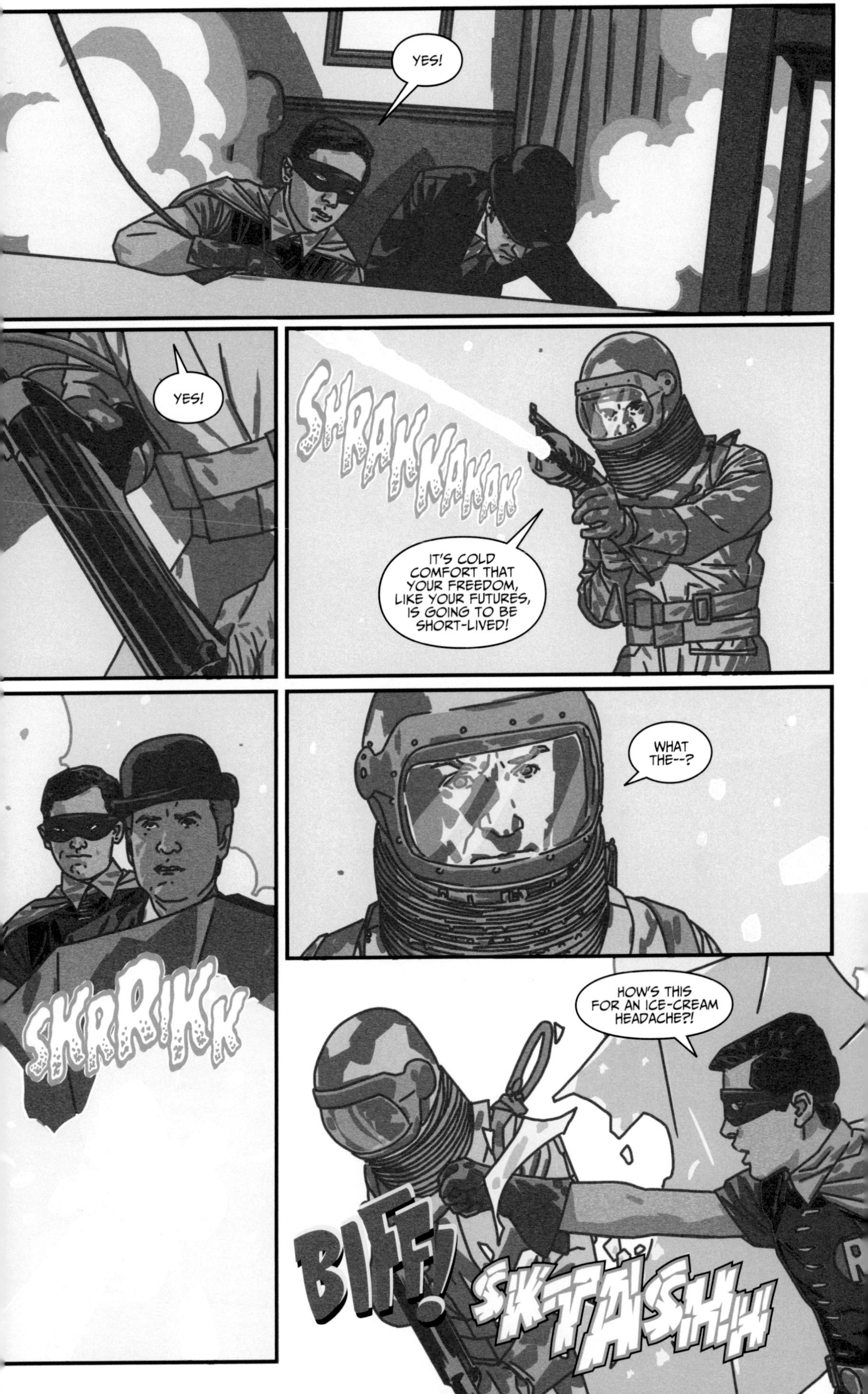

YES!
YES!
SHRAKKAKAK
IT'S COLD COMFORT THAT YOUR FREEDOM, LIKE YOUR FUTURES, IS GOING TO BE SHORT-LIVED!
SKRRIKK
WHAT THE--?
HOW'S THIS FOR AN ICE-CREAM HEADACHE?!
BIFF!
SKTASHH

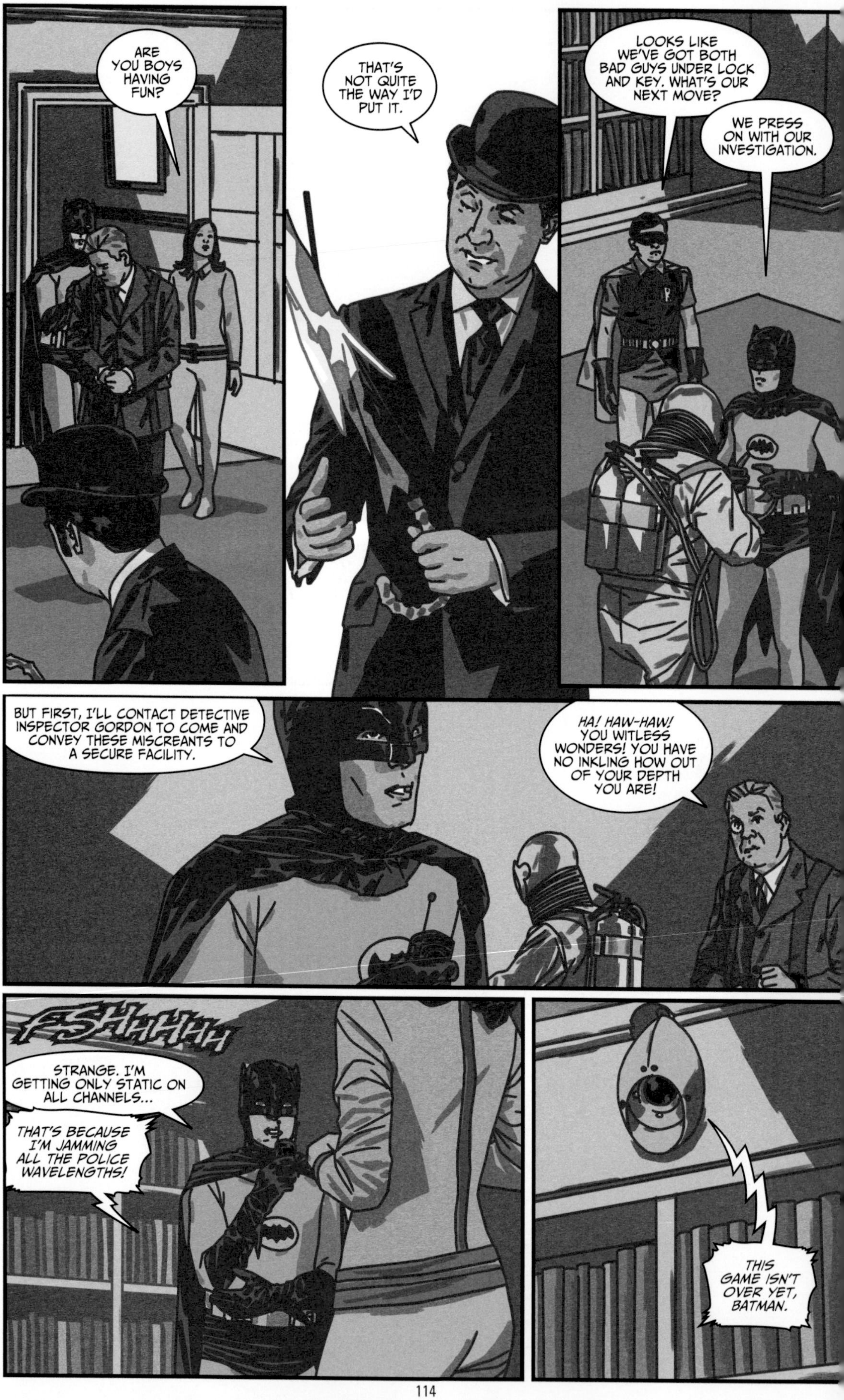
ARE YOU BOYS HAVING FUN?
THAT'S NOT QUITE THE WAY I'D PUT IT.
LOOKS LIKE WE'VE GOT BOTH BAD GUYS UNDER LOCK AND KEY. WHAT'S OUR NEXT MOVE?
WE PRESS ON WITH OUR INVESTIGATION.
BUT FIRST, I'LL CONTACT DETECTIVE INSPECTOR GORDON TO COME AND CONVEY THESE MISCREANTS TO A SECURE FACILITY.
HA! HAW-HAW! YOU WITLESS WONDERS! YOU HAVE NO INKLING HOW OUT OF YOUR DEPTH YOU ARE!
FSHHHHHH
STRANGE. I'M GETTING ONLY STATIC ON ALL CHANNELS...
THAT'S BECAUSE I'M JAMMING ALL THE POLICE WAVELENGTHS!
THIS GAME ISN'T OVER YET, BATMAN.

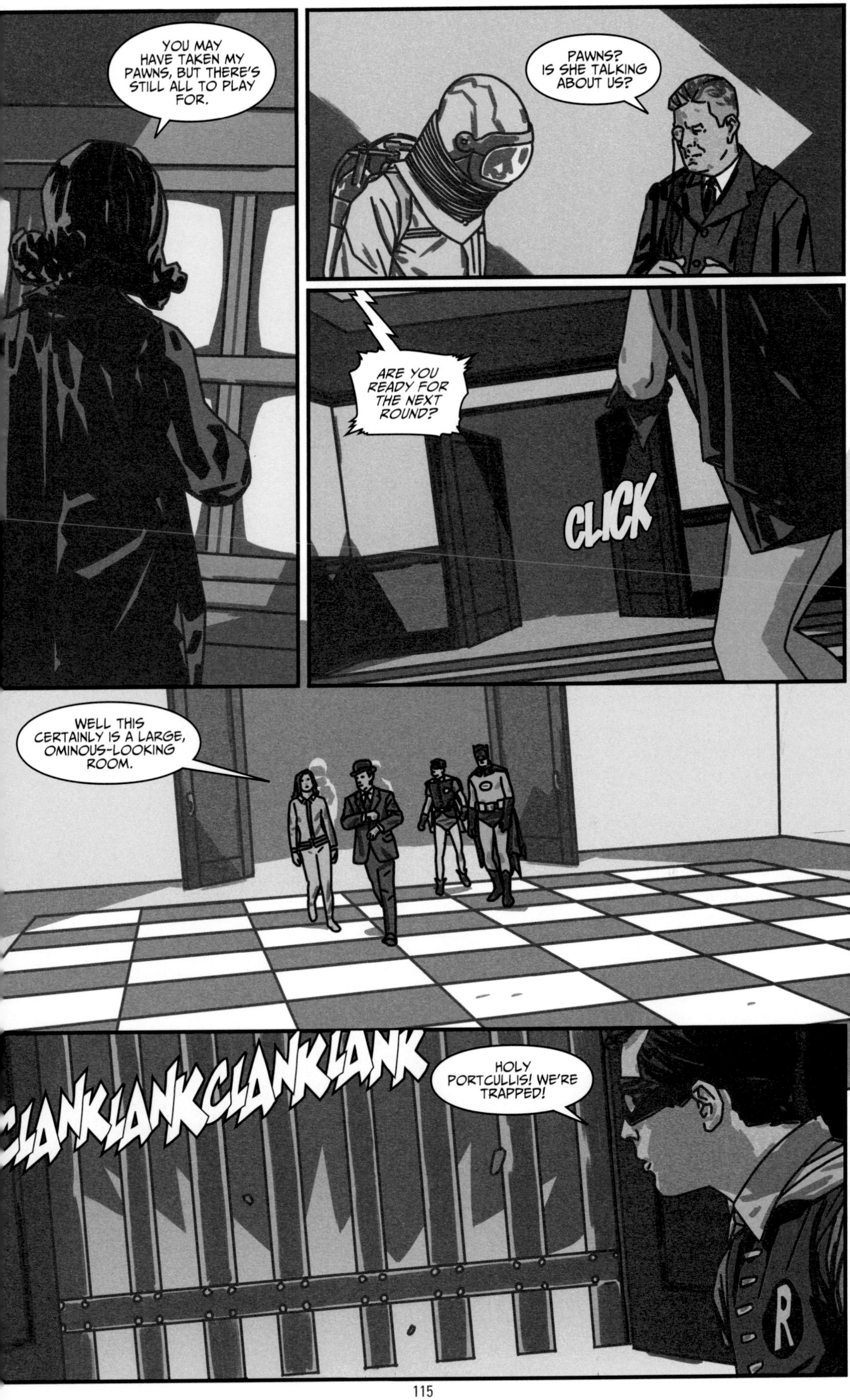
YOU MAY HAVE TAKEN MY PAWNS, BUT THERE'S STILL ALL TO PLAY FOR.
PAWNS? IS SHE TALKING ABOUT US?
ARE YOU READY FOR THE NEXT ROUND?
CLICK
WELL THIS CERTAINLY IS A LARGE, OMINOUS-LOOKING ROOM.
CLANKLANKCLANKLANK
HOLY PORTCULLIS! WE'RE TRAPPED!

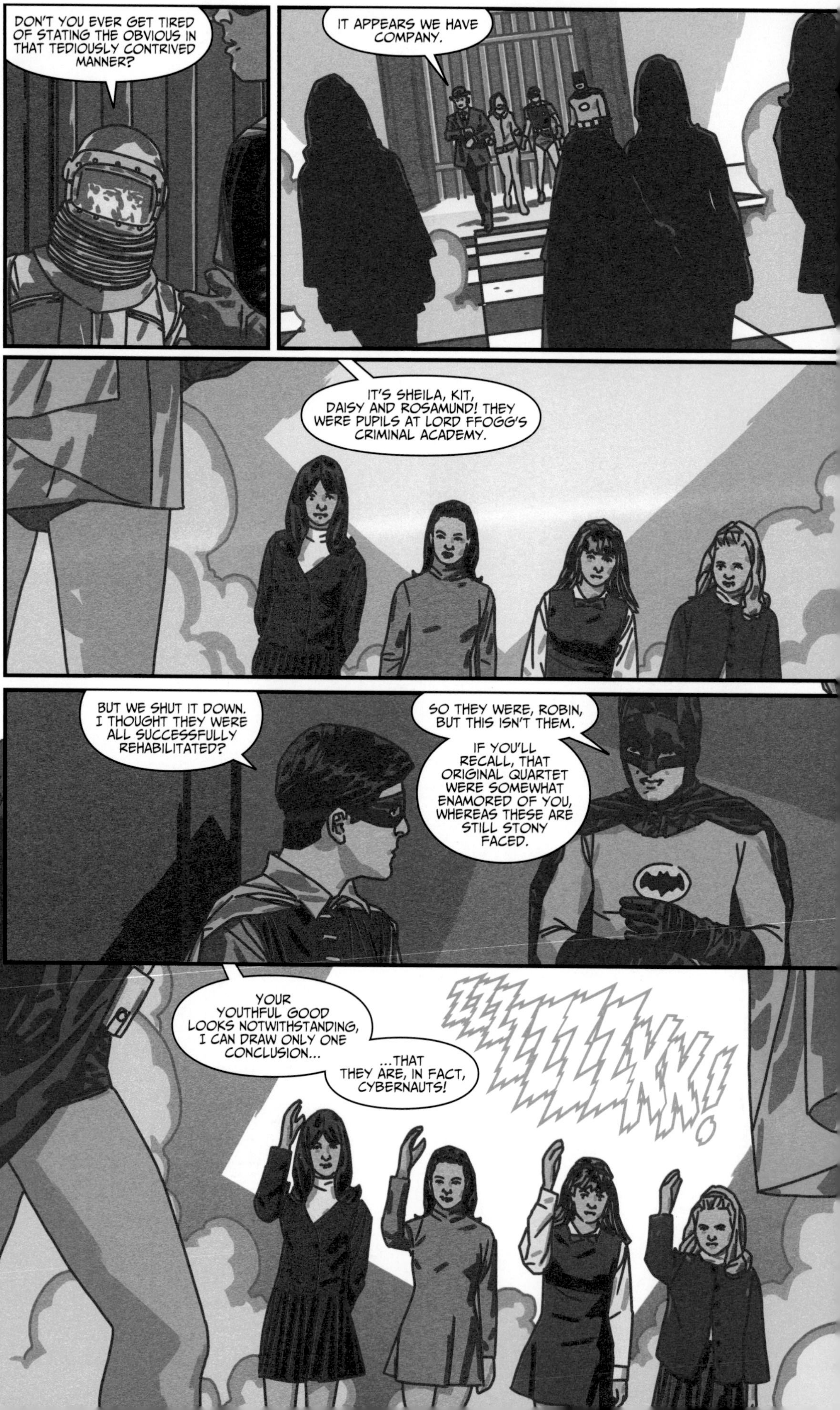
DON'T YOU EVER GET TIRED OF STATING THE OBVIOUS IN THAT TEDIOUSLY CONTRIVED MANNER?
IT APPEARS WE HAVE COMPANY.
IT'S SHEILA, KIT, DAISY AND ROSAMUND! THEY WERE PUPILS AT LORD FFOGG'S CRIMINAL ACADEMY.
BUT WE SHUT IT DOWN. I THOUGHT THEY WERE ALL SUCCESSFULLY REHABILITATED?
SO THEY WERE, ROBIN, BUT THIS ISN'T THEM.
IF YOU'LL RECALL, THAT ORIGINAL QUARTET WERE SOMEWHAT ENAMORED OF YOU, WHEREAS THESE ARE STILL STONY FACED.
YOUR YOUTHFUL GOOD LOOKS NOTWITHSTANDING, I CAN DRAW ONLY ONE CONCLUSION...
...THAT THEY ARE, IN FACT, CYBERNAUTS!
SHHKK!

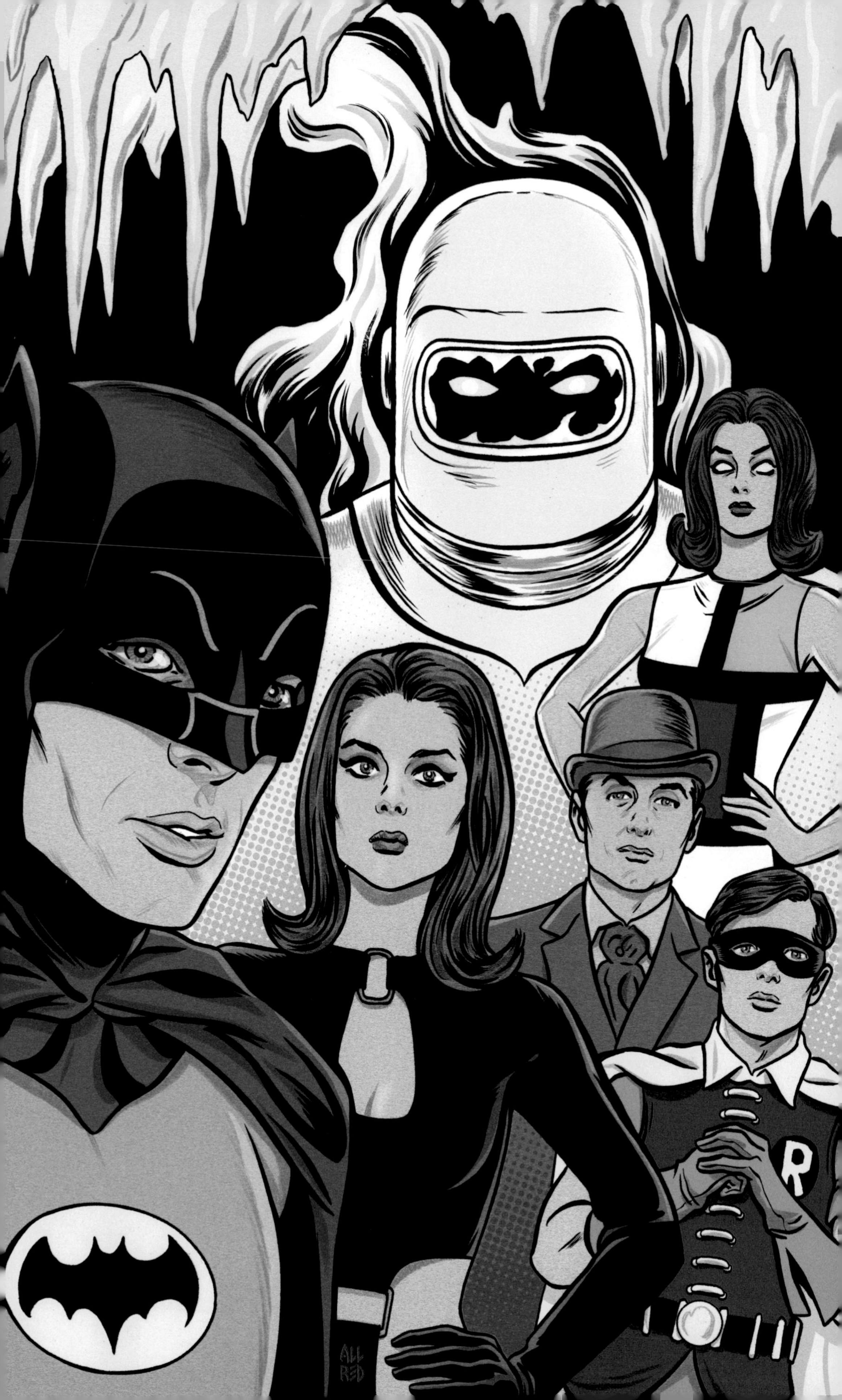
ALL
RED

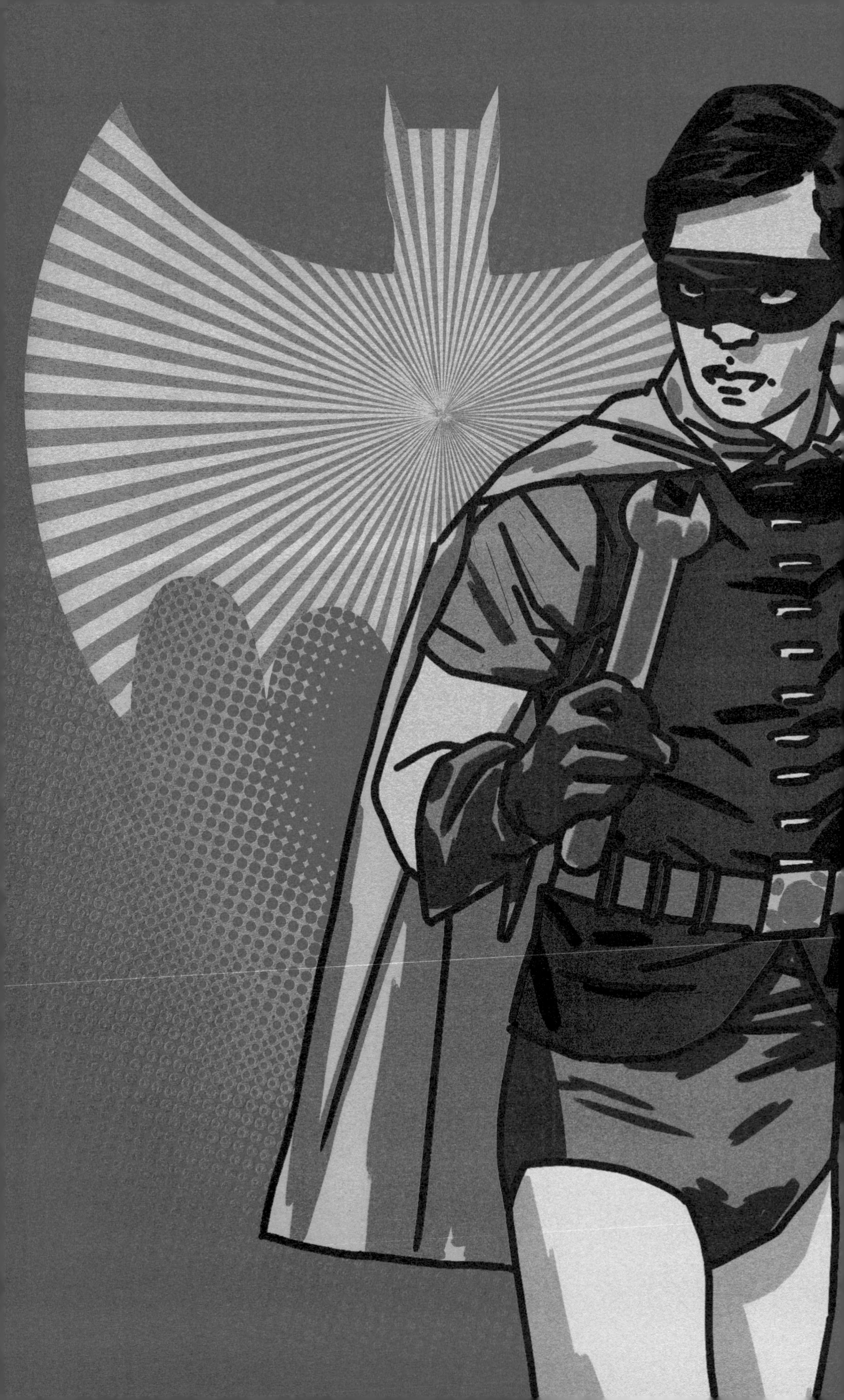

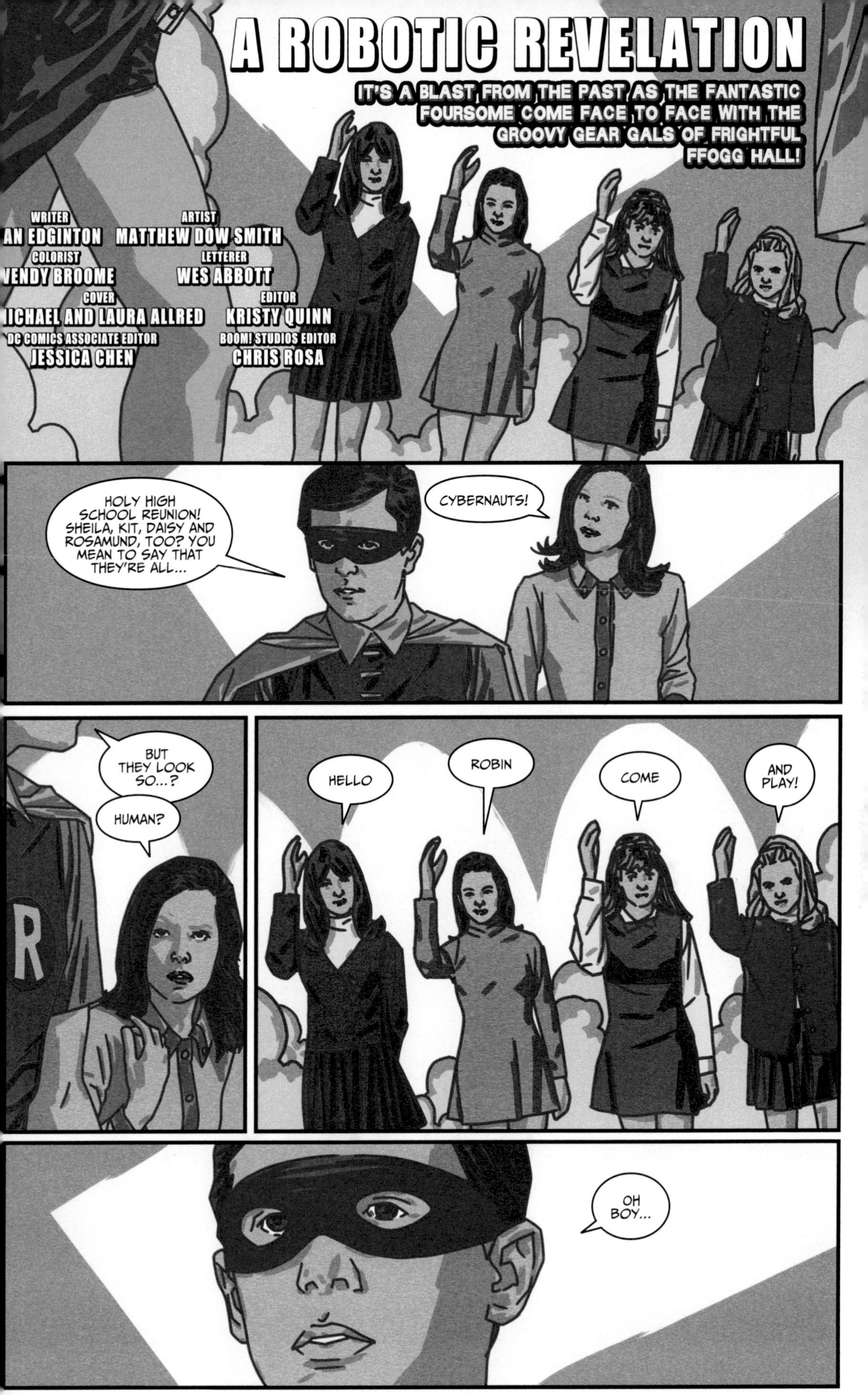
A ROBOTIC REVELATION
IT'S A BLAST FROM THE PAST AS THE FANTASTIC FOURSOME COME FACE TO FACE WITH THE GROOVY GEAR GALS OF FRIGHTFUL FFOGG HALL!
WRITER
AN EDGINTON
ARTIST
MATTHEW DOW SMITH
COLORIST
VENDY BROOME
LETTERER
WES ABBOTT
COVER
ICHAEL AND LAURA ALLRED
EDITOR
KRISTY QUINN
DC COMICS ASSOCIATE EDITOR
JESSICA CHEN
BOOM! STUDIOS EDITOR
CHRIS ROSA
HOLY HIGH SCHOOL REUNION! SHEILA, KIT, DAISY AND ROSAMUND, TOO? YOU MEAN TO SAY THAT THEY'RE ALL...
CYBERNAUTS!
BUT THEY LOOK SO...?
HUMAN?
HELLO
ROBIN
COME
AND PLAY!
OH BOY...

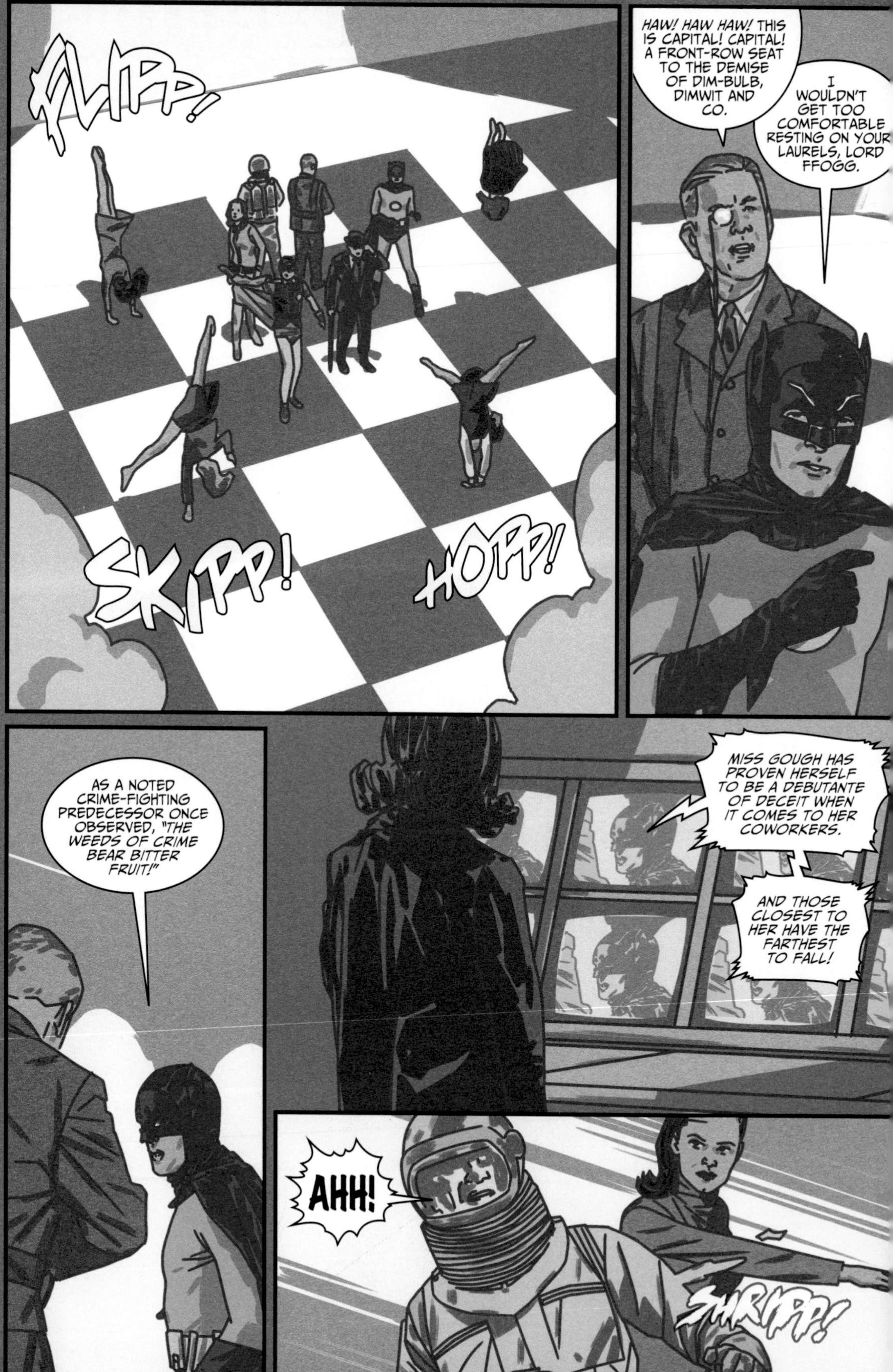
FLIPP!
SKIPP!
HOPP!
HAW! HAW HAW! THIS IS CAPITAL! CAPITAL! A FRONT-ROW SEAT TO THE DEMISE OF DIM-BULB, DIMWIT AND CO.
I WOULDN'T GET TOO COMFORTABLE RESTING ON YOUR LAURELS, LORD FFOGG.
AS A NOTED CRIME-FIGHTING PREDECESSOR ONCE OBSERVED, "THE WEEDS OF CRIME BEAR BITTER FRUIT!"
MISS GOUGH HAS PROVEN HERSELF TO BE A DEBUTANTE OF DECEIT WHEN IT COMES TO HER COWORKERS.
AND THOSE CLOSEST TO HER HAVE THE FARTHEST TO FALL!
AHH!
SHRIPP!

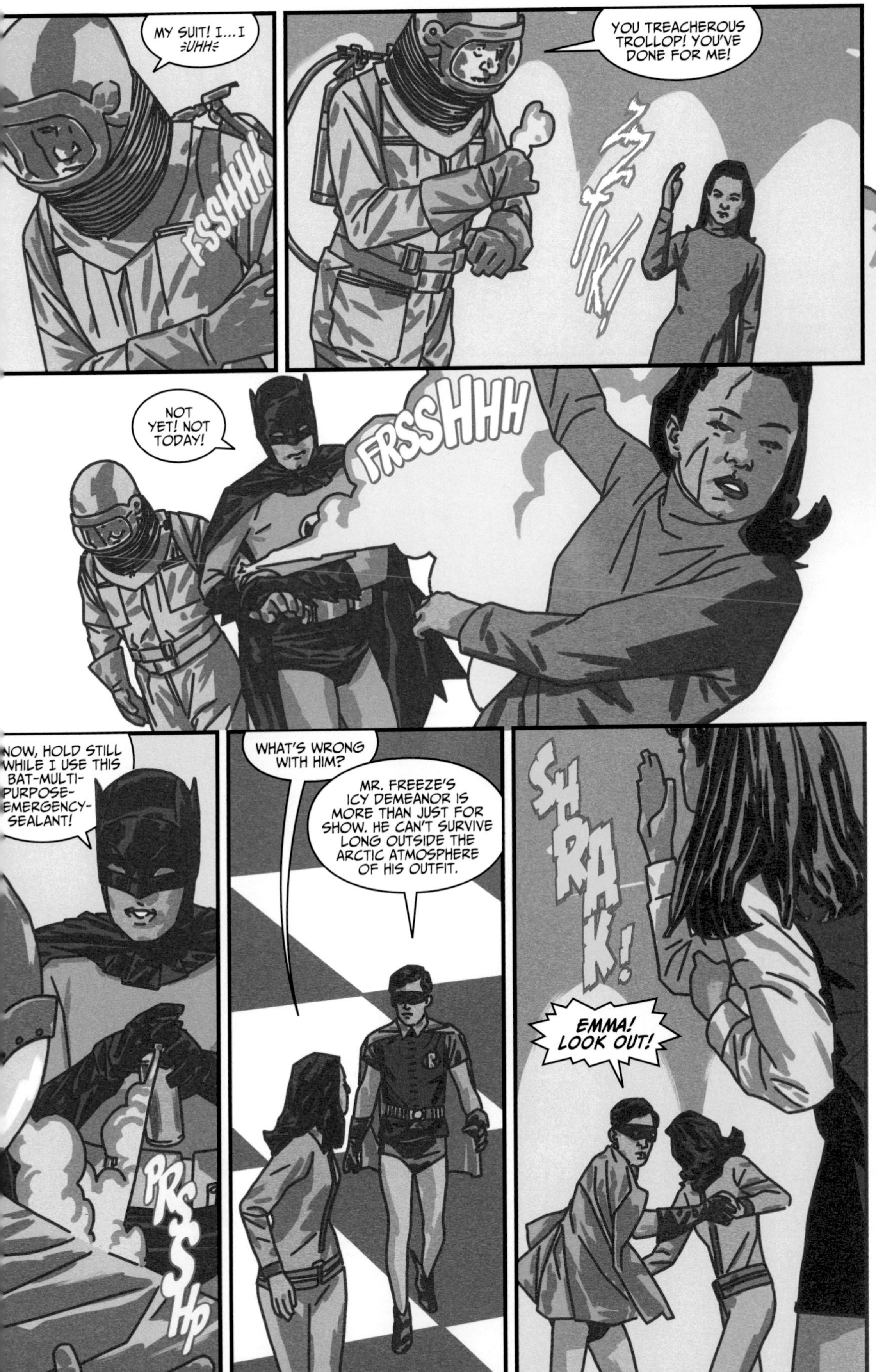
MY SUIT! I...I
=UHH=
FSSHHH
YOU TREACHEROUS TROLLOP! YOU'VE DONE FOR ME!
ZZTK!
NOT YET! NOT TODAY!
FRSSHHH
NOW, HOLD STILL WHILE I USE THIS BAT-MULTI-PURPOSE-EMERGENCY-SEALANT!
PRSSHP
WHAT'S WRONG WITH HIM?
MR. FREEZE'S ICY DEMEANOR IS MORE THAN JUST FOR SHOW. HE CAN'T SURVIVE LONG OUTSIDE THE ARCTIC ATMOSPHERE OF HIS OUTFIT.
SHRAK!
EMMA! LOOK OUT!

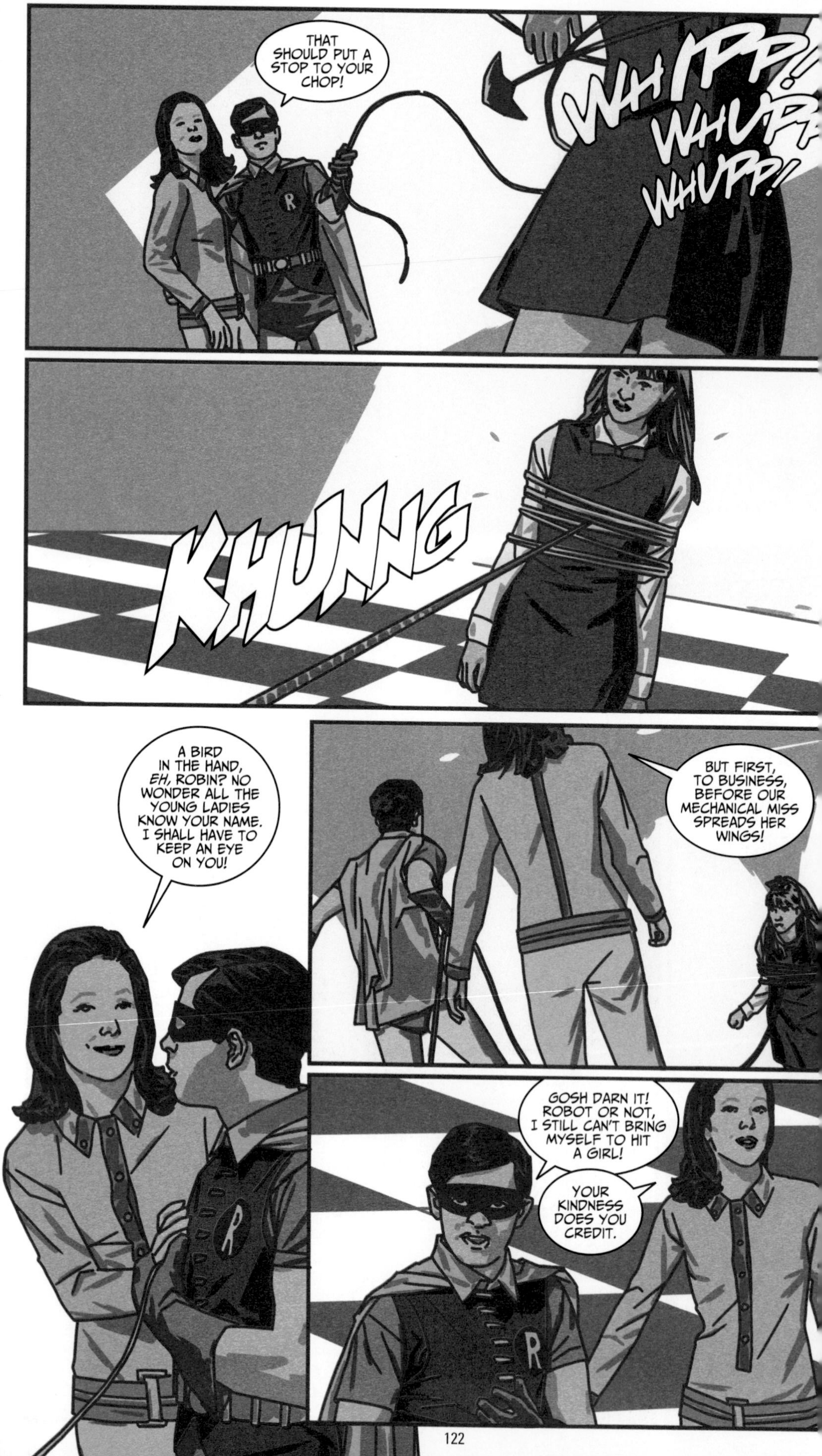
THAT SHOULD PUT A STOP TO YOUR CHOP!
WHIPP! WHUPP! WHUPP!
KHUNNG
A BIRD IN THE HAND, *EH,* ROBIN? NO WONDER ALL THE YOUNG LADIES KNOW YOUR NAME. I SHALL HAVE TO KEEP AN EYE ON YOU!
BUT FIRST, TO BUSINESS, BEFORE OUR MECHANICAL MISS SPREADS HER WINGS!
GOSH DARN IT! ROBOT OR NOT, I STILL CAN'T BRING MYSELF TO HIT A GIRL!
YOUR KINDNESS DOES YOU CREDIT.

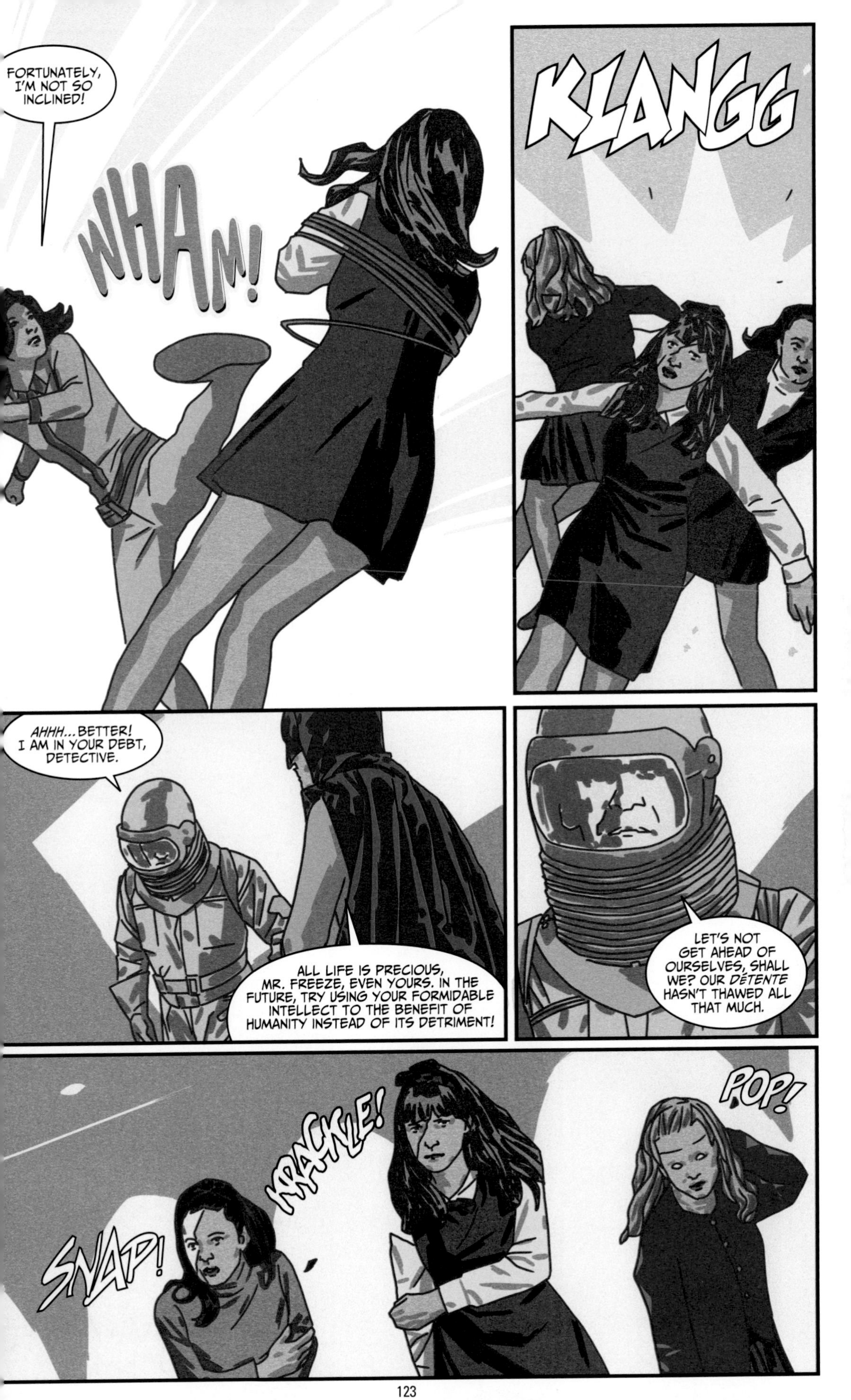

FORTUNATELY, I'M NOT SO INCLINED!
WHAM!
KLANGG
AHHH...BETTER! I AM IN YOUR DEBT, DETECTIVE.
ALL LIFE IS PRECIOUS, MR. FREEZE, EVEN YOURS. IN THE FUTURE, TRY USING YOUR FORMIDABLE INTELLECT TO THE BENEFIT OF HUMANITY INSTEAD OF ITS DETRIMENT!
LET'S NOT GET AHEAD OF OURSELVES, SHALL WE? OUR DÉTENTE HASN'T THAWED ALL THAT MUCH.
SNAP!
KRACKLE!
POP!

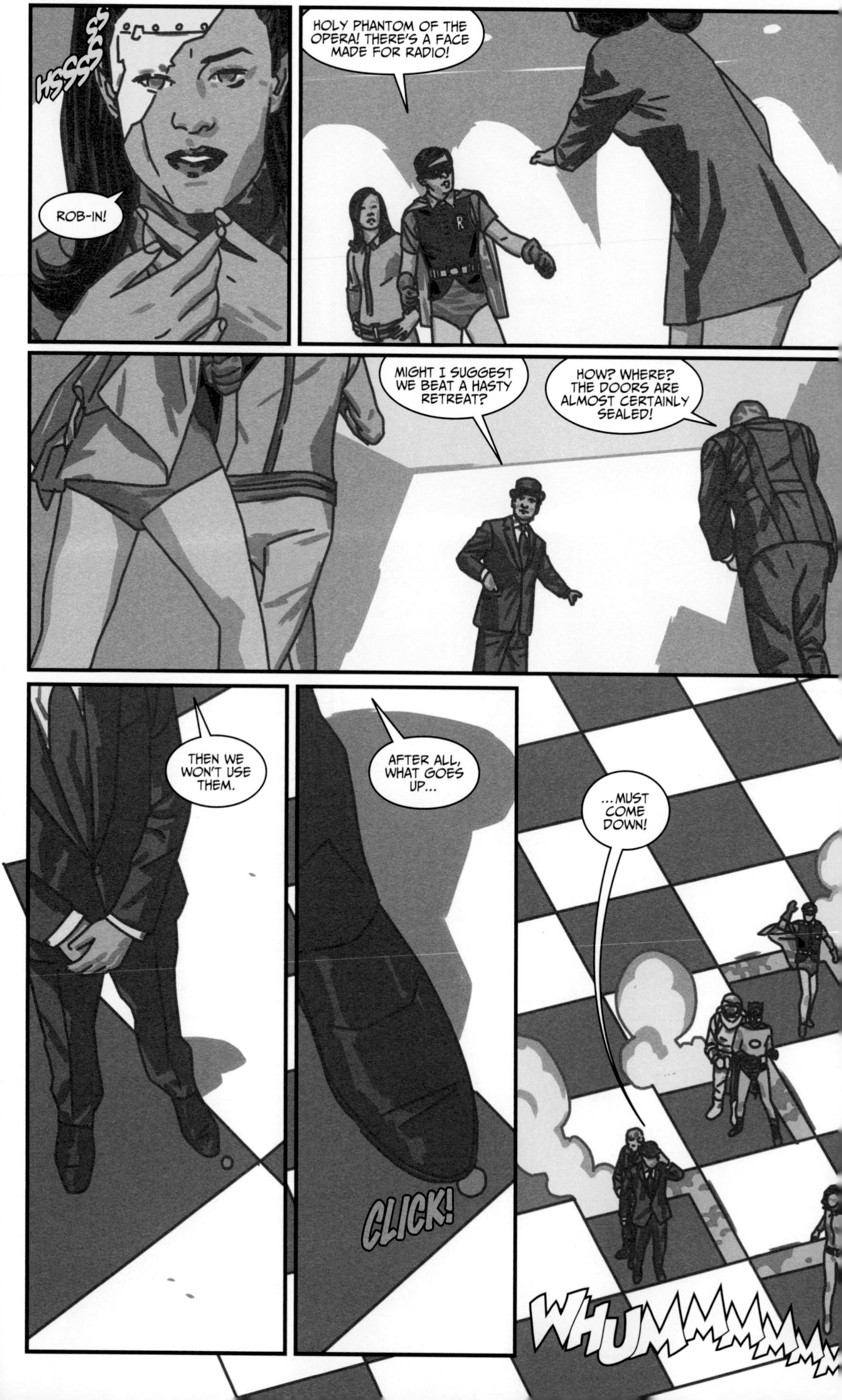
HSSSSS
ROB-IN!
HOLY PHANTOM OF THE OPERA! THERE'S A FACE MADE FOR RADIO!
MIGHT I SUGGEST WE BEAT A HASTY RETREAT?
HOW? WHERE? THE DOORS ARE ALMOST CERTAINLY SEALED!
THEN WE WON'T USE THEM.
AFTER ALL, WHAT GOES UP...
CLICK!
...MUST COME DOWN!
WHUMMMMMMM

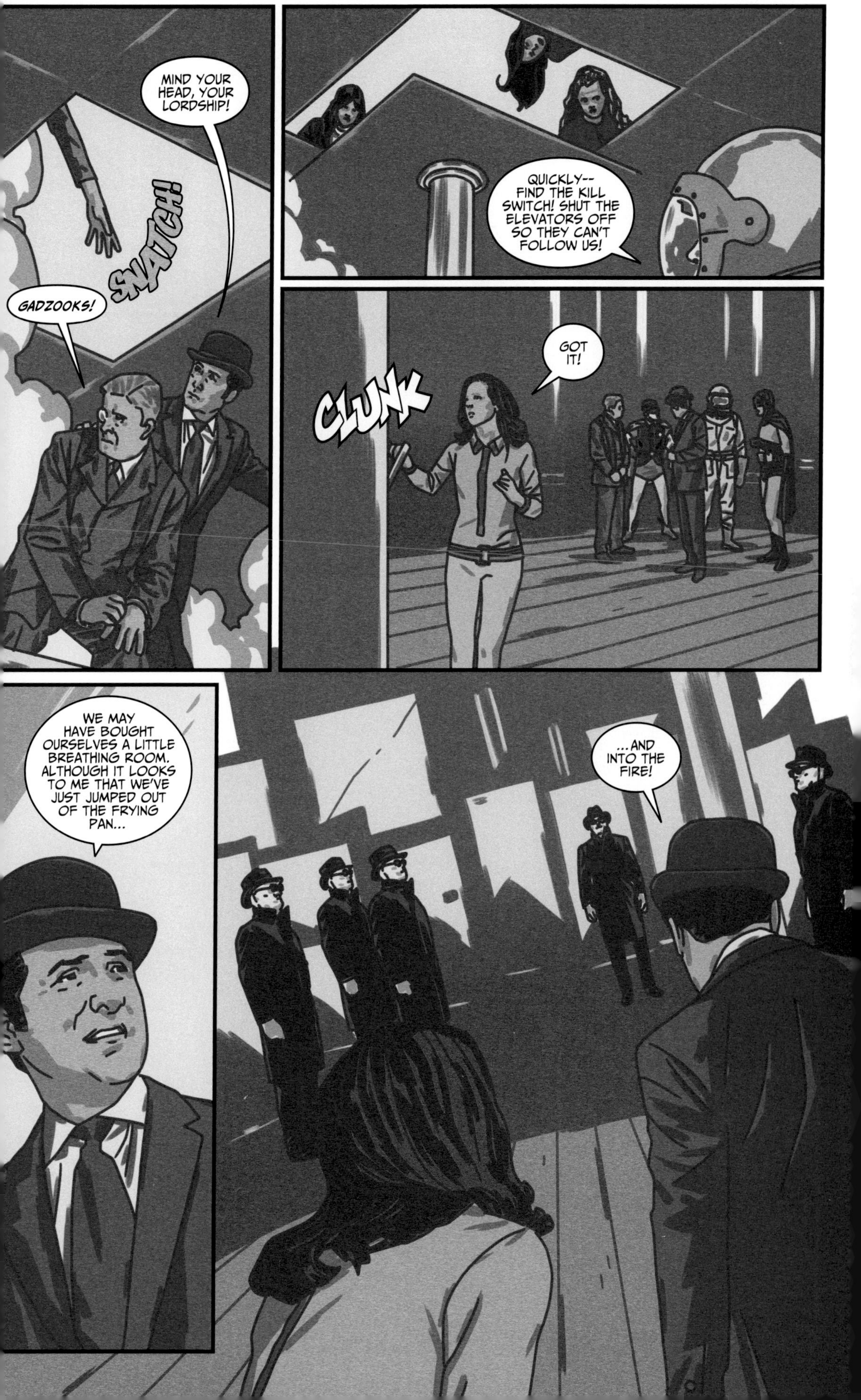
MIND YOUR HEAD, YOUR LORDSHIP!
SNATCH!
GADZOOKS!
QUICKLY-- FIND THE KILL SWITCH! SHUT THE ELEVATORS OFF SO THEY CAN'T FOLLOW US!
CLUNK
GOT IT!
WE MAY HAVE BOUGHT OURSELVES A LITTLE BREATHING ROOM. ALTHOUGH IT LOOKS TO ME THAT WE'VE JUST JUMPED OUT OF THE FRYING PAN...
...AND INTO THE FIRE!

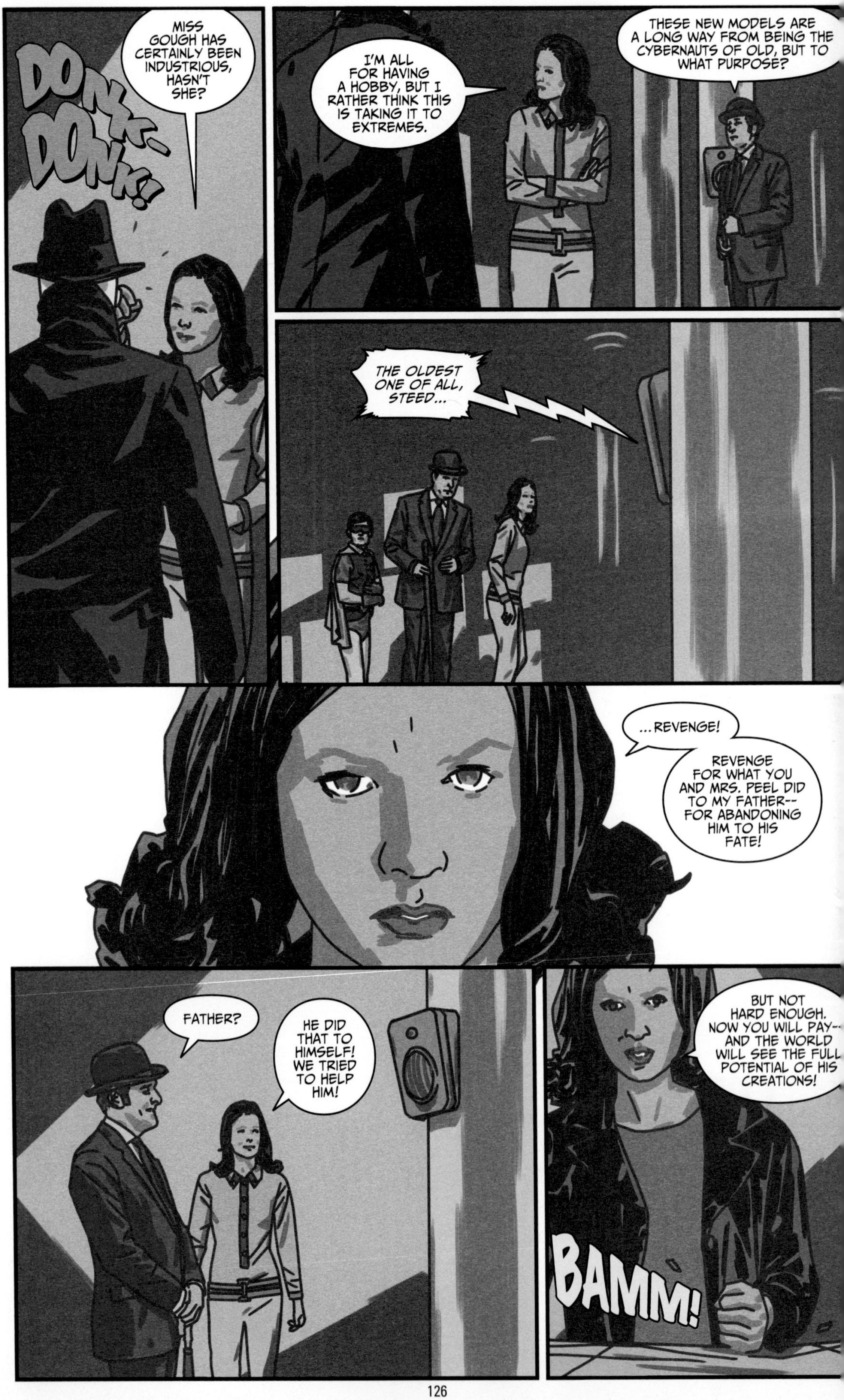
DONK-DONK!
MISS GOUGH HAS CERTAINLY BEEN INDUSTRIOUS, HASN'T SHE?
I'M ALL FOR HAVING A HOBBY, BUT I RATHER THINK THIS IS TAKING IT TO EXTREMES.
THESE NEW MODELS ARE A LONG WAY FROM BEING THE CYBERNAUTS OF OLD, BUT TO WHAT PURPOSE?
THE OLDEST ONE OF ALL, STEED...
...REVENGE!
REVENGE FOR WHAT YOU AND MRS. PEEL DID TO MY FATHER-- FOR ABANDONING HIM TO HIS FATE!
FATHER?
HE DID THAT TO HIMSELF! WE TRIED TO HELP HIM!
BUT NOT HARD ENOUGH. NOW YOU WILL PAY-- AND THE WORLD WILL SEE THE FULL POTENTIAL OF HIS CREATIONS!
BAMM!

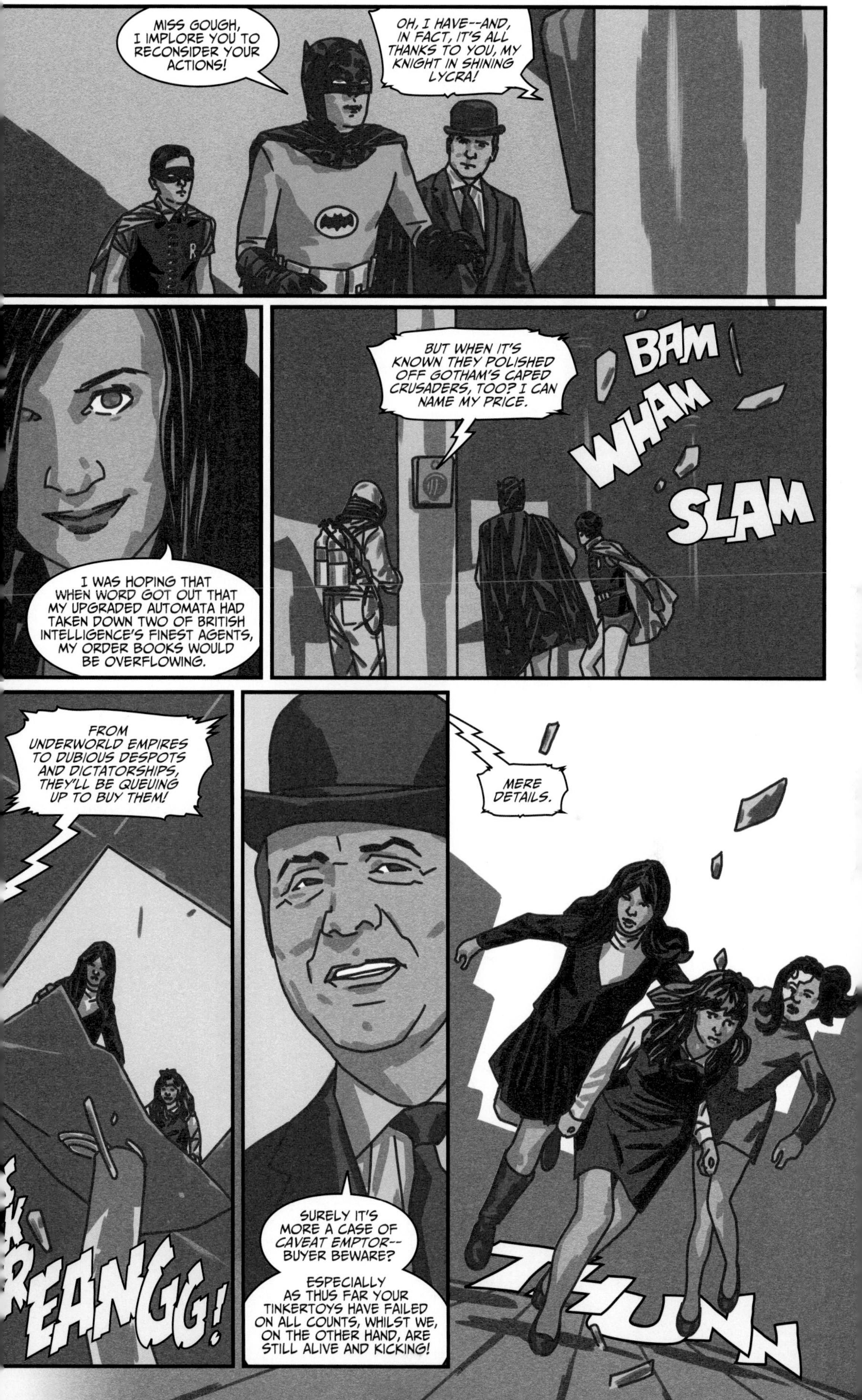

MISS GOUGH, I IMPLORE YOU TO RECONSIDER YOUR ACTIONS!
OH, I HAVE--AND, IN FACT, IT'S ALL THANKS TO YOU, MY KNIGHT IN SHINING LYCRA!
I WAS HOPING THAT WHEN WORD GOT OUT THAT MY UPGRADED AUTOMATA HAD TAKEN DOWN TWO OF BRITISH INTELLIGENCE'S FINEST AGENTS, MY ORDER BOOKS WOULD BE OVERFLOWING.
BUT WHEN IT'S KNOWN THEY POLISHED OFF GOTHAM'S CAPED CRUSADERS, TOO? I CAN NAME MY PRICE.
BAM
WHAM
SLAM
FROM UNDERWORLD EMPIRES TO DUBIOUS DESPOTS AND DICTATORSHIPS, THEY'LL BE QUEUING UP TO BUY THEM!
REANGG!
MERE DETAILS.
SURELY IT'S MORE A CASE OF CAVEAT EMPTOR-- BUYER BEWARE?
ESPECIALLY AS THUS FAR YOUR TINKERTOYS HAVE FAILED ON ALL COUNTS, WHILST WE, ON THE OTHER HAND, ARE STILL ALIVE AND KICKING!
ZHUNN

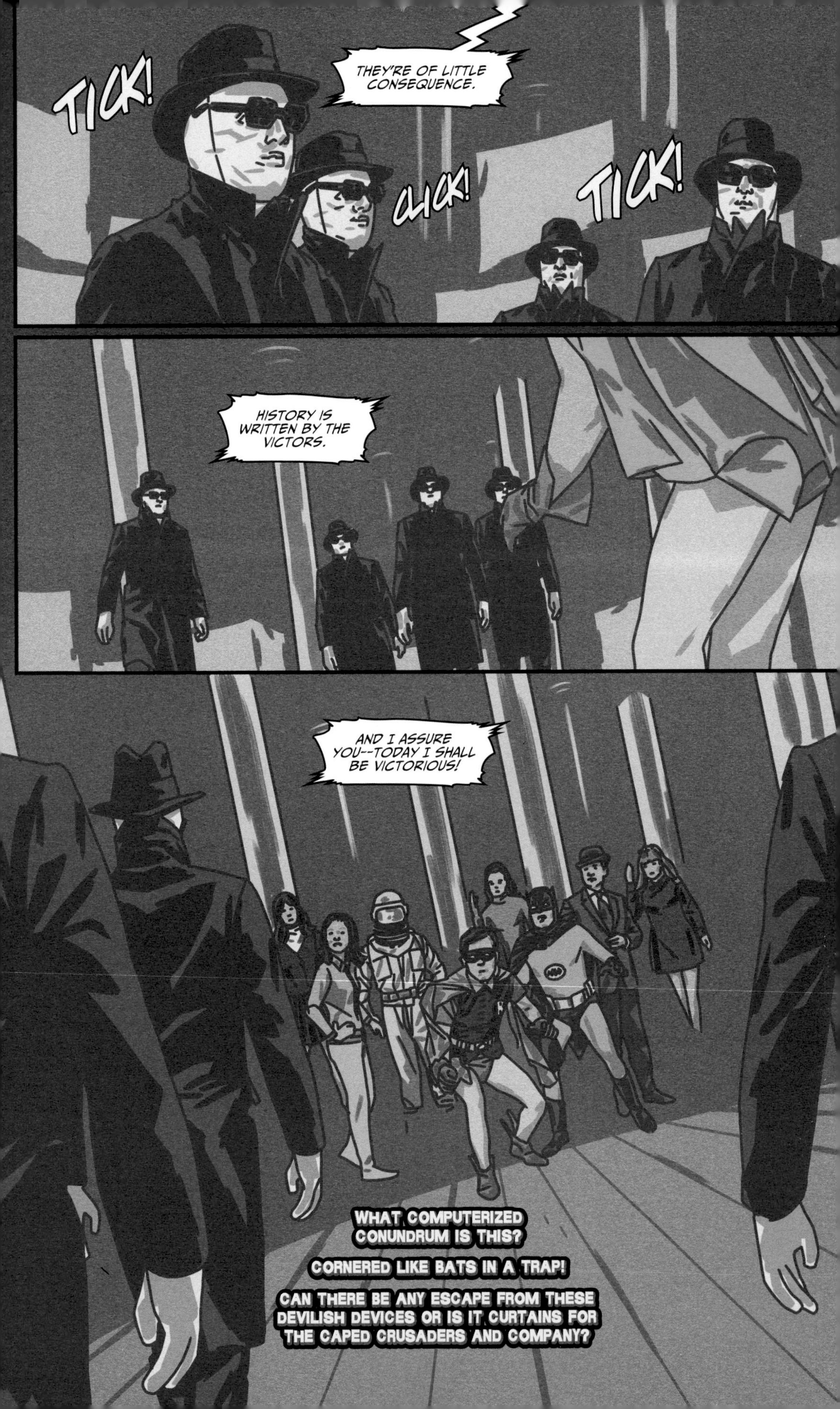
THEY'RE OF LITTLE CONSEQUENCE.
TICK!
CLICK!
TICK!
HISTORY IS WRITTEN BY THE VICTORS.
AND I ASSURE YOU--TODAY I SHALL BE VICTORIOUS!
WHAT COMPUTERIZED CONUNDRUM IS THIS?
CORNERED LIKE BATS IN A TRAP!
CAN THERE BE ANY ESCAPE FROM THESE DEVILISH DEVICES OR IS IT CURTAINS FOR THE CAPED CRUSADERS AND COMPANY?

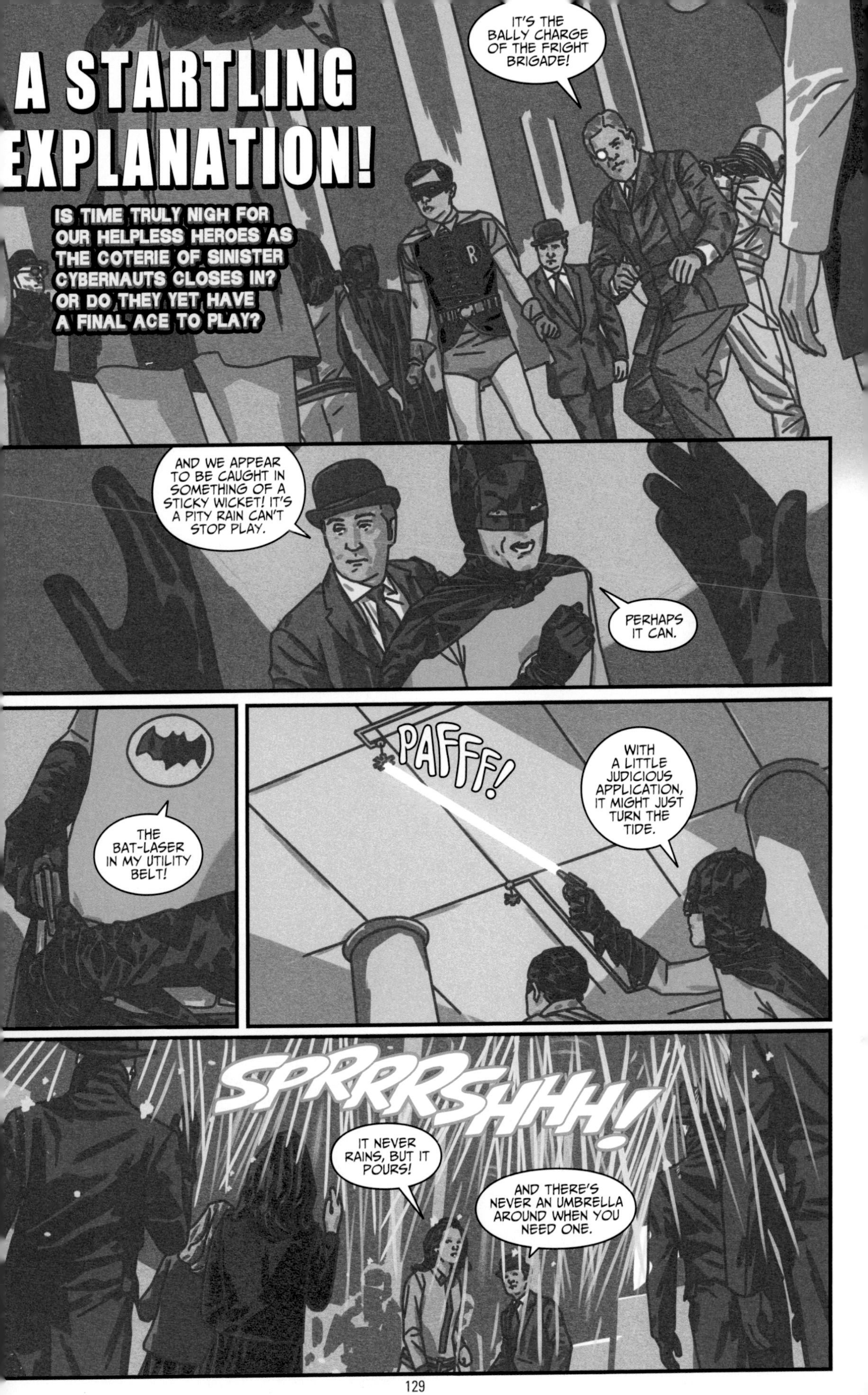
A STARTLING EXPLANATION!
IS TIME TRULY NIGH FOR OUR HELPLESS HEROES AS THE COTERIE OF SINISTER CYBERNAUTS CLOSES IN? OR DO THEY YET HAVE A FINAL ACE TO PLAY?
IT'S THE BALLY CHARGE OF THE FRIGHT BRIGADE!
AND WE APPEAR TO BE CAUGHT IN SOMETHING OF A STICKY WICKET! IT'S A PITY RAIN CAN'T STOP PLAY.
PERHAPS IT CAN.
THE BAT-LASER IN MY UTILITY BELT!
PAFFF!
WITH A LITTLE JUDICIOUS APPLICATION, IT MIGHT JUST TURN THE TIDE.
SPRRRSHHH!
IT NEVER RAINS, BUT IT POURS!
AND THERE'S NEVER AN UMBRELLA AROUND WHEN YOU NEED ONE.

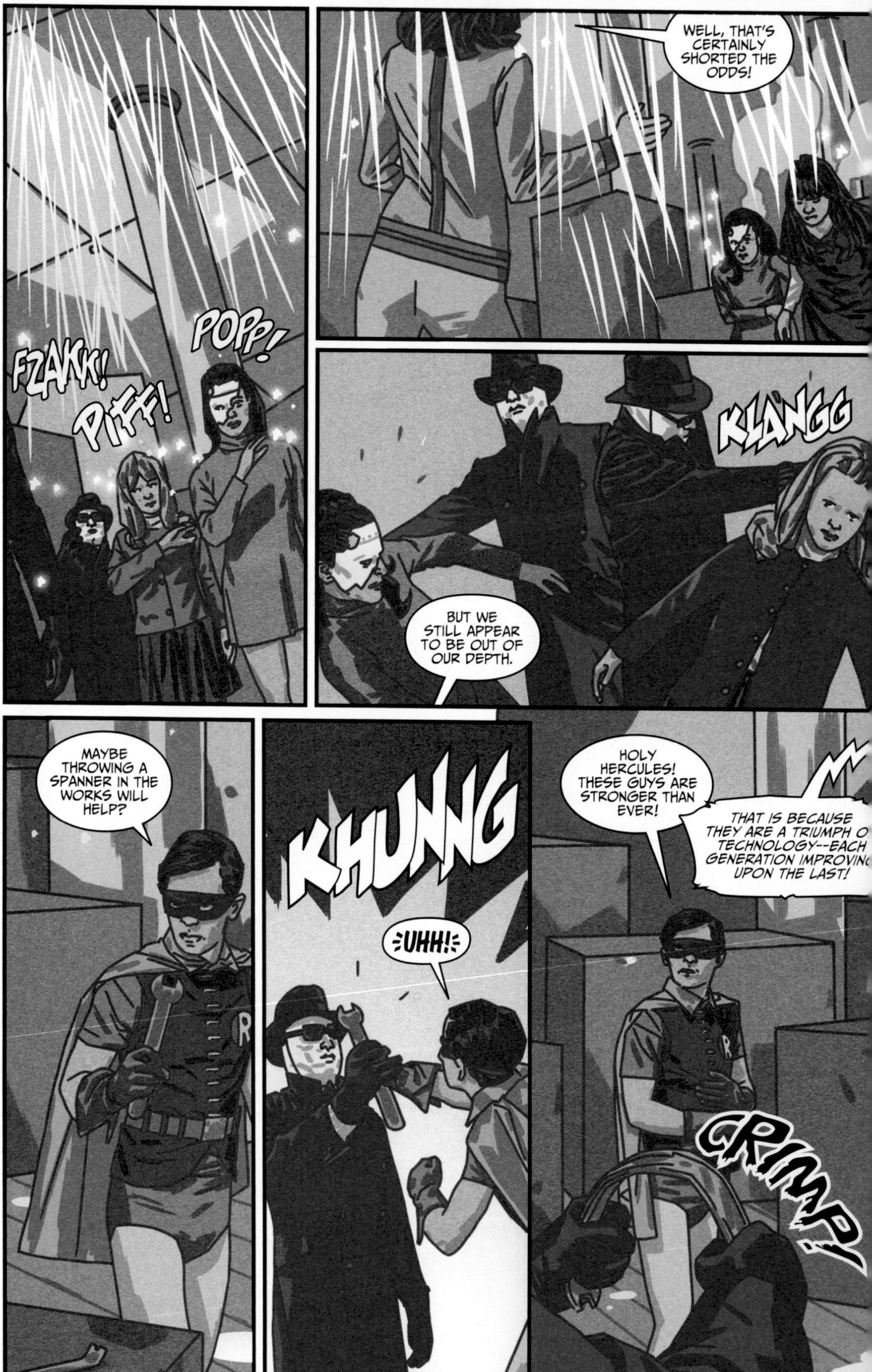
FZAKK!
PIFF!
POPP!
WELL, THAT'S CERTAINLY SHORTED THE ODDS!
KLANGG
BUT WE STILL APPEAR TO BE OUT OF OUR DEPTH.
MAYBE THROWING A SPANNER IN THE WORKS WILL HELP?
KHUNNG
UHH!
HOLY HERCULES! THESE GUYS ARE STRONGER THAN EVER!
THAT IS BECAUSE THEY ARE A TRIUMPH O TECHNOLOGY--EACH GENERATION IMPROVIN UPON THE LAST!
CRIMP!

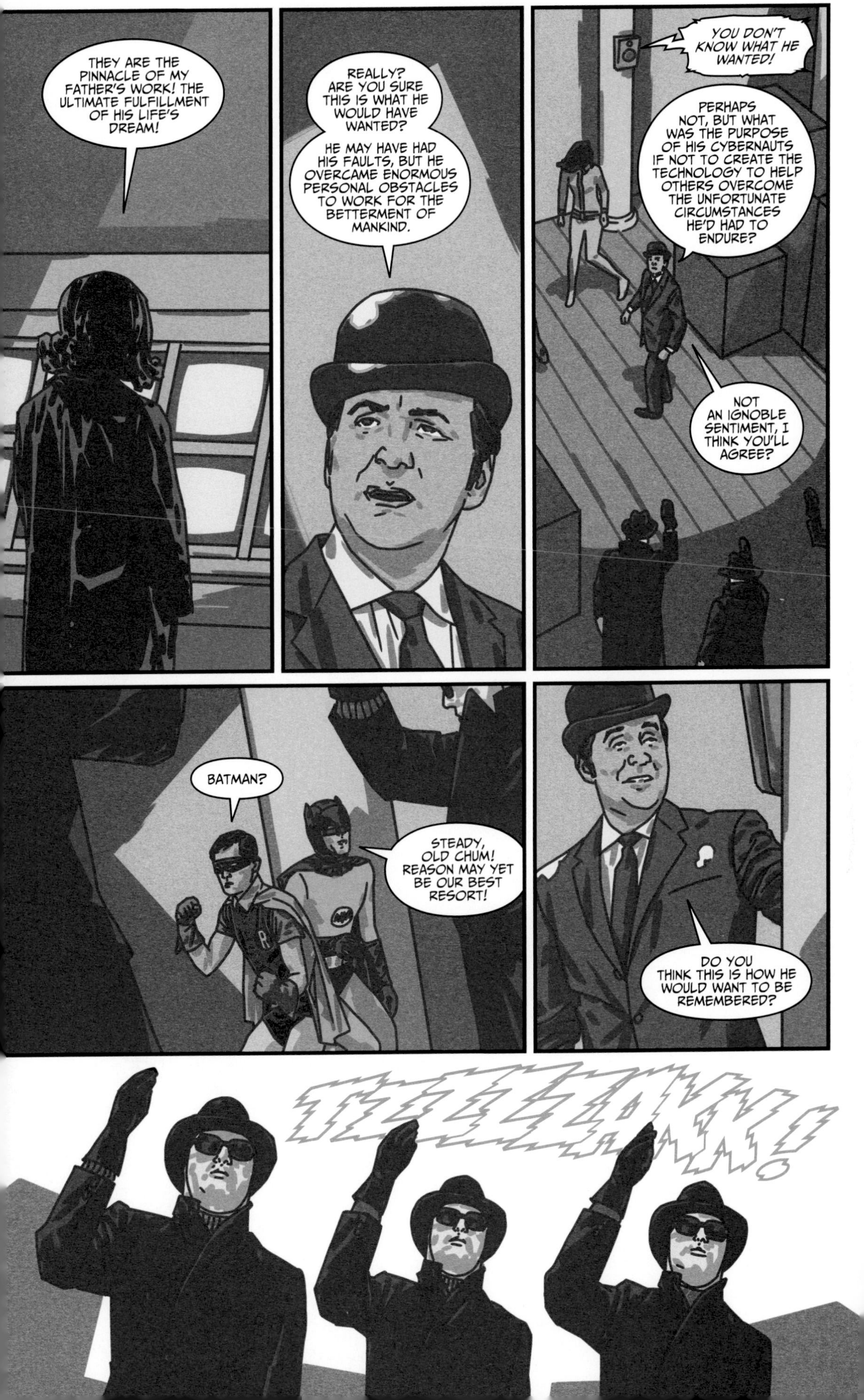
THEY ARE THE PINNACLE OF MY FATHER'S WORK! THE ULTIMATE FULFILLMENT OF HIS LIFE'S DREAM!
REALLY? ARE YOU SURE THIS IS WHAT HE WOULD HAVE WANTED?
HE MAY HAVE HAD HIS FAULTS, BUT HE OVERCAME ENORMOUS PERSONAL OBSTACLES TO WORK FOR THE BETTERMENT OF MANKIND.
YOU DON'T KNOW WHAT HE WANTED!
PERHAPS NOT, BUT WHAT WAS THE PURPOSE OF HIS CYBERNAUTS IF NOT TO CREATE THE TECHNOLOGY TO HELP OTHERS OVERCOME THE UNFORTUNATE CIRCUMSTANCES HE'D HAD TO ENDURE?
NOT AN IGNOBLE SENTIMENT, I THINK YOU'LL AGREE?
BATMAN?
STEADY, OLD CHUM! REASON MAY YET BE OUR BEST RESORT!
DO YOU THINK THIS IS HOW HE WOULD WANT TO BE REMEMBERED?
TZZAK!

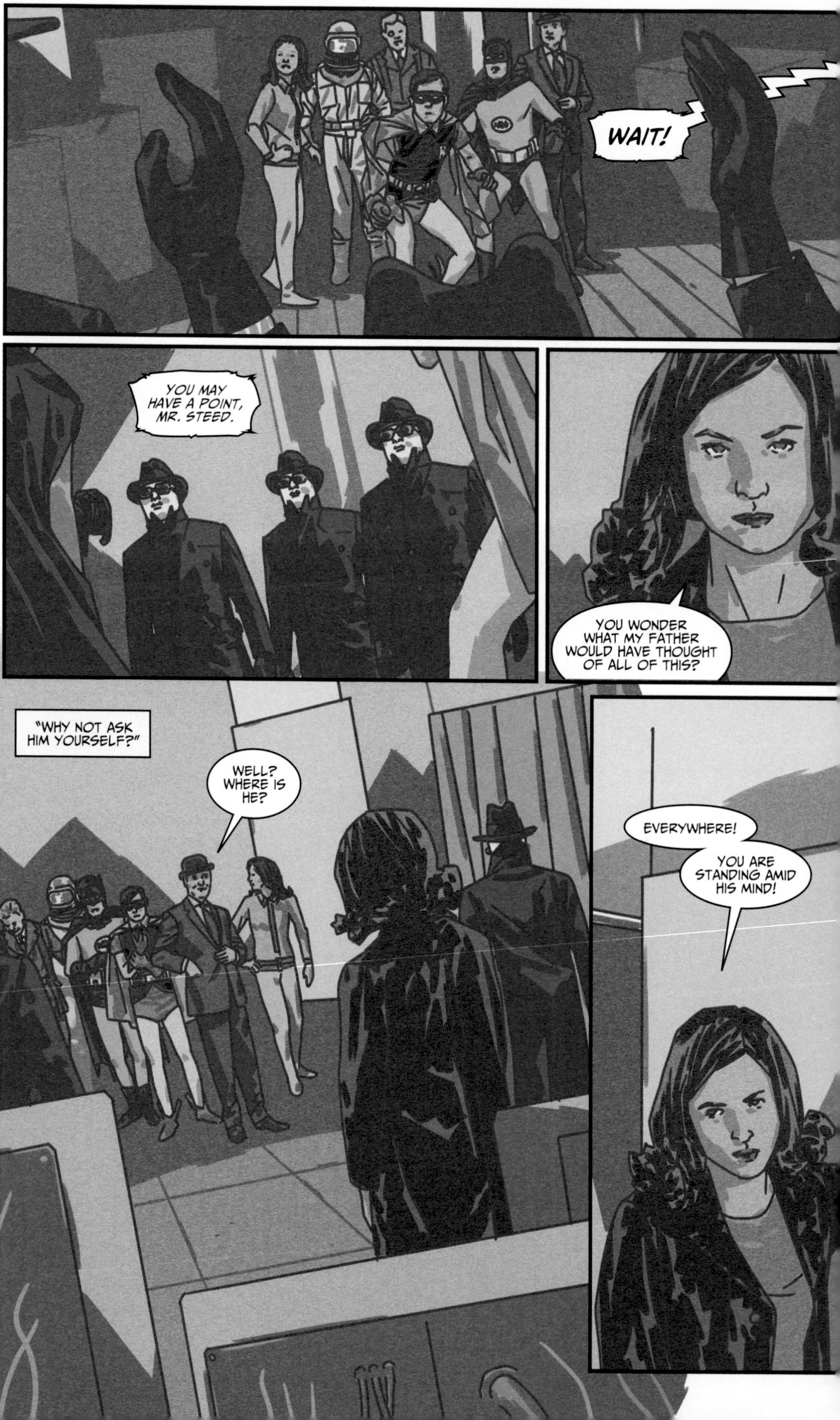
WAIT!
YOU MAY HAVE A POINT, MR. STEED.
YOU WONDER WHAT MY FATHER WOULD HAVE THOUGHT OF ALL OF THIS?
"WHY NOT ASK HIM YOURSELF?"
WELL? WHERE IS HE?
EVERYWHERE!
YOU ARE STANDING AMID HIS MIND!

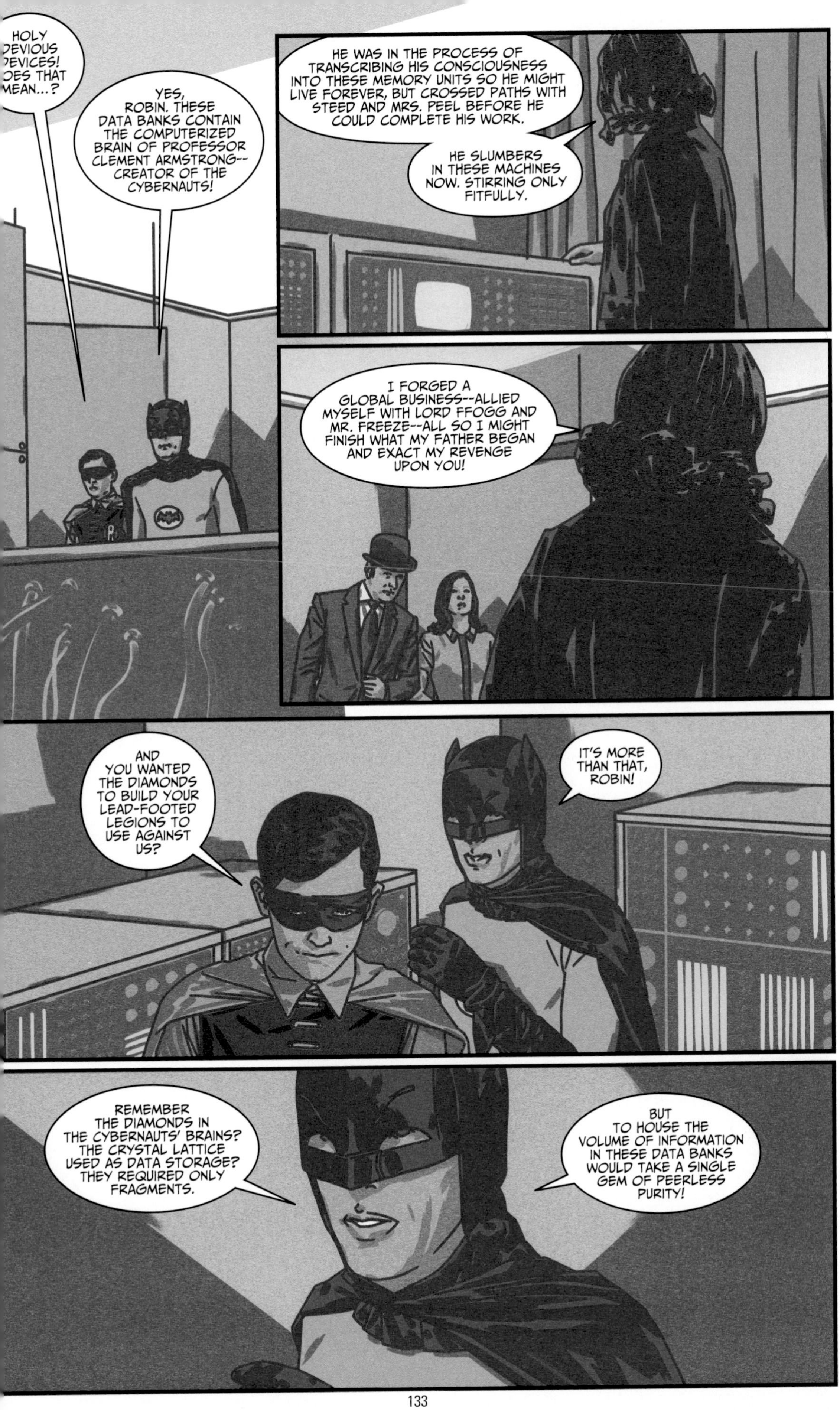
HOLY DEVIOUS DEVICES! DOES THAT MEAN...?
YES, ROBIN. THESE DATA BANKS CONTAIN THE COMPUTERIZED BRAIN OF PROFESSOR CLEMENT ARMSTRONG--CREATOR OF THE CYBERNAUTS!
HE WAS IN THE PROCESS OF TRANSCRIBING HIS CONSCIOUSNESS INTO THESE MEMORY UNITS SO HE MIGHT LIVE FOREVER, BUT CROSSED PATHS WITH STEED AND MRS. PEEL BEFORE HE COULD COMPLETE HIS WORK.
HE SLUMBERS IN THESE MACHINES NOW. STIRRING ONLY FITFULLY.
I FORGED A GLOBAL BUSINESS--ALLIED MYSELF WITH LORD FFOGG AND MR. FREEZE--ALL SO I MIGHT FINISH WHAT MY FATHER BEGAN AND EXACT MY REVENGE UPON YOU!
AND YOU WANTED THE DIAMONDS TO BUILD YOUR LEAD-FOOTED LEGIONS TO USE AGAINST US?
IT'S MORE THAN THAT, ROBIN!
REMEMBER THE DIAMONDS IN THE CYBERNAUTS' BRAINS? THE CRYSTAL LATTICE USED AS DATA STORAGE? THEY REQUIRED ONLY FRAGMENTS.
BUT TO HOUSE THE VOLUME OF INFORMATION IN THESE DATA BANKS WOULD TAKE A SINGLE GEM OF PEERLESS PURITY!

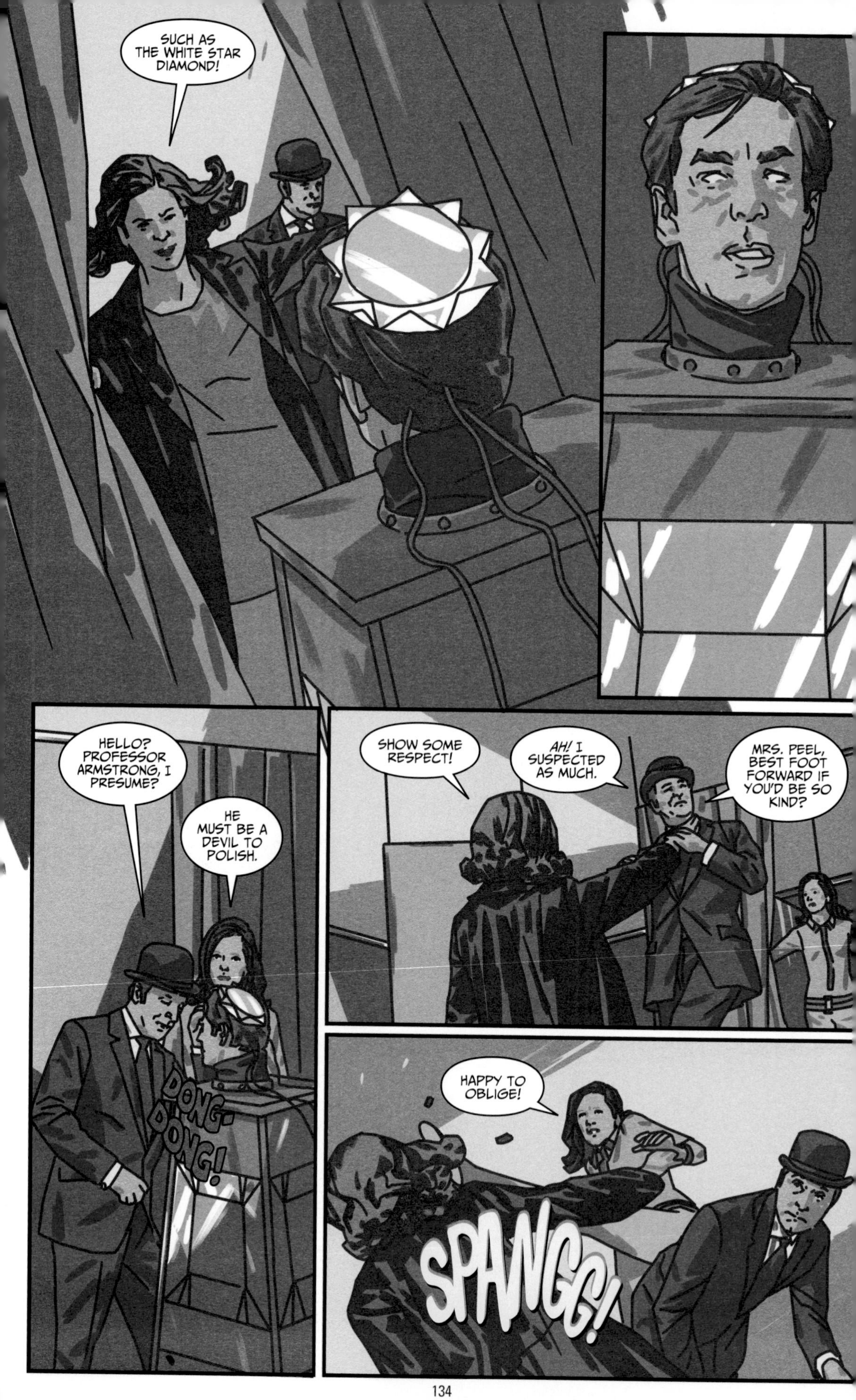

SUCH AS THE WHITE STAR DIAMOND!
HELLO? PROFESSOR ARMSTRONG, I PRESUME?
HE MUST BE A DEVIL TO POLISH.
DONG-DONG!
SHOW SOME RESPECT!
AH! I SUSPECTED AS MUCH.
MRS. PEEL, BEST FOOT FORWARD IF YOU'D BE SO KIND?
HAPPY TO OBLIGE!
SPANGG!

WHAT THE DICKENS?

OF COURSE!

NO WAY!

SHE'S A CYBERNAUT?

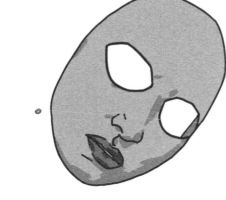

PROFESSOR ARMSTRONG NEVER HAD A DAUGHTER. HE WAS NEVER MARRIED.

YET SHE WAS MORE THAN FAMILIAR WITH HIS WORK, WHICH COULD MEAN ONLY ONE THING.

WHAT?

WHAT ARE YOU SAYING?

I'M NOT A MACHINE!

I-I--I'M MY FATHER'S DAUGHTER!

I...NO! THAT CAN'T BE!

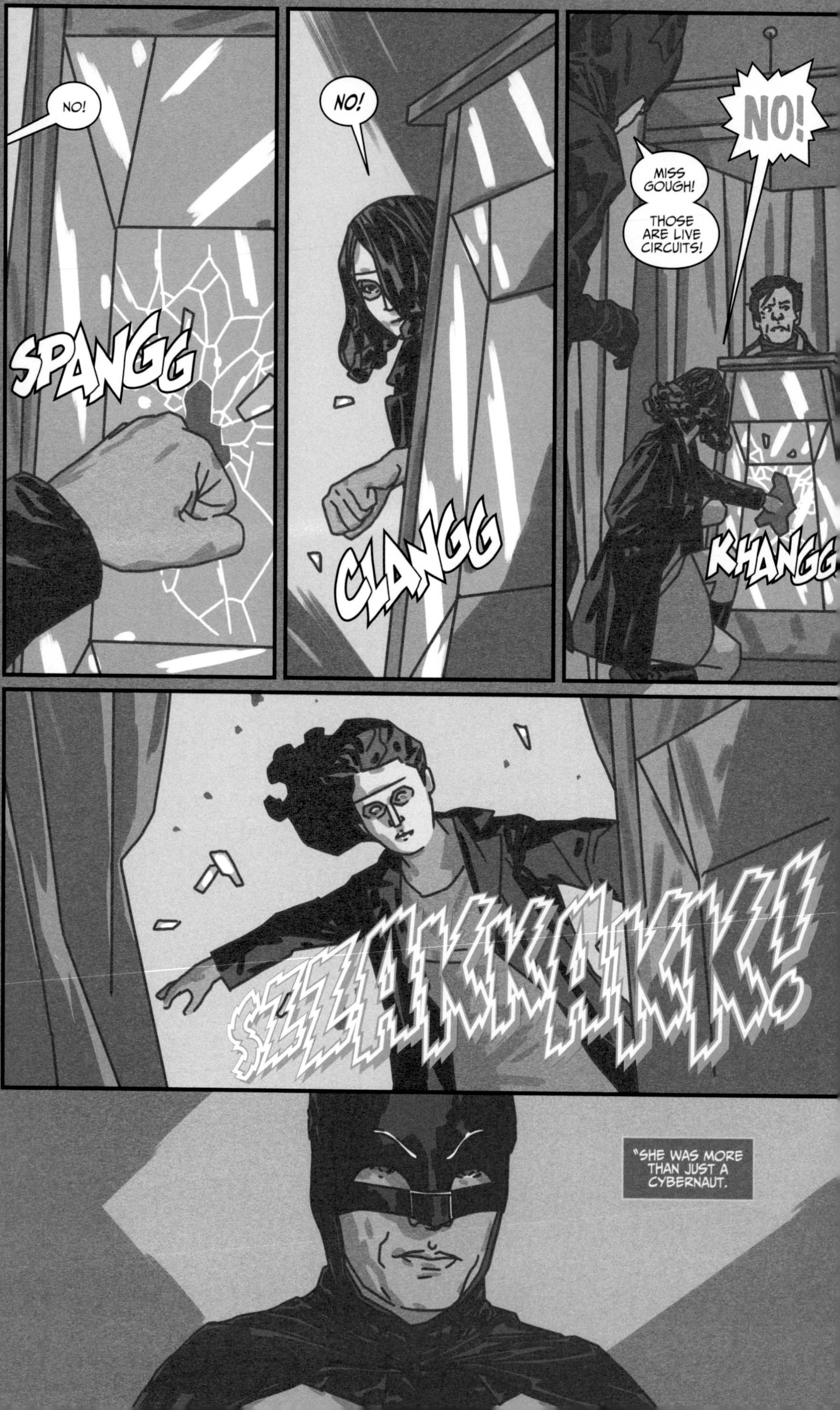
NO!
SPANGG
NO!
CLANGG
MISS GOUGH!
THOSE ARE LIVE CIRCUITS!
NO!
KHANGG
SZZAKKAKKK!
"SHE WAS MORE THAN JUST A CYBERNAUT.

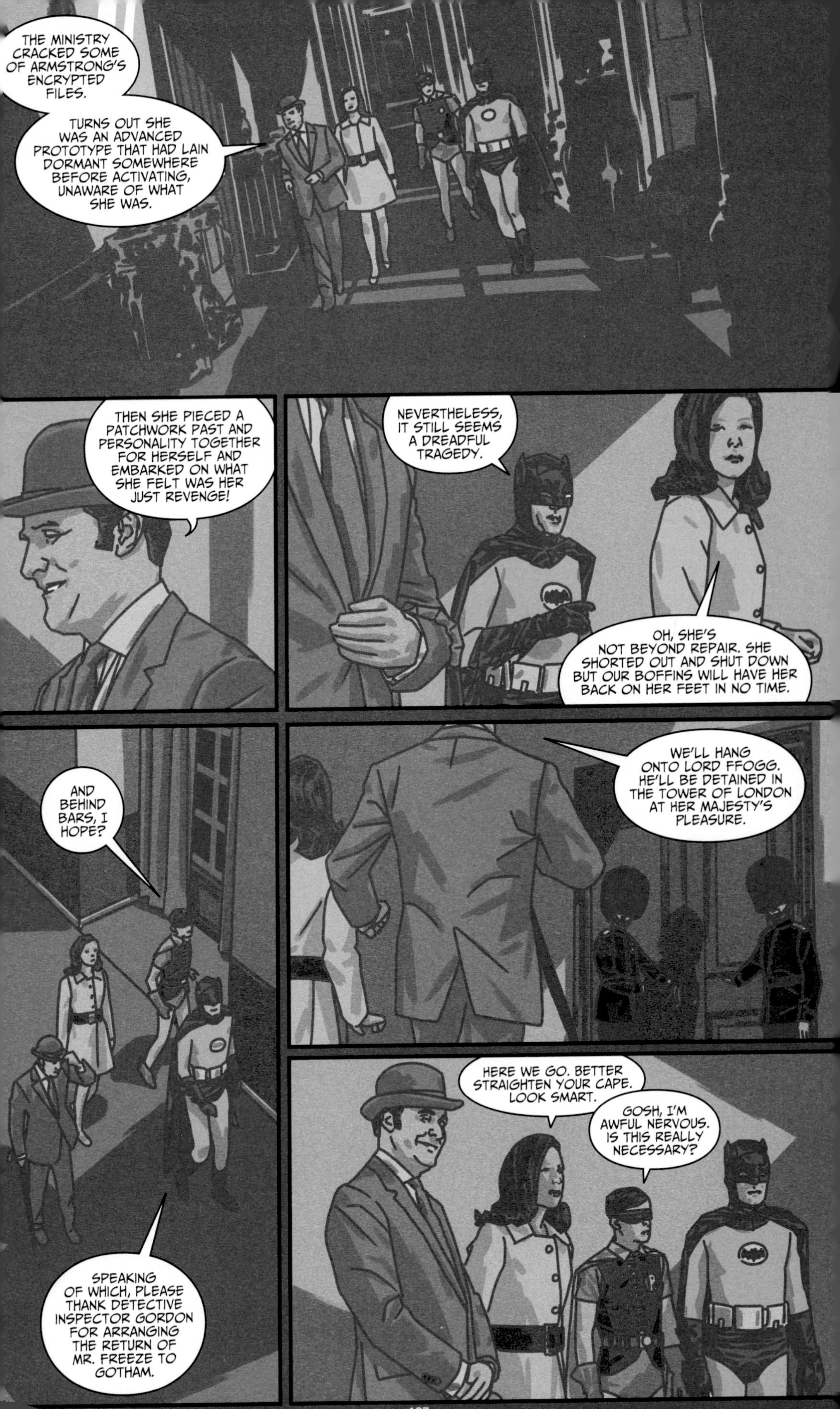
THE MINISTRY CRACKED SOME OF ARMSTRONG'S ENCRYPTED FILES.
TURNS OUT SHE WAS AN ADVANCED PROTOTYPE THAT HAD LAIN DORMANT SOMEWHERE BEFORE ACTIVATING, UNAWARE OF WHAT SHE WAS.
THEN SHE PIECED A PATCHWORK PAST AND PERSONALITY TOGETHER FOR HERSELF AND EMBARKED ON WHAT SHE FELT WAS HER JUST REVENGE!
NEVERTHELESS, IT STILL SEEMS A DREADFUL TRAGEDY.
OH, SHE'S NOT BEYOND REPAIR. SHE SHORTED OUT AND SHUT DOWN BUT OUR BOFFINS WILL HAVE HER BACK ON HER FEET IN NO TIME.
AND BEHIND BARS, I HOPE?
WE'LL HANG ONTO LORD FFOGG. HE'LL BE DETAINED IN THE TOWER OF LONDON AT HER MAJESTY'S PLEASURE.
SPEAKING OF WHICH, PLEASE THANK DETECTIVE INSPECTOR GORDON FOR ARRANGING THE RETURN OF MR. FREEZE TO GOTHAM.
HERE WE GO. BETTER STRAIGHTEN YOUR CAPE. LOOK SMART.
GOSH, I'M AWFUL NERVOUS. IS THIS REALLY NECESSARY?

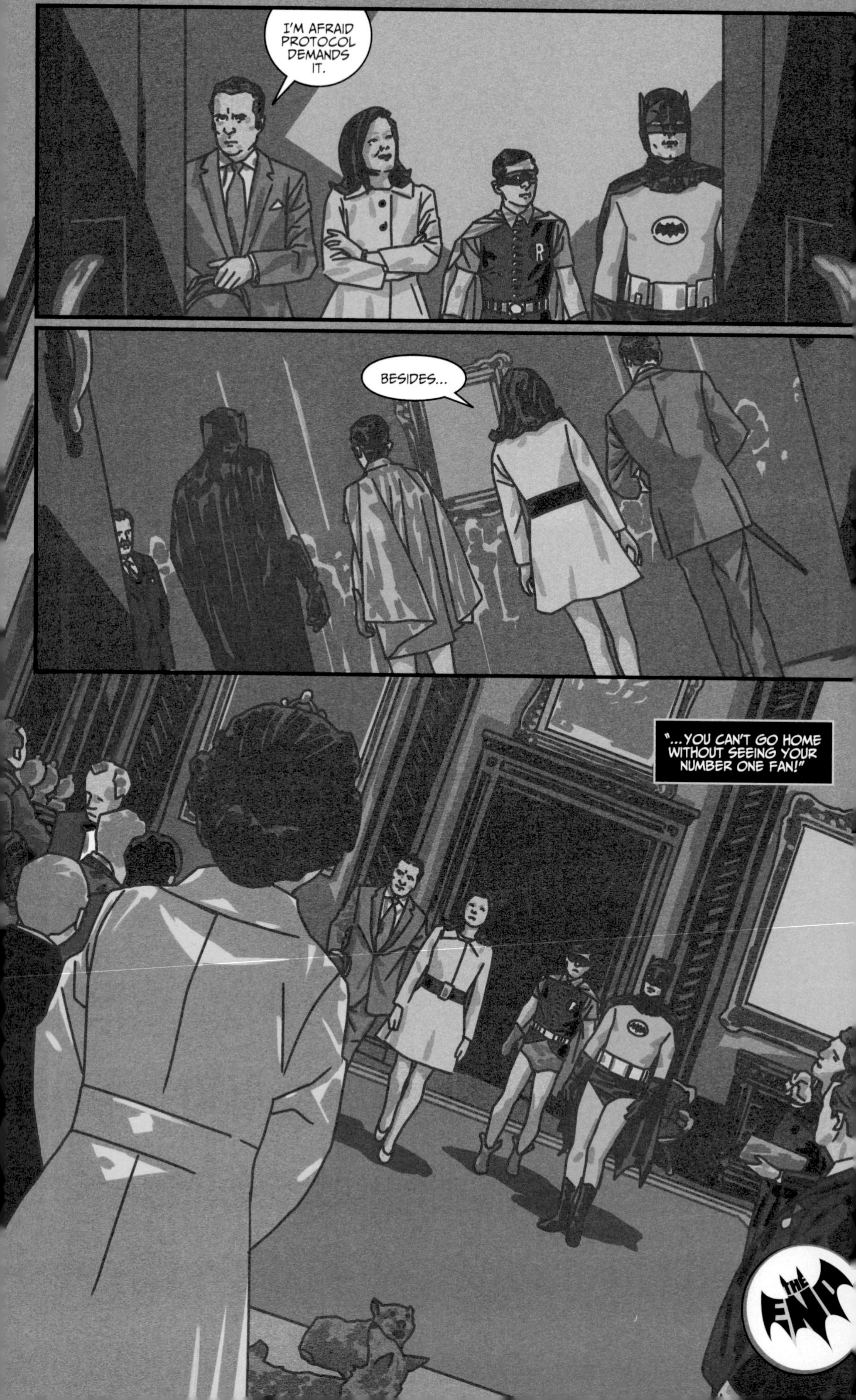
I'M AFRAID PROTOCOL DEMANDS IT.
BESIDES...
"...YOU CAN'T GO HOME WITHOUT SEEING YOUR NUMBER ONE FAN!"
THE END

BATMAN '66 MEETS STEED AND MRS. PEEL #1 variant cover by Cat Staggs

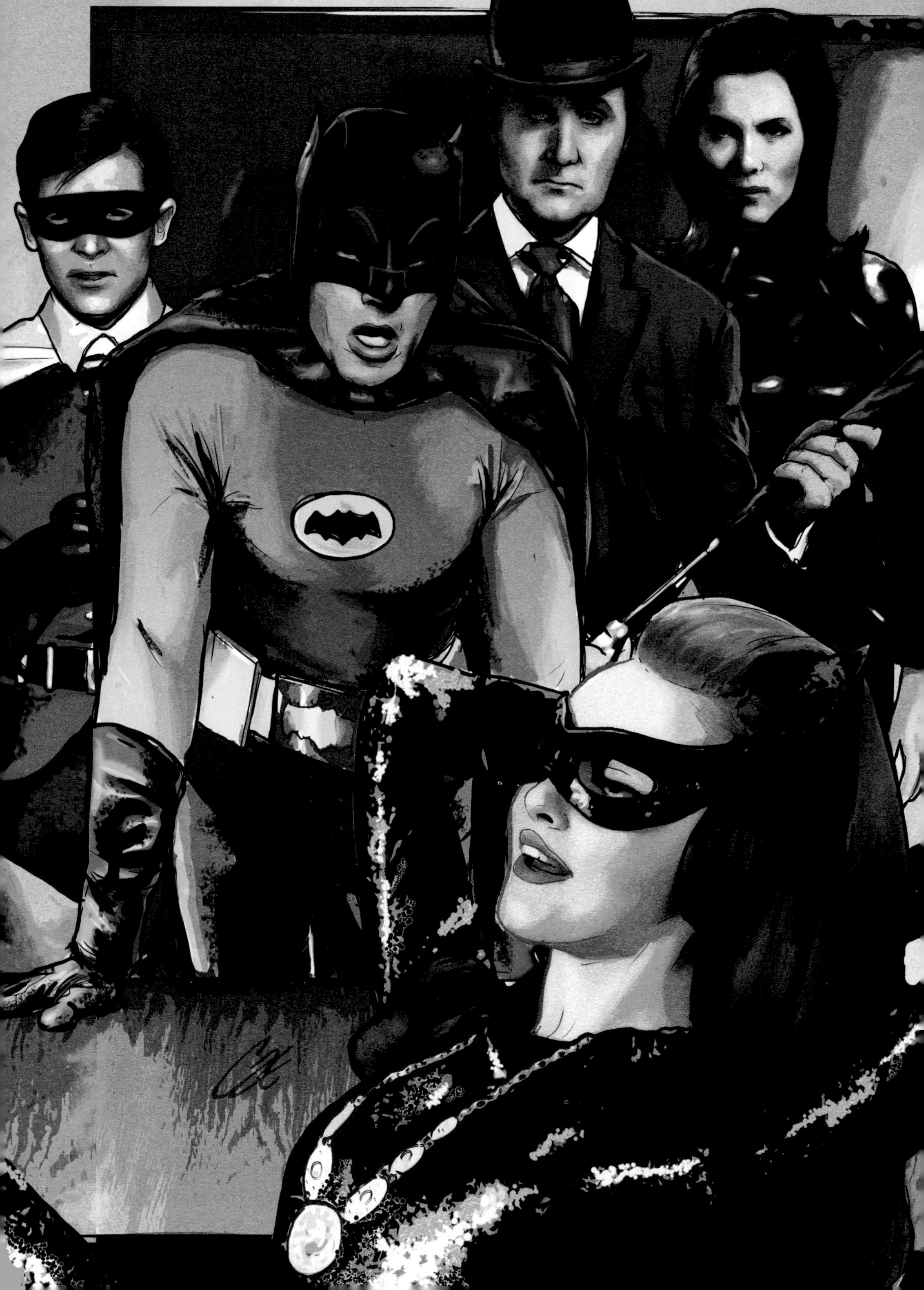

character designs by MATTHEW DOW SMITH

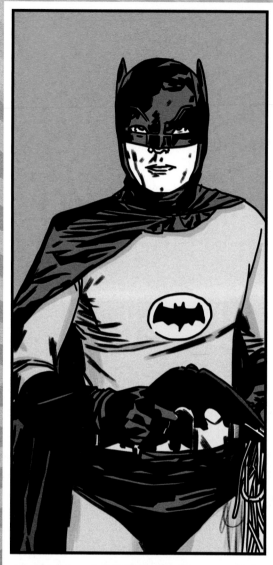

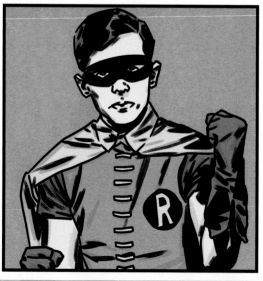

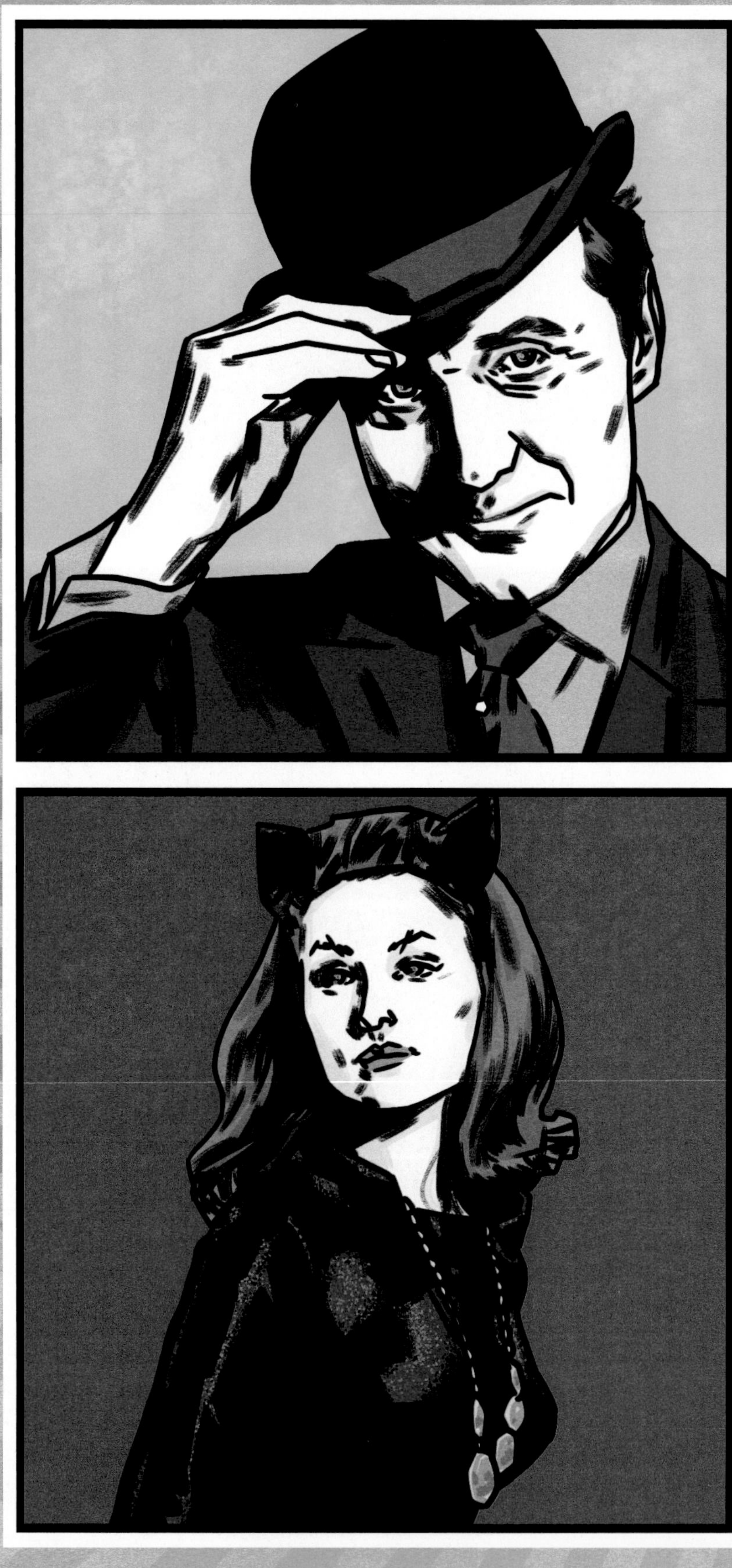

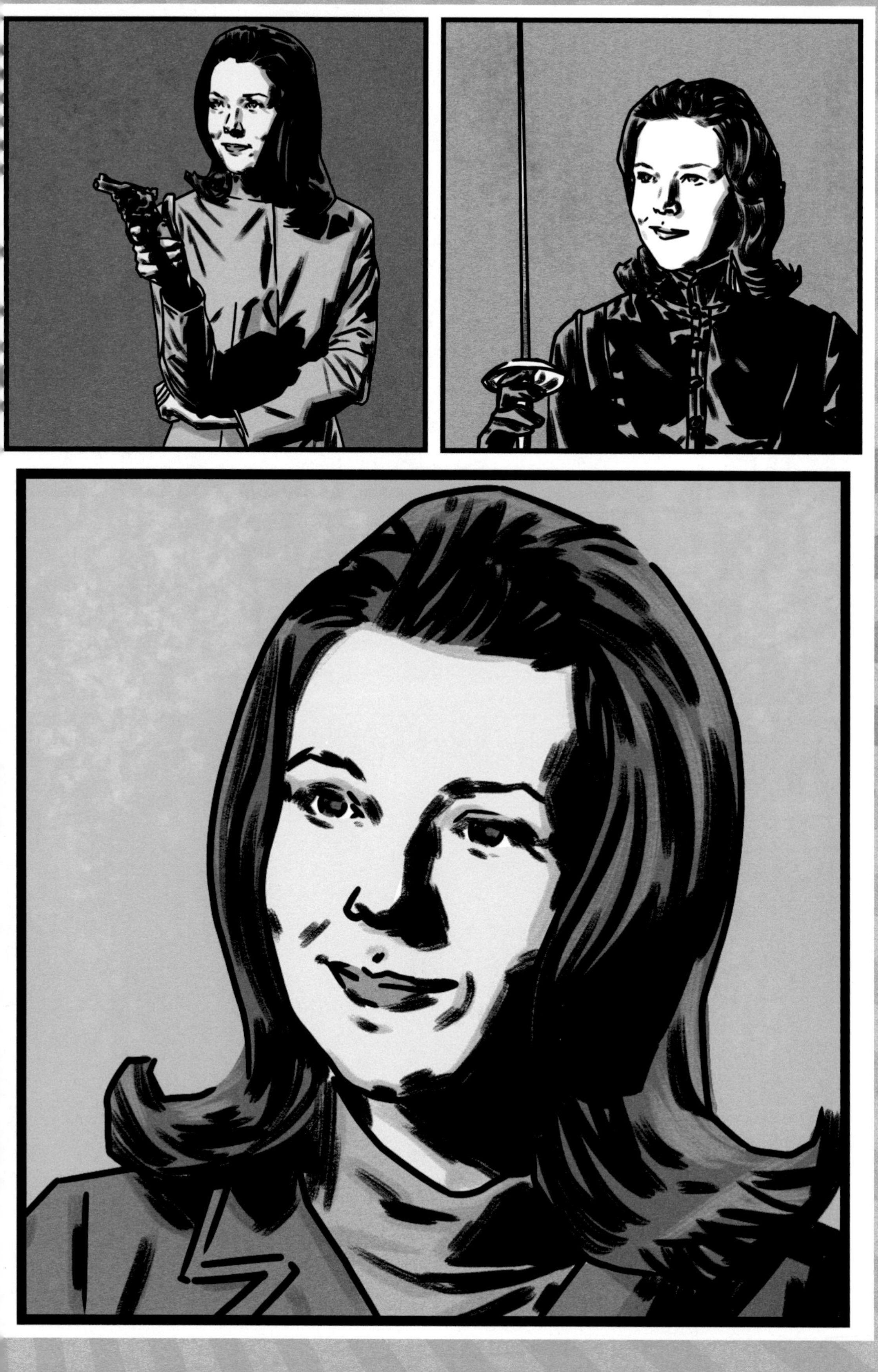

THE FIRST VOLUME OF GRANT MORRISON'S LEGENDARY BATMAN RUN!

"Game-changing redefining of the Caped Crusader."
—ENTERTAINMENT WEEKLY SHELF LIFE

"One of the most exciting eras in Batman history."
—IGN

"Terrifically exciting." —Variety

FROM *NEW YORK TIMES*
#1 BEST-SELLING WRITER

GRANT
MORRISON

with ANDY KUBERT,
J.H. WILLIAMS III
and TONY S. DANIEL

GRANT MORRISON   ANDY KUBERT   J.H. WILLIAMS III   TONY S. DANIEL

BATMAN AND SON

BATMAN: R.I.P.
with TONY S. DANIEL

BATMAN: THE RETURN
OF BRUCE WAYNE
with FRAZER IRVING & RYAN SOOK

BATMAN: TIME AND THE BATMAN
with TONY S. DANIEL

Get more DC graphic novels wherever comics and books are sold!